THAI
FOR TRAVELLERS

THAI
FOR TRAVELLERS

สุรพงศ์ กาญจนนัค
Suraphong Kanchananaga

ASIA BOOKS

Published and distributed by
Asia Books Co., Ltd.
5 Sukhumvit Road Soi 61
Bangkok 10110, Thailand
P. O. Box 40
Tel. 391-2680, 391-0590
Fax. (662) 381-1621, 391-2277

Copyright ©1992, Asia Books

Typeset by COMSET Limited Partnership

Printed in Thailand by Darnsutha Press

ISBN 974-8303-04-7

Foreword

This small handbook is not intended for a methodic study of the Thai language. Its object is more modest: to give simple and practical sentences and phrases on the most usual subjects of daily conversation, to enable the foreigner with little or no knowledge of Thai, as well as the beginner in its study, to express his thoughts in intelligible words and style when speaking with Thais. It will not teach you to speak like a native, but it certainly will provide you with the requisites for making yourself understood and your wishes known.

This book contains more than 2,000 immediately usable sentences and phrases based upon travel and life experiences: Customs, train travels, buses and taxis, hotels, local foods and native dishes, meeting people, inquiring the way, money matters, sight-seeing, going shopping, calling on a friend, social conversations, emergencies, and other situations that occur in daily life. A feature of the book is its transliteration with Thai characters in romanized spelling so that the student is gradually familiarized with the appearance of the language as well as with its sound.

To insure the correct pronunciation of the romanized Thai words and phrases, corresponding words and phrases in Thai characters are given. Follow the instructions first thing and practice talking by yourself or ask educated Thais to read the words and phrases over to you two or three times. They are intended merely as a help to those who have not yet had the opportunity of listening to the living tongue spoken by Thais as well as those who wish to learn the language as it is written with the Thai alphabet.

FOREWORD

Due regard has been paid in arranging the contents of this book, with the result that the required sentence or phrase can be found almost instantly.

It may be added, however, that even the advanced student may find in this modest work, something new to him, something that may increase his linguistic knowledge, as the sentences and phrases it contains are of the colloquial speech used everyday by Thais, many of which are generally overlooked or omitted in books for a methodic study of the language.

The knowledge of Thai may be wanted at any moment. One may be going to Thailand for holiday. One may meet charming Thai speaking ladies there, and wish to converse with them. Businessmen too, would find great advantage in becoming familiar with Thai, not only for use in their negotiations but also in the key it provides to the way the Thais think.

We, the publishers, wish you a most enjoyable trip, and trust this little book will be helpful.

ASIA BOOKS CO., LTD.
Publishers

CONTENTS

CONTENTS

CONTENTS

INTRODUCTION

Introducing Thailand

Location: The Kingdom of Thailand is strategically situated in the middle of the Indochinese Peninsula and is bordered by Laos, Myanmar, Malaysia, Cambodia, the Gulf of Thailand and the Andaman Sea. The Eastern border is partly separated from Cambodia and Southern Laos by the Mekhong River.

Area: The total area is 513,115 square kilometres, approximately the size of France.

Thailand is the only country in Southeast Asia never to have been colonized by Western powers. This undoubtedly accounts for its unique character, continually developed during more than 700 years of cherished independence.

Population: 56.9 million with an annual growth rate of 1.7 percent increase each year in the Kingdom.

Ethnic composition: Thai 85 percent; Chinese 6–10 percent; Malay over 3 percent.

Government: The government of Thailand is established on the lines of parliamentary democracy.

Democratic government is a form of government in which the people rule by discussion and compromise. Free elections, in which the people choose their government representatives, and the secret ballot, which gives them absolute freedom of choice, are prized possessions of Thais.

INTRODUCTION

The Government of Thailand firmly supports the purposes and principles of the United Nations Charter, because they embody the true conception of peace as the Thai people understand it, namely, the positive peace which includes freedom and economic advancement.

It emphasizes belief in God, Nationalism, Respect for Humanity, Democratic Practices and Social Justice. The freedom to choose his own church and faith and to worship according to his own conscience is the right of every Thai.

Bangkok, the capital of Thailand, seat of the Government, residence of the King and Queen, is a focal point of international travel and cultures — a city of many fascinating contrasts and beauty. Her cosmopolitan population of nearly 6 million includes thousands of foreign residents. Well appointed with hotels of every class and kind, Bangkok provides a unique trading location and has become the largest convention and trade show centre of Southeast Asia.

Language: Thai. A modern, dynamic and progressive language which has shown its capability in many fields, especially in education. English is widely spoken and becoming universal and widespread.

Religion: Buddhism is the State Religion and the great majority of the Thai people are Buddhists, e.g. 95 percent Theravada Buddhist, 4 percent Moslem and 0.6 percent Christian. However the Thai Government of every period has bestowed upon people freedom to profess any faith they like, and has been pleased to welcome any missionary of any faith to preach its tenets anywhere in Thailand. In practice, the Thai Government has accorded people not only religious freedom but also full support in

11

INTRODUCTION

their faiths. The State deems the patronage of religion one of its affairs. Moreover, under the Constitution the King is obliged to be a Buddhist and the Upholder of Religion, which includes any faith professed by his subjects whether it be Islam, Hinduism or Christianity or any religion whatsoever.

Thailand is the only country in the world literally living in Buddhism.

Unhampered by racial or religious prejudice and aided by a natural penchant for eclectically adopting values and, through simplification and embellishment, making them unmistakably "Thai", Thailand has maintained a uniformly high level of development throughout its history.

Economy: The country is blessed with fine gifts of nature: lush jungles in the mountains of the north, fertile green plains in the heartland, shimmering beaches and crystal seas in the south.

Thailand has always been known as a beautiful and scenic land endowed with some of the world's richest natural resources, and the land can produce a great abundance of rice, tin, rubber, sugarcane, cassava, maize, mungbean and other agricultural products. Its 740 kilometre Indian Ocean sea coast and 1,875 kilometre Gulf of Thailand shore-line teem with marine life, and its fishing fleet is the world's seventh largest.

Thailand is an agricultural economy with a very strong agricultural base. It is one of the world's few net food exporting nations. The country is blessed with a large quantity of highly fertile soil and is endowed with abundant mineral resources, particularly tin, rock-salt, potash and natural gas. In addition, it also has cheap labour, and unskilled, and large market potential. Foreign investment is playing an important role in Thailand,

INTRODUCTION

because it is both capital and labour intensive and encourages the transfer of technology necessary to develop the country's industries. Those who have the foresight to view Thailand as a viable manufacturing base will discover a lot of untapped potential. Thailand has a lot of advantages over other countries as far as industrial investment is concerned. Thailand remains largely a rural country, and His Majesty the King has created a chain of processes that have brought to the Thai people an uninterrupted good life and an accumulation of national prosperity that never existed in the past. His Majesty the King is a symbol of national unity as well as a tower of strength behind which the Thai people rally together. He is genuinely loved and deeply respected by his loyal subjects throughout the Kingdom for his dedication to their welfare and interests. Thailand has witnessed an irreversible march towards progress.

A predominantly Buddhist kingdom, Thailand today enjoys its own distinctive culture, its own language, its own cuisine, its own martial arts, its own beliefs and attitudes. Thai sculptors, architects and painters have contributed some of the world's expressive and enduring Buddhist art, and its artisans are recognized world-wide for their craftsmanship.

The Thais are a naturally free people as the name implies. Thais are respectful, quiet, always ready with a smile. Centuries-old traditions are still handed down from generation to generation in Thailand. The quality of life is noticeably different up-country, and more so if you could stay a while in the real countryside.

The people of Thailand are renowned for their friendliness and hospitality in welcoming foreign visitors and making them feel relaxed and comfortable. Visitors are always treated with courtesy and respect.

Thailand, Asia's most exotic destination, offers the visitor many unique and unforgettable experiences.

PRONUNCIATION

Guide to Pronunciation

Vowels

In the Thai translations, the words are pronounced as in the French or Italian languages.

Consonants are approximately pronounced as in English. Vowels are pronounced as follows:

- **a** is pronounced as "a" in *hard, arm, father.*
- **aa** is pronounced as "a" in *barn,* i.e. slightly longer sound.
- **ai** is pronounced like "i" in *high,* or in *fine.*
- **ao** is pronounced like "ow" in *bow,* or in *down.*
- **ee** is pronounced like "ee" in *bee.*
- **eu** is pronounced like "u" in *burn* and almost exactly like "eu" in the French word *"feu".*
- **é** this marked "e" is pronounced either like "a" in *able, mate* or like "ai" in *air.*
- **i** the vowel "i" is pronounced like "ee" in *bee,* or *police, machine;* short as "i" in *hit, fin, thin.*
- **o** approaches the sound of "o" in *go, more,* or in *original.*
- **oo** as "oo" in *book, soon, hoot.*
- **ou** is to be pronounced as in *you.*
- **ow** is always to be pronounced as in *cow* and not as in *show.*
- **u** is pronounced like "oo" in *full, foot,* or "u" in *pull, rule, flute.*

Consonants

b, d, f, k,
l, m, p, s,   Normally these are pronounced as in English.
v, w, y.

PRONUNCIATION

The letter "c" is pronounced like English.

ch a palatal, nearly as *church, chat.*

sh pronounced as in *Shanghai, shell.*

 d initial d like English d; final "d" like "t" in *cat.*

 g as in *gun, get,* but not as in *gem, germ* or gin.

ng as in *singing, banging,* never as in *tingle, sponging.* It is pronounced exactly like English "ing" with "i" cut off. Quite a few words begin with "**ng**", e.g. **ngo** (stupid), **ngarm** (pretty) and **ngou** (snake).

Tones

The Thai language is tonal with five primary tones. No two voices are alike for the simple reason that no two people hear them exactly alike. If a person would learn to speak Thai correctly he must learn the correct pronunciation from a native speaker or ask an educated Thai to read the Thai character or words over to him two or three times.

Special Notes

When two or more words are joined with a hyphen, it means that these words are intimately connected and pronounced in one breath.

The mark (~) above words in this book denotes high tonal words. The high tone in Thai corresponds very closely to the intonation we use when asking questions, as for example when we say *"Really?"* Further examples are:

sẽe– สี –colour	**mãw**– หมอ –doctor
phõm– ผม –I	**sũan**– สวน –garden

15

THAI GRAMMAR

A Bit of Thai Grammar

The Thai language has a simple grammatical construction, a great paucity of word forms and a vivid, picturesque way of forming cumulative nouns from other words which describe the object; it also has a wealth of idiomatic expressions. These unique characteristics make the Thai language very easy to learn.

Generally speaking, spoken grammar is simple. The basic structure of Thai sentences is subject-verb-object with adjectives following nouns. Each Thai word is complete inasmuch as there are no Thai suffixes, genders, articles, declensions or plurals. Tenses are indicated by standard auxiliaries, e.g. **pai** (go) with the auxiliary **kamlang** becomes **kamlang pai** (is going); and with the auxiliary **laew** becomes **pai laew** (go already or went). In many cases, verbs can be changed into nouns with the use of a prefix, e.g. **khid** (think) with the prefix **khwam** becomes **khwam-khid** (thought), etc.

In conventional spoken Thai, two or more words are often combined to form literal descriptions of common objects. Thus, "ice" is **narm-khãeng** (hard water) and "match" is **mai-kheed-fai** (stick/strike/fire).

Although satisfactory for common objects, this system is inadequate for coining new Thai words that can accurately convey western concepts of recent scientific terms.

Parts of speech for a given word appear in the following order: article, noun, pronoun, verb, adjective, adverb, preposition, conjunction and interjection.

THAI GRAMMAR

Article

There is no article definite or indefinite in Thai. However, there are a few seeming exceptions:

When it is desired to indicate particular objects, the place of the definite article is taken by demonstrative pronouns **ni** (this, these) and **nanh** (that, those). In most cases the article can be omitted as unnecessary.

Noun

The Thai noun undergoes no inflection to denote gender, number or case. Gender is defined by placing the word **shaai** (male) and **yĭng** (female) after nouns denoting persons, e.g. **dek-shaai** (boy) and **dek-yĭng** (girl). For animals the word **tua-phu** is used to denote the males and **tua-mia** to denote females after the nouns, e.g.

a bull	=	woa tua-phu
a cow	=	woa tua-mia
a cat	=	maew
a male cat	=	maew tua-phu
a female cat	=	maew tua-mia

The Thai noun may be singular or plural according to context:
I eat peanuts   =   **Shãn kin thua li-sõng**

When it is necessary to indicate plural, this is done in the following ways:

(a) By numerals and numeral coefficients, e.g.
   I have five hens   =   **Shãn mi kai ha tua**
   Eight slices of bread   =   **Khanõm-pang paed phaen**

17

THAI GRAMMAR

(b) By *words* expressing quantity, such as:
   There are many people in that house.
   Mi khon lāai khon nai baan nanh.

(c) By *reduplication* to form a plural with variety in it, e.g.
   Children like cakes.
   Dek-dek shob khanõm.
   Everybody knows about it.
   Khrai-khrai kaw roo.

"**Dek**" means a child; a youth; a boy; or a girl.
"**Dek-dek**" means children; youths; boys; or girls.

Numeral Coefficients

Numeral Coefficients are used to qualify Nouns which denote
living and material objects. For example:

For ten women	**yĭng sib khon**	หญิงสิบคน
For ten oxen	**wua sib tua**	วัวสิบตัว
For ten houses	**baan sib lang**	บ้านสิบหลัง

The following are the numeral coefficients most commonly in use.

anh	อัน	for small objects; things (in general).
shabab	ฉบับ	for letters; newspapers.
shaw	ช่อ	for bunches of flowers.
baan	บาน	for windows; doors; picture frames; mirrors.
bai	ใบ	for round hollow objects; leaves.

18

dawk	ดอก	for flowers.
duang	ดวง	for stars; postage stamps.
fawng	ฟอง	for poultry eggs.
haw	ห่อ	for bundles; parcels.
kaew	แก้ว	for drinking glasses, tumblers.
kham	คำ	for words; mouthful of food.
khanh	คัน	for vehicles; umbrellas.
khon	คน	for a person; a child; human beings.
khoo	คู่	for pairs of articles; forks and spoons.
klak	กลัก	for match-boxes.
konn	ก้อน	for lumps of sugar; stones.
krabawk	กระบอก	for guns; cannon.
kawng	กอง	for piles or heaps of stones, sand.
lamh	ลำ	for boats; ships; aeroplanes.
lang	หลัง	for houses; mosquito nets.
lem	เล่ม	for books; candles; scissors.
med	เม็ด	for smaller things; fruit pits; pills.
muan	มวน	for cigarettes.
ong	องค์	for holy personages; kings; also for monks.
phaen	แผ่น	for sheets of paper; pieces of planks.
phõl	ผล	for fruits.
phũen	ผืน	for blankets; carpets; mats.
reuan	เรือน	for clocks; watches.
roup	รูป	for monks and novices.
sãai	สาย	for roads; waterways; belts; necklaces.
sawng	ซอง	for envelopes.

19

THAI GRAMMAR

senh	เส้น	for hairs of the heads; lines drawn in ink.
si	ซี่	for teeth; ribs.
thuai	ถ้วย	for ceramic cups.
tonh	ต้น	for trees; plants; posts.
tua	ตัว	for animals; insects; fishes; tables and chairs; shirts; pants; coats; other living creatures.
wẽe	หวี	for a bunch of bananas.
wong	วง	for rings; bracelets; a circle.

The following are examples:

1. I want two glasses of cold water.
   Shãn tongkarn narm-yen sõng kaew.
2. Five bicycles.
   Rot chakra-yarn ha khanh.

It is not necessary to use the coefficient when the context does not require specification or numerical definition, e.g.

I want to buy (some) cigarettes.
Shãn tongkarn sue buri.

Pronoun

The following is a table of personal pronouns and their uses:

THAI GRAMMAR

Person Speaking	I	WE	YOU	HE, SHE THEY
Husband to wife	Shãn	Raow	Theu	Khow
Elder brother to younger sister	Shãn	Raow	Kae	Khow
Intimate and close friends	Shãn	Raow	Theu or Kae	Khow
Superiors to inferiors	Shãn	Raow	Kae	Khow
Thais to foreigners	Phõm (male) Di-shãn (fem.)	Raow	Khun/ Thanh	Khun/Nai
Thai gentry to one another	Phõm (male) Di-shãn (fem.)	Raow	Khun	Khow
Commoners to nobleman, a prime minister, a minister of state or person of rank	Kraphõm (male) Di-shãn (fem.)	Raow	Tai-thao or Thanh	Thanh

Khun is a form of address when speaking to a Thai if his name is not known. It is used both in written form and also in conversation; it is applied indiscriminately to men and women, either young or old.

21

THAI GRAMMAR

Nai, the official title for male "Commoners", is rapidly becoming replaced by **Khun**, which is a more polite form. Both mean Mister (Mr.). **Nai** is, however, still used in all official documents for men and **Nang** (Mrs.) or **Nang-saõ** (Miss) for women.

Phõm (male) and **Di-shãn** or **Ee-shãn** (female) paired with **Khun** (You). These are deferential terms used among equals or when speaking to superiors. **Phõm** is nowadays the most used personal pronoun in the first person, taking the place of **Shãn**, which is used mostly when speaking to an inferior like a servant or sometimes used familiarly as when talking to one's spouse.

When a woman is speaking to a nobleman, a prime minister, a minister of State, a superior, or an equal: **Di-shãn**, or sometimes colloquially: **Ee-shãn**.

Raow used as the common term for "We". In addition it is sometimes used to mean "I" when speaking to oneself or to intimates and inferiors.

Kanh (I), male speaks to male, paired with **Kae** (you) used among intimates of the same sex, otherwise insulting.

Manh (He, She, It, They) a derogatory term when used of people. The common term when speaking of animals (and occasionally of things). In vulgar usage or to express contempt: **Kha** or **Ku**.

Theu is perfectly polite and is used for "You" between husband and wife, brother or sister, friends and colleagues. But remember also that **Theu** can be used only to those very junior to you in age and status; to anyone else it would be downright rude.

Kraphŏm and Tai-thao. In general, when speaking with nobility or people of high rank use **Kraphŏm** (I) and **Tai-thao** to serve as the pronoun "You".

Mom is a title attached to the name of a lady who has married a prince. For a female speaker when speaking to the Sovereign, a Royal Highness, or a Serene Highness: **Mom-shăn**.

Khun-yĭng those who have become successful in their careers or the wives of senior government officials.

Nŭ or Nŏo is often used when the speaker is a child or a young women. Unmarried Thai ladies are usually addressed as **Khun Nŭ**. For Thai married women, they prefer and it is proper to address them **Khun-nai or Mae-nai**.

For Chinese born in Thailand, they are usually addressed as **Ah-Check** to the males and **Ah-Sim** to the females. A young Chinese boy is called **Ah-Tee** and a girl **Ah-Muăi** or simply **Muăi**. Rich Chinese storekeepers, estate owners and bankers are usually addressed as **Thow-kay, Sia and Chao-sŭa** respectively according to the value of his worth.

You should always address a Thai policeman or private constable as **Mou or Moo**, and for a Police Officer **Phu-Muad**; in the case of a Chief Police Officer you may address him **Phu Kam-kab**.

Do you know how to say "You" to the cook, the gardener, the office boy, the canteen girl? If the person is much older than you, say **Loung** (uncle) or **Pa** (auntie). For a woman a little older than you, say **Na**.

THAI GRAMMAR

When Thais speak among themselves, if the context and circumstances admit of no doubt, they omit the personal pronouns.

For example:

When Thais speak among themselves, if the context and circumstances (are you) going? The other replies **Pai Changwad** (I'm off to town).

The Thais will use nouns denoting real or politely fictitious relationships, between speaker and person addressed or spoken of in the third person. Common words so used are:

Paternal Grandfather	**Pou**
Paternal Grandmother	**Ya**
Maternal Grandfather	**Ta**
Maternal Grandmother	**Yaai**
Father / Mother	**Phaw / Mae**
Uncle / Aunt	**Loung / Pa**
Younger brother or sister of one's mother	**Na**
Younger brother or sister of one's father	**Ah**

A young person wanting to ask where are you going? or where is he (or she) going? will address or speak of any elderly man **Loung pai nai?** of any elderly woman **Na** (or **Pa**) **pai nai?** of any girl, older or younger than himself, if he desires to preserve a platonic distance, **Phee pai nai?** of his sweetheart, younger or older than himself, **Nong pai nai?** Any youth or girl will address a man, not old enough to be called "father", **Phee pai nai?** a girl will so address a casual acquaintance or real brother or lover. Each will reply, according to his or her standing "I am going home", **Klab baan chah phee**, **Klab baan chah loung**, **Klab baan chah yaai** (or more probably as explained above, any one of them will reply simply **Klab baan chah**).

If the person addressed or spoken of has a title or age, rank or profession, then that title will be used instead of pronouns of second or third person. Examples:

The Governor of a province	Thanh phu-wa
Deputy Chief	Thanh palad
Commune Headman	Thanh Kamnan
District Chief	Thanh Nai Ampheu
An Assemblyman	Thanh phu-thaen
Village headman	Thanh phu-yai baan
Aged Buddhist monk	Luang-phaw
Abbot of a monastery	Thanh Sŏmpharn

Verb

When constructing a sentence the principle order is: subject-verb-object. The order of words in a simple sentence is as follows:

1.	I	eat	rice
	Shan	kin	khao
2.	He	goes	to the Fair
	Khow	pai	ngarn

There is no change in the form of the Thai verb to indicate person or number. Examples:

THAI GRAMMAR

1. I drink water.   **Shãn duem narm.**
2. Pongthip drinks water.   **Pongthip duem narm.**
3. The children drink water.   **Dek-dek duem narm.**

The verb TO BE and the verb TO HAVE is **Mi**, which means to exist and having. Examples:

1. There are Thais in Chicago.   **Thi Chicago mi shao Thai.**
2. Have you a telephone book?   **Khun mi samud thorasab mãi?**

The **present tense** in the Thai language is formed by using the ordinary verb without reflecting any change to it. For example:

1. Suraphong goes to the airport.   **Suraphong pai thi sanãrm-bin.**

The **present continuous tense** is formed by placing the word **kamlang** or **yang** meaning "still" before the verb. Examples:

1. I am eating rice.   **Shan kamlang kin khao.**
2. Chutharat is still sleeping.   **Chutharat yang nonn you.**

The **past tense** is formed by placing the word **laew** meaning "finished" or "completed" after the verb. Examples:

1. I ate rice.   **Shãn kin khao laew.**
2. He drank (his) tea.   **Khõw duem narm-sha laew.**
3. I had seen this picture already. **Shãn dai hẽn pharb ni laew.**

The **future tense** is formed by placing the word **chah** meaning "shall" or "will" before the verb. Examples:

1. I shall go.   **Shan chah pai.**

2. They will come.	Khow chah ma.
3. Thawatchai will be going to New York.	Thawatchai chah pai New York.

Context determines the voice of the Thai verb, though the simple verb generally expresses the active. Examples:

1. Please look at the new house.	Shern shom baan lang mai.
2. Don't throw away today's newspaper.	Ya thing nǎngsūe-phim wan-ni.

The particle **mai**, placed after a word, has the function of a question mark, e.g. Will he go? (**Khõw chah pai mai?**) In Thai, the same verbal expression is used for all persons, singular or plural, so that, for instance, may mean I, You, They have, There is or There are.

There is no Copula in Thai. The word **penh** must never be used to translate the auxiliary verb of: is, am, are, was, were, etc.

1. I (am) sick.	Shan mai sabaai.
2. He (is) dead.	Khow taai.
3. It is not right.	Mai thouk tong.

Adjective

As attribute, the adjective follows the noun it qualifies; the demonstrative pronoun, if employed, coming behind it. Examples:

1. Thin man or men	Khon phõmm
2. That tall man	Khon sõung
3. Fat woman	Yǐng ouan

27

THAI GRAMMAR

4. This large house   **Baan yai lāng ni**

When speaking Thai, you need a few basic rules. Adjectives always follow the noun. Example: **Baan** (house) and **yai** (large) together as **baan yai** mean "a large house" and so on.

There is no word for the verb TO BE in Thai, when it is merely a copula, or link, joining a word to its description. When the adjective is used predicatively, it may be put in front of the noun if it is necessary to emphasize it. Example:

> **Toh yai tua-ni.**   This is a large table or
>   merely "This table is large."

You have already used the words **ni** and **nanh** as demonstrative adjectives, after the noun, e.g.

> **Sunak tua-ni**   this dog
> **Sunak laow-ni**   these dogs
> **Maew tua-nanh**   that cat
> **Maew laow-nanh**   those cats

Any adjective which comes after the **nanh** is predicative, e.g.

> **Ling tua-nanh duh.**   That (or the) monkey is wicked.
> **Thuai nanh taek.**   That (or the) cup is broken.

When the words **ni** and **nanh** precede the noun they are not adjectives but pronouns, e.g.

> **Ni toh.**   This is a table.

Adverb

The rules for the adverb are identical with those for the adjective.

(a) a word attached to a verb, to indicate time, place or manner, e.g.

He came *immediately*.	Khõw ma *thanh-thi*.
Park the car *here*.	Chawd rot *thi-ni*.
She dances *well*.	Knõw tenh *di*.

(b) a word attached to an adjective or to another adverb, to indicate degree, e.g.

It is *very* warm.	**Ronn** *maak*.
He was driving *rather* fast.	**Khow khab-rot** *khonn-khang* **reow**.

Adjectives can be used as adverbs. In addition to root forms like very (**maak**); suddenly (**thanh-thi**), nearly (**keuab**), we get adverbs formed by reduplication, e.g.

early (**nern-nern**)	always (**samẽu-samẽu**)
daily (**thouk-thouk wanh**)	nearly (**keuab-keuab**)

Preposition

A word that shows the relationship (usually time or place relationship) between some word (usually a verb or an adjective) and a noun, e.g.

THAI GRAMMAR

1. He was sitting *on* the chair.   **Khow nang** *bonh* **kao-ee.**
2. Wait *until* tomorrow.   **Khoi** *thŭeng* **phroung-ni.**

Conjunction

A joining word.

(a) joining words of equal weight, i.e. a co-ordinating conjunction, e.g.

   1. cups *and* saucers   **thuai** *lae* **chaan-rawng**
   2. foolish *but* kind   **ngo** *tae* **chai-di**
   3. black or white   **damh** *rŭe* **khão**

(b) attaching an explanatory statement (expressing condition, time, reason, etc.) to a main statement, or an object clause to its verb, i.e. a subordinating conjunction, e.g.

   1. I will ring up *if* I can't come.
     Chah thoh ma bawk *tha* **shãn ma mai-dai.**
   2. She said *that* she was tired.
     Theu bawk *wa* **theu neui (phlia raeng).**
   3. Saensak is a boxer *but* Thanongsak a singer.
     Sãensak penh nak-muai *tae* **Thanongsak penh nak-rawng.**

Interjections

These will be found in the Vocabulary of useful words. They call for no remark.

When You Enter Thailand

Salutations and Greetings

The Thai method of Greeting is the "Wai" (to show respect) which is executed by bringing the palms of both hands together and raising them to the level of one's face, the finger tips about eye level and the head bent slightly forward.

A woman will "wai" first during introduction in which a man is represented. When you are introduced to someone, the usual greeting is "Sawadee". If you meet someone to whom you have already been introduced, "Sawadee" is customary. The younger or lower in the station of life begins the greeting. When taking leave, the same word and procedure are repeated.

Good Morning.
Good Afternoon.
Good Evening.
Good Night.
$\left.\right\}$ In greeting the word **Sawadee** is commonly used.

Good-bye.	**La-konn.**	ลาก่อน
How are you?	**Khun sabaai dee rũe?**	คุณสบายดีหรือ
I am fine, thanks.	**Phõm sabaai dee, khob-khun.**	ผมสบายดี ขอบคุณ
What is your name, please?	**Khun shue a-rai?**	คุณชื่ออะไร

ENTERING

My name is Robert Lee.	Phõm shue Robert Lee.	ผมชื่อ โรเบิร์ต ลี
Where are you from?	Khun ma chaak nãi?	คุณมาจากไหน
I am from Hong Kong.	Phõm ma chaak Hongkong.	ผมมาจากฮ่องกง
When did you arrive?	Khun ma tang tae meua-rai?	คุณมาตั้งแต่เมื่อไร
I arrived only last week.	Phõm ma meua sap-da konn.	ผมมาเมื่อสัปดาห์ก่อน
Good luck.	Shoke dee.	โชคดี
You're welcome.	Yindi tonn rab.	ยินดีต้อนรับ
I hope that we will meet again.	Phõm wãng wa khong chah phob kanh ik.	ผมหวังว่าคงจะพบกันอีก

Customs Inspection

The following few phrases are some that you are likely to encounter at the Customs checkpoints:

Customs house	Darn phasĩ/Rong phasĩ	ด่านภาษี/โรงภาษี
Customs official	Phanak-ngarn phasĩ Sũlkarak	พนักงานภาษี ศุลการักษ์
Customs duty	Kha-thamniam phasĩ	ค่าธรรมเนียมภาษี

Where is Customs?	Darn-phasĭ you thi-nãi?	ด่านภาษีอยู่ที่ไหน
Here is my baggage.	Ni penh krapão dernthang phõm.	นี่เป็นกระเป๋าเดินทางผม
Here is my passport.	Ni nãngsŭe dern-thang phõm.	นี่หนังสือเดินทางผม
Here is my identification card.	Ni batt-pracham-tua phõm.	นี่บัตรประจำตัวผม
Have you anything to declare?	Mi arai tong sĩa phasĩ mãi?	มีอะไรที่ต้องเสียภาษีไหม
Nothing but wearing apparel.	Mai mi, mi tae seua-pha.	ไม่มี มีแต่เสื้อผ้า
Which is your suitcase?	Heep bai-nãi penh khong khun?	หีบใบไหนเป็นของคุณ
These are for my own private use.	Khõng laow-ni-penh khong shai suan tua.	ของเหล่านี้เป็นของใช้ส่วนตัว
What is in that bag?	Mi arai you nai krapãow nanh?	มีอะไรอยู่ในกระเป๋านั้น
You may open it.	Shern perd-dou dai.	เชิญเปิดดูได้
I have......	Phõm mi......	ผมมี......
– 200 cigarettes	– buri sõng-roi muan	– บุหรี่สองร้อยมวน

33

ENTERING

– a bottle of whisky	– **whisky nueng khuad**	– วิสกี้หนึ่งขวด
– a portable radio	– **vithayu**	– วิทยุ
– a home computer	– **computer sãmrap dek**	– คอมพิวเตอร์ สำหรับเด็ก
– a typewriter	– **phim-deed**	– พิมพ์ดีด
– a photographic camera	– **klong thaai pharb**	– กล้องถ่ายภาพ
– a bottle of perfume	– **narm-hõmn**	– น้ำหอม
– the jewellery is not new.	– **Khreuang-petch shai laew.**	– เครื่องเพชรใช้แล้ว
Do I have to pay duty on these things?	**Phõm tong sĩa phasĩ duai rue?**	ผมต้องเสียภาษีด้วยหรือ
I will take these things back with me when I leave the country.	**Phõm chah aow-klab meua dern-thang awk pai.**	ผมจะเอากลับเมื่อเดินทาง ออกไป
How much is the duty?	**Kha-thamniam phasĩ thaorai?**	ค่าธรรมเนียม ภาษีเท่าไร
I don't have enough money with me.	**Phõm mai mi ngoen phaw.**	ผมไม่มีเงินพอ
Here is my passport.	**Ni nãng-sũe-dern-thang phõm.**	นี่หนังสือเดินทางผม

34

| Have you finished? | Truad laew rŭe-khrap? | ตรวจแล้วหรือครับ |

Immigration Inspection

An immigration official will check your passport, your visa, and other official papers. Have these papers in your hand as you land. Do not leave them in your baggage because your baggage will be taken to a different place.

If your papers are complete, your landing card will be stamped to permit you to enter Thailand. The following phrases are some that you are likely to encounter at the Immigration checkpoints: —

Are the passports asked for here?	Thi-ni truad nãngsŭe dern-thang shai-mãi?	ที่นี่ตรวจหนังสือเดินทางใช่ไหม
What is your name?	Khun shue a-rai?	คุณชื่ออะไร
My name is Yamamoto.	Phõm shue Yamamoto.	ผมชื่อยามาโมโต
What nationality are you ?	Khun sãn-shard a-rai?	คุณสัญชาติอะไร
I am......	Phõm Penh......	ผมเป็น......
– an American	– shao American	– ชาวอเมริกัน
– an Australian	– shao Australian	– ชาวออสเตรเลียน
– a British	– shao Angkrit	– ชาวอังกฤษ
– a Burmese	– shao Phama	– ชาวพม่า

ENTERING

– a Canadian	– shao Khanada	– ชาวคานาดา
– a Dutch	– shao Hawlanda	– ชาวฮอลันดา
– a Filipino	– shao Filippine	– ชาวฟิลิปปินส์
– a French	– shao Farangset	– ชาวฝรั่งเศส
– a German	– shao Jerman	– ชาวเยอรมัน
– an Indonesian	– shao Indonesia	– ชาวอินโดนีเซีย
– an Italian	– shao Itali	– ชาวอิตาลี
– a Japanese	– shao Yipun	– ชาวญี่ปุ่น
– a Korean	– shao Kaolī	– ชาวเกาหลี
– a Malaysian	– shao Malaysia	– ชาวมาเลเซีย
– a Nepalese	– shao Nepal	– ชาวเนปาล
– a New Zealander	– shao New Zealand	– ชาวนิวซีแลนด์
– a Norwegian	– shao Norway	– ชาวนอร์เวย์
– a Pakistani	– shao Paki stărn	– ชาวปากีสถาน
– a Portuguese	– shao Portuguez	– ชาวปอร์ตุเกส
– a Singaporean	– shao Sĭngkhapo	– ชาวสิงคโปร์
– a Singhalese	– shao Sĭnghol/ Silon	– ชาวสิงหล/ซีลอน
– a Swedish	– shao Sweden	– ชาวสวีเดน
– a Taiwanese	– shao Taiwăn	– ชาวไต้หวัน
What is your occupation?	Khun mi ar-sheep a-rai?	คุณมีอาชีพอะไร
I am……	Phõm penh……	ผมเป็น……
– a school teacher	– khru rong-rian	– ครูโรงเรียน
– a student	– nak-rian/nak auek-sa	– นักเรียน/นักศึกษา

– a doctor	– phaed/maw	– ทนายความ
– a newsman	– phu sue khao nãng-sũe phim	– ผู้สื่อข่าว หนังสือพิมพ์
– a trade consultant	– thi pruek sã karn kha	– ที่ปรึกษาการค้า
– a book publisher	– phu chad phim nãngsũe	– ผู้จัดพิมพ์หนังสือ
– an engineer	– visava-korn	– วิศวกร
– an embassy counsellor	– thi-prueksa satharn-thoud	– ที่ปรึกษาสถานทูต
– a commission merchant	– nak thurakich	– นักธุรกิจ
What is the purpose of your visit?	Khun ma tham a–rai?	คุณมาทำอะไร
Your Identity Card.	Batt pracha–chon.	บัตรประชาชน
Do you intend to make some stay here?	Khun tongkarn you narn thao rai?	คุณต้องการอยู่นานเท่าไร
Where are you now staying?	Dião-ni phak thi-nãi?	เดี๋ยวนี้พักที่ไหน
I am for the present staying at the Amarin Hotel.	Khana-ni phak thi Rongraem Amarin	ขณะนี้พักที่โรงแรม อัมรินทร์

37

ENTERING

Changing Money

The currency system used in Thailand is very simple and can be mastered in a short time. The monetary unit is the Thai Baht, divided into 100 satangs.

The value is inscribed in Thai figures on all coins and paper money. There are coins for 50 satangs, 1 Baht, 2 Baht and 5 Baht, while bank notes come in denominations of 10 Baht, 20 Baht, 50 Baht, 100 Baht and 500 Baht.

I want to change some money.	Phõm tongkam laek ngoen.	ผมต้องการแลกเงิน
Is there a bank near here?	Thãew ni mi thanakharn mãi?	แถวนี้มีธนาคารไหม
Which is the way to the Bangkok Bank?	Thanakharn Krungthep pai thang nãi?	ธนาคารกรุงเทพไป ทางไหน
Can you change this, please?	Phõm laek ngoen ni dai mãi?	ผมแลกเงินนี้ได้ไหม
I would like to cash this cheque.	Phõm tongkarn laek shek bai ni.	ผมต้องการแลกเช็คใบนี้
Here is my passport.	Ni nãngsũe dern-thang phõm.	นี่หนังสือเดินทางผม
Can you cash a personal cheque?	Shek suan-tua laek dai mãi?	เช็คส่วนตัวแลกได้ไหม

I want to cash a travellers' cheque.	Phõm tongkam laek shek dern-thang.	ผมต้องการแลกเช็คเดินทาง
What is the rate of exchange today?	Attra laek-plian wan-ni pen yang-rai?	อัตราแลกเปลี่ยนวันนี้เป็นอย่างไร
I have a letter of credit.	Phõm mi L / C (Letter of Credit).	ผมมี แอล ซี (เล็ตเตอร์ออฟเครดิต)
I have a bankers' draft.	Phõm mi draft thanakharn.	ผมมีดราฟต์ธนาคาร
I have a credit card.	Phõm mi credit card.	ผมมีเครดิตการ์ด
Is there a money changer near here?	Thaew ni mi raan laek ngoen mãi?	แถวนี้มีร้านแลกเงินไหม
I have American dollars.	Phõm mi dollar american.	ผมมีดอลลาร์อเมริกัน
How much can you give for an American dollar?	Khun chah hai dollar-lah ki Baht?	คุณจะให้ดอลลาร์ละกี่บาท
I'd like to change Singapore dollars into Baht.	Phõm tongkam laek rĩan Singkhapo penh Baht.	ผมต้องการแลกเหรียญสิงคโปร์เป็นบาท
Please let me have......	Karuna hai phõm......	กรุณาให้ผม......
– two 500 Baht notes	– thanabat ha-roi Baht sõng bai	– ธนบัตรห้าร้อยบาทสองใบ

39

ENTERING

– fifty 20 Baht notes	– thanabat yi-sib Baht ha-sib bai	– ธนบัตรยี่สิบบาท ห้าสิบใบ
– fifty 10 Baht notes	– thanabat sib Baht ha-sib bai	– ธนบัตรสิบบาท ห้าสิบใบ
Please give me some small change.	Khaw ngoen-pleek hai phõm bang.	ขอเงินปลีกให้ผมบ้าง
Can I change money here at the hotel?	Laek ngoen thi rongraem dai mai?	แลกเงินที่โรงแรมได้ไหม
Do you have change for a hundred Baht?	Mi ngoen laek roi Baht mãi?	มีเงินแลกร้อยบาทไหม

Inquiries in the Street

Excuse me.	Khãw-thode.	ขอโทษ
Can you help me please?	Karuna shuai phõm noi dai mai?	กรุณาช่วยผม หน่อยได้ไหม
I am lost/I have lost my way.	Phõm lõng-thang/ Phõm pai mai thouk.	ผมหลงทาง ผมไปไม่ถูก
I thought the French Embassy was around here.	Phõm khid-wa Sathãrn-thout Farangset you thãew-thãew ni.	ผมคิดว่าสถานทูต ฝรั่งเศสอยู่แถวๆ นี้

40

English	Thai (romanized)	Thai
But I can't find it anywhere.	Tae phõm hã mai phob.	แต่ผมหาไม่พบ
I've been trying to get a taxi to take me there.	Phõm phaya-yarm hã taxi pai song phõm thi nanh.	ผมพยายามหาแท็กซี่ไปส่งผมที่นั่น
But they don't seem to know where I want to go.	Tae dou-mẽuan khõw mai-saab wa phõm tongkarn pai thi-dai.	แต่ดูเหมือนเขาไม่ทราบว่าผมต้องการไปที่ใด
I'm afraid my Thai pronunciation is very poor.	Khid-wa Khõw fang mai rou-reuang.	คิดว่าเขาฟังไม่รู้เรื่อง
How far is it from here to......?	Chaak-ni pai...... ik kiai mãi?	จากนี้ไป.......อีกไกลไหม
– Lumbhini Gardens	– Sũan Lumbhini	– สวนลุมพินี
– Silom Plaza	– Sĩlom Plaza	– สีลม พลาซ่า
– Suphakarn Shopping Centre	– Sõon-karn kha Suphakarn	– ศูนย์การค้าศุภาคาร
– the Bangkok Metropolitan Administration	– Kaw-Thaw-Maw (Thesabarn Nakhorn Krungthep)	– กทม. (กรุงเทพมหานคร)
– the Tourist Information Centre	– Sõon Shuai-lẽua Nak thong-thiao	– ศูนย์ช่วยเหลือ นักท่องเที่ยว

41

ENTERING

– the United Nations offices	– Sãmnak-ngarn Saha Prasha-chart	– สำนักงานสหประชาชาติ
– the General Post Office	– Praisani Thoralek Klang	– ไปรษณีย์โทรเลขกลาง
– the Police Headquarters	– Kongbansha-karn Krom Tamruat	– กองบัญชาการกรมตำรวจ
– the Railway Station	– Sathãni Rot-fai	– สถานีรถไฟ
– the Commercial Relations Dept	– Krom Phanich Sãmphand	– กรมพาณิชย์สัมพันธ์
– the Bangkok International Airport	– Tha Akassayarn Krungthep	– ท่าอากาศยานกรุงเทพฯ
– The Royal Folk Arts & Craft Centre, Bangsai	– Sõon Silapa–sheep Phiset Bangsai	– ศูนย์ศิลปาชีพพิเศษบางไทร
– Suan Luang Rama IX Public Gardens	– Sũan Lũang Raw Kao	– สวนหลวง ร.9
– Chulalongkorn University	– Chulalongkorn Mahã Vithayalai	– จุฬาลงกรณ์มหาวิทยาลัย
– Asian Institute of Technology (AIT)	– Sathãban Technology Haeng Asia	– สถาบันเทคโนโลยีแห่งเอเชีย

42

Is there a bus which goes direct to……?	Mi rot prachamthang pai…… mãi?	มีรถประจำทางไป……ไหม
– the Australian Embassy	– Sathãrn-thout Australia	– สถานทูตออสเตรเลีย
– the Canadian Embassy	– Sathãrn-thout Canada	– สถานทูตคานาดา
– the American Chamber of Commerce	– Hãw karn-kha American	– หอการค้าอเมริกัน
– the British Embassy	– Sathãrn-thout Angkrit	– สถานทูตอังกฤษ
– USAID Office	– Sãmnak-ngarn USOM	– สำนักงานยูซอม
– the Department of Immigration	– Krom truadkhon khow meuang	– กรมตรวจคนเข้าเมือง
– Office of the Board of Investment	– Sãmnak-ngarn Songsẽrm Karn Long-thoun	– สำนักงานส่งเสริมการลงทุน
Is this the right way to……?	Pai thang-ni thouk mai?	……ไปทางนี้ถูกไหม
– the Post Office	– Sãmnak-ngarn Praisani	– สำนักงานไปรษณีย์
– the City Hall	– Sãla Klang	– ศาลากลาง
– the Bus Terminal	– Sathãni Khõn-Song	– สถานีขนส่ง

43

ENTERING

– the Municipal Office	– Sãmnak-ngarn Thesabarn	– สำนักงานเทศบาล
– the District Officer's Office	– Sãmnak-ngarn Nai Ampheu	– สำนักงานนายอำเภอ
Have I to go......?	Phõm tong ......shai mai?	ผมต้อง......ใช้มั้ย
– straight on	– trong-pai	– ตรงไป
– to the right	– pai thang khwã	– ไปทางขวา
– to the left	– pai thang saai	– ไปทางซ้าย
Is it this way/that way?	Thang ni/thang nanh?	ทางนี้/ทางนั้น
Is it on this side of the street?	Thang daan-ni khong thanõn shai mai?	ทางด้านนี้ของถนนใช้มั้ย
Is it on the other side?	You thang daan none shai mai?	อยู่ทางด้านโน้นใช้มั้ย
Is there a bus-stop somewhere around here?	Mi paai chawd-rot pracham-thang thãew ni mãi?	มีป้ายจอดรถประจำทาง แถวนี้ไหม
What bus number should I take?	Phõm khuan khuen-rot beur a-rai?	ผมควรขึ้นรถเบอร์อะไร
Does the bus stop here?	Rot chawd thi-ni mãi?	รถจอดที่นี่ไหม
Is there a post office near here?	Thãew ni mi Praisani mãi?	แถวนี้มีไปรษณีย์ไหม

44

| What is your name? | Khun shue a-rai? | คุณชื่ออะไร |
| Thanks very much for your help. | Khob-khun maak thi karuna shuai lẽua. | ขอบคุณมากที่กรุณาช่วยเหลือ |

Taxicab

Do you speak/ understand some English?	Khun phoud/ khaochai angkrit bang mãi?	คุณพูด/เข้าใจอังกฤษไหม
Where can I get a taxi?	Hã rot taxi dai thi-nãi?	หารถแท็กซี่ได้ที่ไหน
Take me to this address, please.	Pha phõm pai-song thi-ni......	พาผมไปส่งที่นี่......
Do you know where this place is?	Khun rou-mãi wa ni thi nãi?	คุณรู้ไหมว่านี่ที่ไหน
What is the fare to......	Pai thi......aow thao-rai?	ไปที่......เอาเท่าไร
– the American Embassy	– Sathãrn-thout American	– สถานทูตอเมริกัน
– the Japanese Club	– Samosõrn Yipun	– สโมสรญี่ปุ่น
– Sharn Issara Tower	– Akharn Sharn Issarah	– อาคารชาญอิสสระ

ENTERING

– Mah Boonkrong Centre	– **Sŏon karn-kha Mah Boonkrong**	– ศูนย์การค้า มาบุญครอง
– City Square	– **Chaturat Nakhorn Lŭang**	– จตุรัสนครหลวง
– Siam Centre	– **Sayăm Centre**	– สยามเซ็นเตอร์
I will give you 100 Baht.	**Phŏm hai roi Baht.**	ผมให้ร้อยบาท
I cannot pay more.	**Phŏm hai thao-nanh.**	ผมให้เท่านั้น
May I stop at Pratu Narm on the way?	**Chawd thi Pratu Narm dai măi?**	จอดที่ประตูน้ำได้ไหม
Please help me with my luggage.	**Shuai-phŏm yok khăwng.**	ช่วยผมยกของ
Is there room for everything?	**Mi thi-waang phaw măi?**	มีที่ว่างพอไหม
Put these parcels next to you in the car.	**Aow haw lao-ni waang nai rot klai tua khun.**	เอาห่อเหล่านี้วางในรถ ใกล้ตัวคุณ
I will take the small bag.	**Phŏm aow krapăo-lek.**	ผมเอากระเป๋าเล็ก
I/We have altogether six parcels.	**Khăwng mi thang-mod hok shin.**	ของมีทั้งหมดหกชิ้น
Where can I find the W.C. /Toilet?	**Thi-năi mi hong suam/ hong narm?**	ที่ไหนมีห้องส้วม/ห้องน้ำ

46

Is the toilet free or does one have to pay?	Free rũe tong sĩa ngoen?	ฟรีหรือต้องเสียเงิน
Can you drive any faster?	Khab reow ik-nid dai mãi?	ขับเร็วอีกนิดได้ไหม
Drive on! Don't stop!	Khab-taw-pai! Mai-tong yout!	ขับต่อไป/ไม่ต้องหยุด
Could you please drive more slowly?	Khab sha-sha dai mãi?	ขับช้าๆ ได้ไหม
What is that tall building over there?	A-kharn sõung nanh a-rai?	อาคารสูงนั่นอะไร
How far is it to the Sathorn Thani Building?	A-kharn Sãthorn Thani yang ik klai mãi?	อาคารสาธรธานี ยังอีกไกลไหม
Where is the World Trade Centre?	World Trade Centre you thi-nãi?	เวิลด์ เทรดเซ็นเตอร์ อยู่ที่ไหน
Slow down! Stop here!	Sha-sha noi! Yout thi-ni!	ช้า-ช้าหน่อย! หยุดที่นี่
Wait here until I come back.	Raw thi-ni chon kwa phõm klab.	รอที่นี่จนกว่าผมกลับ
How long have I kept you?	Phõm nang-rot khun narn ki shua-mong?	ผมนั่งรถคุณนานกี่ชั่วโมง

ENTERING

How much do I have to pay you?	Phõm tong-chaai thao-rai?	ผมต้องจ่ายเท่าไร
I am giving you too much.	Phõm hai maak laew.	ผมให้มากแล้ว
You are trying to over-charge me.	Khun phaya yarm khoud-reed aow kab phu-doai-sãrn.	คุณพยายามขูดรีดเอากับผู้โดยสาร
Drive me to the Police Station!	Pai phoud kanh kanh thi rong-phak!	ไปพูดกันที่โรงพัก

48

Checking in at a Hotel

Your accommodations may be a deluxe hotel, a modest hotel, a guesthouse, or whatever, but it is important to be able to express your needs to be sure you get what you want. Outside Bangkok, of course, few people are likely to be able to help you if you do not speak Thai, so we have given you the most useful expressions to cover most situations. They may make the difference between getting the room you want and having to settle for something less.

On Arrival — Engaging a Room

Can you recommend a small hotel?	Nae-nam rongraem ra-kha yaow hai dai mãi?	แนะนำโรงแรมราคาเยา ให้ได้ไหม
I like this hotel.	Phõm shob rongraem ni.	ผมชอบโรงแรมนี้
Is any accommodation available?	Mi hong wang mãi?	มีห้องว่างไหม
I want two rooms.	Phõm tongkarn sõng hong.	ผมต้องการสองห้อง
I want two adjoining rooms.	Phõm tongkarn sõng hong shid kanh.	ผมต้องการสองห้อง ชิดกัน
I want......	Phõm tongkarn	ผมต้องการ......
– a single-bed room	– hong tiang diao	– ห้องเตียงเดียว

49

HOTEL

– a room with two beds	– hong sōng tiang	– ห้องสองเตียง
– a room with a double bed	– hong tiang diao nonn sōng khon	– ห้องเตียงเดียวนอนสองคน
– a room with bathroom attached	– hong mi thi ab-narm khang nai	– ห้องมีที่อาบน้ำข้างใน
– an air-conditioned room	– hong mi khreuang prab-akas	– ห้องมีเครื่องปรับอากาศ
Can I see the room?	Khāw dou hong dai mãi?	ขอดูห้องได้ไหม
Have you a room on the second floor?	Hong-wang bonh shanh thi-sōng mi mãi?	ห้องว่างบนชั้นที่สองมีไหม
I want a quiet room.	Phōm tongkam hong ngiap-ngiap.	ผมต้องการห้องเงียบๆ
No, I don't like this room.	Hong ni phōm mai shob.	ห้องนี้ผมไม่ชอบ
The room is too small.	Hong lek pai.	ห้องเล็กไป
Show me another one.	Khāw dou ik hong.	ขอดูอีกห้อง
What is the price of this room?	Hong ni ra-kha thao-rai?	ห้องนี้ราคาเท่าไร

That is too expensive.	Phaeng maak pai.	แพงมากไป
Do you have any cheaper rooms?	Hong thouk kwa-ni mi mãi?	ห้องถูกกว่านี้มีไหม
I will take this room.	Phõm aow hong ni.	ผมเอาห้องนี้
Where is ......?	......you nãi?	......อยู่ไหน
– the toilet	– hong suam	– ห้องส้วม
– the bathroom	– hong abb-narm	– ห้องอาบน้ำ
– the elevator	– lift	– ลิฟต์
– the telephone	– thorasab	– โทรศัพท์
Is there a shower?	Mi fak-bua nai hong-narm mãi?	มีฝักบัวในห้องน้ำไหม
How can I call the boy?	Riak dek rab-shai yang rai?	เรียกเด็กรับใช้อย่างไร
Is there an electric bell?	Mi krading fai-fa riak mãi?	มีกระดิ่งไฟฟ้าเรียกไหม
Do you serve meals in the hotel?	Mi a-hãrn khãai mãi?	มีอาหารขายไหม
Do you have overnight laundry service?	Mi borikarn sak-reed wan-diao set mãi?	มีบริการซักรีดวันเดียวเสร็จไหม
Where shall I keep my car?	Phõm chah kep rot dai thi nãi?	ผมจะเก็บรถได้ที่ไหน
Do you have garage / parking facilities?	Mi ou-rot /thi chawd rot mãi?	มีอู่รถ/ที่จอดรถไหม

HOTEL

At what time does the hotel close?	Pratou rongraem pid ki mong?	ประตูโรงแรมปิดกี่โมง
Is the hotel open all night?	Rongraem perd talawd khuen rũe?	โรงแรมเปิดตลอดคืนหรือ
What is the number of my room?	Hong phõm beur a-rai?	ห้องผมเบอร์อะไร
What is the telephone number?	Thorasab beur a-rai?	โทรศัพท์เบอร์อะไร
My room key, please.	Khãw kunchae hong hai phõm.	ขอกุญแจห้องให้ผม

With Hotel Attendants — During Stay

Please ask the room-boy to come up.	Karuna riak dek-raub-shai ma thi-ni.	กรุณาเรียกเด็กรับใช้มาที่นี่
Who is it?	Nanh khrai?	นั่นใคร
Just a minute!	Khoi pra-dĩao!	คอยประเดี๋ยว!
Come in!	Khao-ma dai!	เข้ามาได้!
Can I have ……?	Phõm khãw……	ผมขอ……
– an ash-tray	– thi khia-buri	– ที่เขี่ยบุหรี่
– an extra towel and soap	– pha shed-tua lae sabu	– ผ้าเช็ดตัวและสบู่
– an extra pillow	– mõnn ik bai	– หมอนอีกใบ

52

– an extra chair	– kao-ee ik tua	– เก้าอี้อีกตัว
– an extra blanket	– pha hom-nonn ik phûen	– ผ้าห่มนอนอีกผืน
– some more hangers	– mai khwãen-seua	– ไม้แขวนเสื้อ
– writing paper and envelopes	– kradad lae sawng chod-mãai	– กระดาษจดหมาย และซองจดหมาย
– a waste paper basket	– takra thing kradad	– ตะกร้าทิ้งกระดาษ
– two rolls of bathroom tissue	– kradad sham-rah song muan	– กระดาษชำระสองม้วน
– a pot of Chinese tea	– sha-chine nueng ka	– ชาจีนหนึ่งกา
There are mosquitoes in the room.	Nai hong mi yung.	ในห้องมียุง
Please spray the room with DDT.	Karuna sheed DDT lai yung.	กรุณาฉีดดีดีทีไล่ยุง
This chair is broken.	Kao-ee tua-ni sham-roud.	เก้าอี้ตัวนี้ชำรุด
Please sweep the room.	Karuna kwaad hong.	กรุณากวาดห้อง
Please clean my shoes.	Karuna shed rong-thao.	กรุณาเช็ดรองเท้า
I am a sound sleeper.	Phõm nonn khee-saow.	ผมนอนขี้เซา

53

HOTEL

Can you awaken me at eight o'clock?	Plouk phõm vela paed nalika dai mai?	กรุณาปลุกผมเวลาแปด นาฬิกาได้ไหม
I would like to have......	Phõm tongkarn......	ผมต้องการ......
– breakfast in my room	– tham a-ham shao nai hong	– ทานอาหารเช้าในห้อง
– dinner in the hall	– tham a-hãm yen thi hong rab-khaek	– ทานอาหารเย็นที่ ห้องรับแขก
I am expecting	Phõm kamlang khoi......	ผมกำลังคอย......
– a friend	– pheuan	– เพื่อน
– a lady friend	– pheuan-yĩng	– เพื่อนหญิง
I am going out now.	Phõm chah pai khang-nawk dĩao-ni.	ผมจะไปข้างนอกเดี๋ยวนี้
I don't know what time I shall be back.	Kam-nod mai-dai chah klab ki-mong.	กำหนดไม่ได้จะกลับกี่โมง
If anyone calls for me tell him that I shall be in from one till three.	Tha mi khrai riak hã bawk khão-wa phõm chah you rawang nueng thũeng sãrm mong.	ถ้ามีใครเรียกหาบอกเขา ว่าผมจะอยู่ระหว่าง หนึ่งถึงสามโมง
Call a taxi for me.	Karuna riak taxi.	กรุณาเรียกแท็กซี่

54

Washing and Mending

Do you do any washing in the hotel?	Nai rongraem mi borikarn sak-reed mãi?	ในโรงแรมมีบริการซักรีด ไหม
I want to have these shirts washed.	Phõm tongkarn sak seua-shirt laow-ni.	ผมต้องการซักเสื้อเชิ้ต เหล่านี้
I want these clothes......	Phõm tongkam seua-pha laow ni......	ผมต้องการเสื้อผ้า เหล่านี้......
– washed	– sak	– ซัก
– dry-cleaned	– sak-haeng	– ซักแห้ง
– ironed	– reed	– รีด
When will they be ready?	Meua-rai chah set?	เมื่อไรจะเสร็จ?
I must have them......	Tong hai set......	ต้องให้เสร็จ......
– this afternoon	– baai wan-ni	– บ่ายวันนี้
– tonight / this evening	– khuen-ni / yen ni	– คืนนี้/เย็นนี้
– today	– wan-ni	– วันนี้
– tomorrow	– phrung-ni	– พรุ่งนี้
– before Saturday	– konn Wan-Sãow	– ก่อนวันเสาร์
You must bring back this list.	Tong aow banshi seua-pha ni ma duai.	ต้องเอาบัญชีเสื้อผ้า นี้มาด้วย

HOTEL

English	Thai (romanized)	Thai
Please use some starch.	Long paeng nid-noi.	ลงแป้งนิดหน่อย
Don't use any starch.	Ya long paeng.	อย่าลงแป้ง
Can you get this stain out?	Aow roi-peuan ni awk dai mai?	เอารอยเปื้อนนี้ออกได้ไหม
Can you mend this thing?	Pah rue shoun trong-ni dai mãi?	ปะหรือชุนตรงนี้ได้ไหม
Can you stitch this?	Yeb trong-ni dai mãi?	เย็บตรงนี้ได้ไหม
This is not mine.	Ni mai-shai khong phõm.	นี่ไม่ใช่ของผม

Washing List

English	Thai (romanized)	Thai
Bath robe	Seua ab-harm	เสื้ออาบน้ำ
Bath towel	Pha shed tua	ผ้าเช็ดตัว
Blouse	Seua khãen-sanh	เสื้อแขนสั้น
Boy's shirt	Seua dek-shaai	เสื้อเด็กชาย
Dressing gown	Seua gown phuyĩng	เสื้อกาวน์ผู้หญิง
Gent's shirt	Seua-shirt shaai	เสื้อเชิ้ตชาย
Handkerchief	Pha shed-na	ผ้าเช็ดหน้า
Jeans	Kang-keng jeans	กางเกงยีนส์
Napkin	Pha shed-paak	ผ้าเช็ดปาก
Night gown	Seua-nonn	เสื้อนอน
Panties	Kangkeng nai	กางเกงใน

English	Thai (romanized)	Thai
Pajamas	**Kangkeng nonn**	กางเกงนอน
Petticoat	**Petticoats**	เพ็ตติโค้ท
Shorts	**Kangkeng khã-sanh**	กางเกงขาสั้น
Skirt	**Kaprong**	กระโปรง
Socks	**Thõung-thao sanh**	ถุงเท้าสั้น
Stockings	**Thõung-thao yao**	ถุงเท้ายาว
Trousers	**Kangkeng khã yao**	กางเกงขายาว

In the Office

English	Thai (romanized)	Thai
Shall I enter my name?	**Phõm tong khĩan shue long thabian mãi?**	ผมต้องเขียนชื่อลงทะเบียนไหม
My name is Suraphong Kanchananaga.	**Phõm shue Suraphong Kanchananaga.**	ผมชื่อสุรพงศ์ กาญจนนัค
Here is my passport.	**Ni nãngsũe dern-thang.**	นี่หนังสือเดินทาง
Do you have the correct time?	**Vela khun trong mãi?**	เวลาคุณตรงไหม
Do you have the time-table for trains?	**Mi samud kamnod-vela rot-fai mãi?**	มีสมุดกำหนดเวลารถไฟไหม
Is there any letter or telegram for me?	**Mi chodmãai rue thoralek thũeng phõm mãi?**	มีจดหมายหรือโทรเลขถึงผมไหม

HOTEL

I am expecting......	Phŏm kamlang khoi......	ผมกำลังคอย......
– a registered letter	– chodmăai long thabian	– จดหมายลงทะเบียน
– a gentleman	– pheuan shaai	– เพื่อนชาย
– a young lady	– yĭng săo	– หญิงสาว
Did any one ring up for me?	Mi khrai thorasab hă phŏm mai?	มีใครโทรศัพท์หาผมไหม
Have you any English newspapers?	Khun mi năngsŭe-phim bhasă angkrit măi?	คุณมีหนังสือพิมพ์ภาษา อังกฤษไหม
Is there a money changer near here?	Raan laek-ngoen thăew-ni mi-măi?	ร้านแลกเงินแถวนี้มีไหม
I would like to change Singapore dollars for Thai Baht.	Phŏm tongkarn laek ngoen Sĭngkhapo penh Thai Baht.	ผมต้องการแลกเงิน สิงคโปร์เป็นเงินบาท ไทย
What is the rate of exchange today?	Attra laek plian ngoen wan-ni pen yang-rai?	อัตราแลกเปลี่ยนเงิน วันนี้เป็นอย่างไร
Please give me small change for this.	Khăw laek thanabat ni pen ngoen-yoi.	ขอแลกธนบัตรนี้เป็น เงินย่อย
The air-conditioner in my room doesn't work.	Khreung prab-akas nai hong mai tham ngarn.	เครื่องปรับอากาศในห้อง ไม่ทำงาน

58

HOTEL

The room is dirty.	Hong sokka-prok maak.	ห้องสกปรกมาก
The sheets are not clean.	Pha pou mai sa-ard.	ผ้าปูไม่สะอาด
The sink is blocked.	Ang-narm tanh/ Narm mai-lai.	อ่างน้ำตัน/น้ำไม่ไหล
It's too noisy.	Nuak-hõu maak.	หนวกหูมาก
There's no hot water in the room.	Nai hong mai-mi narm-ronn.	ในห้องไม่มีน้ำร้อน
The bed is too hard.	Thi-nonn khãeng lẽua thon.	ที่นอนแข็งเหลือทน
The bell doesn't ring.	Krading fai-fa mai tham-ngarn.	กระดิ่งไฟฟ้าไม่ทำงาน
I was promised a better room as soon as one became free.	Khun sãnya hai hong thi di-kwa tha mi waang.	คุณสัญญาให้ห้องที่ดีกว่า ถ้ามีว่าง
My room-key is left inside the room.	Phõm luem kunchae wai nai hong.	ผมลืมกุญแจไว้ในห้อง
Can you give me another key?	Khaw kunchae mai phõm dai mãi?	ขอกุญแจใหม่ผมได้ไหม
Can I keep the key?	Phõm keb kunchae ni wai dai mãi?	ผมเก็บกุญแจนี้ไว้ได้ไหม
Where must I leave my key?	Phom chah moob kunchae hai kab khrai/thi-nai?	ผมจะมอบกุญแจให้กับ ใคร/ที่ไหน

HOTEL

At what time does the hotel close?	Rongraem pid pratou ki mong?	โรงแรมปิดประตูกี่โมง
I am leaving tonight.	Khuen ni phõm chah pai.	คืนนี้ผมจะไป
I am leaving tomorrow.	Phõm chah pai phrung ni.	ผมจะไปพรุ่งนี้

With Hotel Attendants – Leaving

Can I see the Proprietor/ Manager?	Phõm khãw phob Thow-kae/Phu chad-karn?	ผมขอพบเถ้าแก่/ ผู้จัดการ
I am leaving tomorrow after breakfast.	Phrung-ni tharn a-harn laew phõm pai.	พรุ่งนี้ทานอาหารแล้ว ผมไป
Please make out my bill.	Karuna tham bill.	กรุณาทำบิล
Make out one bill for us.	Tham bill ruam.	ทำบิลรวม
Make separate bills.	Tham bill yaek.	ทำบิลแยก
This bill is not correct.	Bill ni mai thouk tong.	บิลนี้ไม่ถูกต้อง
The total is wrong.	Chamnuan yawd phid.	จำนวนยอดผิด
We did not have this.	Ni raow mai-dai sang.	นี่เราไม่ได้สั่ง

This must be a mistake.	Ni khid-phid nae-nae.	นี่คิดผิดแน่ๆ
You have charged too much for this.	Ni khun khid phaeng kern pai.	นี่คุณคิดแพงเกินไป
I want to have time to check this.	Phõm khãw vela shek bill.	ผมขอเวลาเช็คบิล
I want to pay now.	Phõm tong-karn sham-rah dĩao-ni.	ผมต้องการชำระเดี๋ยวนี้
Do you accept travellers' cheques?	Khun rab shek-dern-thang mãi?	คุณรับเช็คเดินทางไหม
Will you change these US dollars and give me Malaysian ringgit?	Phõm khãw laek dollar American penh ringgit Malaysia?	ผมขอแลกดอลลาร์อเมริกันเป็นริงงิตมาเลเซีย
Please give me some small change.	Phõm khãw ngoen-pleek bang.	ผมขอเงินปลีกบ้าง
Tell the boy to take down my things.	Proad bawk dek yok khõng phõm long-ma.	โปรดบอกเด็กยกของผมลงมา
Have you got everything?	Aow thouk sing long-ma mod-laew rũe?	เอาทุกสิ่งลงมาหมดแล้วหรือ

61

HOTEL

Please call a taxi for me.	**Karuna riak taxi.**	กรุณาเรียกแท็กซี่
What is the taxi fare to the airport?	**Chaak-ni thueng sa-nãrm-bin thaorai?**	จากที่นี่ถึงสนามบินเท่าไร
Will you post this letter for me?	**Thing chod-mãi ni hai phõm dai mãi?**	ทิ้งจดหมายนี้ให้ผมได้ไหม
Don't forget!	**Ya-luem nah!**	อย่าลืมนะ!
Here is the key of my room.	**Ni kunchae hong phõm.**	นี่กุญแจห้องผม

62

Eating and Drinking

Thai Food

Merely going abroad is thrill enough for some persons, for others the high points of a trip are likely to be the hours spent at the table. Getting to know and appreciate the national cuisine and learning how to order native dishes are extra thrills for many travellers.

Although the leading hotels and restaurants offer cosmopolitan menus, printed in English as well as in Thai, the following are some common Thai foods. With this handy list, you can go into any medium or high-class Thai restaurant and order exactly the food you want. However, sufficient time should be given for the preparation of any one of these dishes.

Kaeng-chued (Bland soups of fresh vegetables)

Kaeng-chued kalampli	แกงจืดกะหล่ำปลี
Kaeng-chued louk-shin nang-moo	แกงจืดลูกชิ้น หนังหมู
Kaeng-chued mõo bah-shaw	แกงจืดหมูบะช่อ
Kaeng-chued naw-mai sod	แกงจืดหน่อไม้สด
Kaeng-chued phak-kard khão	แกงจืดผักกาดขาว
Kaeng-chued taeng-kwa sawd sai	แกงจืดแตงกว่าสอดไส้
Kaeng-chued tao-hu khão	แกงจืดเต้าหู้ขาว
Kaeng-chued woon-sen	แกงจืดวุ้นเส้น

EATING AND DRINKING

Kaeng-phed (Hot curry)

Kaeng hang-lay	แกงฮังเล
Kaeng lĕuang pak-taai	แกงเหลืองปักษ์ใต้
Kaeng khĭao-wāan kai/neua	แกงเขียวหวานไก่/เนื้อ
Kaeng mŏo-yang bai khilek	แกงหมูย่างใบขี้เหล็ก
Kaeng khua sapparot	แกงคั่วสับปะรด
Kaeng liang	แกงเลียง
Kaeng massaman kai/neua	แกงมัสหมั่นไก่/เนื้อ
Kaeng mŏo thé-pho	แกงหมูเทโพ
Kaeng omm marah	แกงอ่อมมะระ
Kaeng pa pla-duk	แกงป่าปลาดุก
Kaeng phed neua/kai	แกงเผ็ดเนื้อ/ไก่
Kaeng shu-shi pla	แกงฉู่ฉี่ปลา

Tom-yam, Kaeng-som (Light hot soup)

Tom-yam mŏo-yang	ต้มยำหมูย่าง
Tom-yam koung/kai or neua	ต้มยำกุ้ง/ไก่/เนื้อ
Tom-yam pla or hŭa-pla	ต้มยำปลา หรือหัวปลา
Poh-taek	โป๊ะแตก
Kaeng-som Krachiab/ Malakaw	แกงส้มกระเจี๊ยบ/มะละกอ
Kaeng-som bai-khae/ Maroom	แกงส้มใบแค/มะรุม
Tom-som plathu sod	ต้มส้มปลาทูสด
Tom-kha kai	ต้มข่าไก่

EATING AND DRINKING

Phad (Stir-frying)

Fak-thong phad khai	ฟักทองผัดไข่
Hoi-laai phad phrik	หอยลายผัดพริก
Kai/neua/mõo phad khing	ไก่/เนื้อ/หมูผัดขิง
Kalampli phad koung/mõo	กะหล่ำปลีผัด กุ้ง หมู
Kai phad phrik/hõmm yai	ไก่ผัดพริก/หอมใหญ่
Kai phad narm-sauce hõi	ไก่ผัดน้ำซ้อสหอย
Kai sab phad kaphrao	ไก่สับผัดกะเพรา
Koung phad hed sod	กุ้งผัดเห็ดสด
Mõo/kai phad phrik-khĭng	หมู/ไก่ ผัดพริกขิง
Mõo/koung phad priao-wãan	หมู/กุ้ง ผัดเปรี้ยวหวาน
Mõo phad phrik-yuak/hed	หมูผัดพริกหยวก/เห็ด
Mõo phad khana/phak kwangtung	หมูผัดคะน้า/ผัดกวางตุ้ง
Phad woon-senh	ผัดวุ้นเส้น
Phad poai-sian	ผัดโป๊ยเซียน
Pladuk phad phed	ปลาดุกผัดเผ็ด
Phad mee-krob	ผัดหมี่กรอบ
Tao-hu khão phad raad-na	เต้าหู้ขาวผัดราดหน้า

Laab, Lonh, Phla, Yam

Laab kai/neua/mõo	ลาบไก่/เนื้อ/หมู
Phla koung/hõi/pou	พล่ากุ้ง/หอย/ปู
Phla pla-duk/pla in-see	พล่าปลาดุก/ปลาอินทรี

65

EATING AND DRINKING

Kapih-khua lonh	กะปิคั่วหลน
Taochiao lõnh	เต้าเจี้ยวหลน
Yam Yai	ยำใหญ่
Yam koung-lũang	ยำกุ้งหลวง
Yam hõi nang-rom	ยำหอยนางรม
Yam hõi-khraeng	ยำหอยแครง
Yam neua narm-tok	ยำเนื้อน้ำตก
Yam ma-muang	ยำมะม่วง
Yam woon-senh	ยำวุ้นเส้น

Narm-phrik

Narm-phrik ong Koung-haeng	น้ำพริกอ่อง น้ำพริกกุ้งแห้ง
Narm-phrik khai poo	น้ำพริกไข่ปู
Narm-phrik ma-muang/makhãrm	น้ำพริกมะม่วง/มะขาม
Narm-phrik pla-thu	น้ำพริกปลาทู

Khao phad (Fried rice)

Khao-phad poo	ข้าวผัดปู
Khao-phad kapih	ข้าวผัดกะปิ
Khao-phad narm-phrik	ข้าวผัดน้ำพริก
Khao-phad koung kari	ข้าวผัดกุ้งกะหรี่
Khao-phad sapparot	ข้าวผัดสับปะรด

66

EATING AND DRINKING

Special dishes

Haw-mok pla/kai	ห่อหมกปลา/ไก่
Haw-mok hed-fang	ห่อหมกเห็ดฟาง
Mōo wǎan	หมูหวาน
Neua-khem fōi phad wǎan	เนื้อเค็มฝอยผัดหวาน
Poo ob woon-senh	ปูอบวุ้นเส้น
Tom kathi saai-bua plathu	ต้มกะทิสายบัวปลาทู
Tom-som sapparot	ต้มส้มสับปะรด
Khanōm-chine narm ya	ขนมจีนน้ำยา
Khanōm-chine narm-phrik	ขนมจีนน้ำพริก
Phad phrik-khǐng	ผัดพริกขิง
Phra Rama long-sǒng	พระรามลงสรง

Thai desserts (**Khǒng Wǎnn**)

Bua-loi khai wǎan	บัวลอยไข่หวาน
Fak-thong kaeng buad	ฟักทองแกงบวด
Khanōm thian/ Khanōm sai-sai	ขนมเทียน/ขนมใส่ไส้
Khanōm khrong-khraeng kaew	ขนมครองแครงแก้ว
Khanōm maw-kaeng/ Louk-tarn sheuam	ขนมหม้อแกง/ลูกตาลเชื่อม
Khanōm thuai/ Khanōm shanh	ขนมถ้วย/ขนมชั้น

EATING AND DRINKING

Khanõm nĩao/Khanõm tom khão	ขนมเหนียว/ขนมต้มขาว
Khaonĩao piak lamyai	ข้าวเหนียวเปียกลำไย
Khaonĩao narm kathi thurian	ข้าวเหนียวน้ำกะทิทุเรียน
Kluai buad shee/Kluai sheuam	กล้วยบวชชี/กล้วยเชื่อม
Sãkhu-piak thua-damh	สาคูเปียกถั่วดำ
Sãngkhayã fak-thong/ Foi-thong	สังขยาฟักทอง/ฝอยทอง
Sake sheuam, thong-yip, thong-yawd	สาเกเชื่อม ทองหยิบ ทองหยอด
Manh kaeng buad/ Pheuak narm-kathi	มันแกงบวด/เผือกน้ำกะทิ
Manh sãmpalãng sheuam	มันสำปะหลังเชื่อม
Pheuak kaeng buad/Med khanõun	เผือกแกงบวด/เม็ดขนุน
Maphrao sãng-khayã	มะพร้าวสังขยา
Woon sãng khayã/ Woon kathi	วุ้นสังขยา/วุ้นกะทิ
Lawd-shong narm kathi/ Tako	ลอดช่องน้ำกะทิ/ตะโก้
Taeng-thai narm kathi	แตงไทยน้ำกะทิ
Pla-krim khai taow	ปลากริมไข่เต่า
Maled bua tom narm-tarn	เมล็ดบัวต้มน้ำตาล
Ruam-mit/Salim	รวมมิตร/ซ่าหริ่ม

68

EATING AND DRINKING

International Food

Wide Variety of Food Dishes for Travellers

Visitors to Thailand will of course find a great variety and excellence in the different culinary styles to be found in the foods served here. The variety of food offered would fill a whole guide book, and to run through a whole gamut in a sampling spree would take a month of hard digestion.

Bangkok, Thailand's 200-year-old metropolis, is a city full of intrigue and oriental mystery, and in its thousands of restaurants one can sample almost any cuisine of the world, ranging from steak and kidney pudding to borscht. There are many fine Chinese specialty restaurants, where menus cover the best of the rest of the northern and southern hemispheres. All five of the great regional cuisines of China — Hunan, Canton, Peking, Shanghai and Szechuan — are superbly represented in Bangkok. Thais are known as the gourmets of the Orient and the food served in Thai first class restaurants is in a class by itself: exotic, excellent, and comparatively inexpensive. If you want to eat like a king and enjoy all the choice dishes offered in Thai language menus, this book will help you discover new, delightful, dining experiences in Thailand.

Some selected specialities that are only to be found in Thailand are listed below for the guidance of newcomers. The restaurant may not serve all the dishes mentioned, but if you indicate the ones you want it will certainly provide something similar.

EATING AND DRINKING

Abalone soup	**Kaeng-chued pow-hue**	แกงจืดเป๋าฮื้อ
Asparagus salad	**Salad naw-mai farang**	สลัดหน่อไม้ฝรั่ง
Barbecued pork	**Mōudaeng sharsiew**	หมูแดงช้าซิ้ว
Beefsteak (Hainanese style)	**Steak Hailam**	สเต็กไหหลำ
Beef stew	**Satu neua**	สตูเนื้อ
Bitter melon stuffed with pork	**Marah sawd sai**	มะระสอดไส้
Boiled legs of pork with star anise	**Kha-mōo pha-lo**	ขาหมูพะโล้
Boiled viscera	**Khreuang nai wua tom-peui**	เครื่องในวัวต้มเปื่อย
Braised beef curry	**Phanaeng neua**	พะแนงเนื้อ
Chicken fried with bamboo shoots	**Kai phad naw-mai**	ไก่ผัดหน่อไม้
Chicken fried with basil leaves	**Kai phad kaphraow**	ไก่ผัดกะเพรา
Chicken fried with shredded ginger	**Kai phad khǐng**	ไก่ผัดขิง
Chicken fried with mushrooms	**Kai phad hed**	ไก่ผัดเห็ด
Chicken fried sweet sour	**Kai phad priao-wǎan**	ไก่ผัดเปรี้ยวหวาน

Chicken in clay pot	Kai ob maw-din	ไก่อบหม้อดิน
Chicken in wine sauce	Kai ob laow daeng	ไก่อบเหล้าแดง
Chicken masala	Kai phad kari haeng	ไก่ผัดกะหรี่แห้ง
Chicken rice	Khao-manh kai	ข้าวมันไก่
Chicken/crab salad	Salad kai/Salad poo	สลัดไก่/สลัดปู
Chop-suey	Phad chap-shaai	ผัดจับฉ่าย
Crab curry	Poo phad kari	ปูผัดกะหรี่
Crab roasted	Poo ob	ปูอบ
Crab fried with celery	Poo phad khuen-shaai	ปูผัดคื่นช่าย
Crabmeat omelette	Poo phad fu-yong-hai	ปูผัดฟูยงฮาย
Deep-fried crab's claws	Karm-poo thawd	ก้ามปูทอด
Deep fried rolls stuffed with minced pork & prawns	Hae kuen	แฮ่กึ๊น
Egg noodles fried with vegetables	Bah-mee phad raad-na	บะหมี่ผัดราดหน้า
Eggs fried & topped with sweet sauce	Khai louk-khẽui	ไข่ลูกเขย

71

EATING AND DRINKING

Fried meat with curry	Neua phad kari	เนื้อผัดกะหรี่
Fried beef with oyster sauce	Neua phad narm-manh hõi	เนื้อผัดน้ำมันหอย
Fried beef with shredded ginger/chillies	Neua phad khĩng/phad phrik	เนื้อผัดขิง/ผัดพริก
Fried fish patties	Thawd-manh pla	ทอดมันปลา
Fried frogs with chillies	Kob phad phed	กบผัดเผ็ด
Fried tao-hu with chopped pork	Phad tao-hu mõo-sab	ผัดเต้าหู้หมูสับ
Fried catfish with red hot chillies	Pla-duk phad phed	ปลาดุกผัดเผ็ด
Fried pomfret in gravy	Pla-charamed chĩan	ปลาจะละเม็ดเจี๋ยน
Fried prawns with red sauce	Koung-phad si-iew	กุ้งผัดซีอิ๊ว
Fried mussels with basil	Hõi-khraeng phad kaphrao	หอยแครงผัดกะเพรา
Fried pork and eggs	Khai-dao mõo-thawd	ไข่ดาว หมูทอด
Fried prawns with garlic and pepper	Koung phad krathiam phrik-thai	กุ้งผัดกะเทียมพริกไทย
Fried red snapper with brown sauce	Pla-kaphong narm-daeng	ปลากะพงน้ำแดง

72

EATING AND DRINKING

Fried rice with crabmeat	Khao-phad poo	ข้าวผัดปู
Fried rice with fishpaste	Khao-phad kapih	ข้าวผัดกะปิ
Morning Glory vegetables stir-fried	Phad phak-boung fai-daeng	ผัดผักบุ้งไฟแดง
Mutton curry	Kari phaeh	กะหรี่แพะ
Omelet (plain)	Khai chiao	ไข่เจียว
Omelet with minced pork	Khai-chiao mõo-sab	ไข่เจียวหมูสับ
Oysters omelette	Hõi thawd	หอยทอด
Ox-tongue stew	Satu lin-wua	สตูลิ้นวัว
Paper-wrapped chicken	Kai haw-kradard	ไก่ห่อกระดาษ
Peking sauce duck	Ped pucking	เป็ดปักกิ่ง
Pork toast	Khanõm-pang na mõo	ขนมปังหน้าหมู
Pig's trotters in brown sauce	Khã-mõo narm daeng	ขาหมูน้ำแดง
Popiah (pork rolls)	Popiah sai mõo	เปาะเปี๊ยะไส้หมู
Pork fried with garlic and pepper	Moo tha kathiam phrik-thai thawd	หมูทากระเทียมพริกไทยทอด
Pork fried with cloudears mushrooms	Mõo phad hed hõo-nõu	หมูผัดเห็ดหูหนู

73

EATING AND DRINKING

Potato soft balls	**Manh yat sai thawd**	มันยัดไส้ทอด
Poultry stuffed with ground mixture	**Kai sawd-sai ob**	ไก่สอดไส้อบ
Prawn/fish hot curry	**Kaeng-phed koung/pla**	แกงเผ็ดกุ้ง/ปลา
Prawn salad	**Salad koung**	สลัดกุ้ง
Prawns in shell grilled or boiled	**Koung phãow/ tom chim narm-pla**	กุ้งเผา/ต้ม จิ้มน้ำปลา
Pineapple fried rice	**Khao phad sapparot**	ข้าวผัดสับปะรด
Roast chicken/ roast duck	**Kai ob/Ped od**	ไก่อบ/เป็ดอบ
Roast pork/grilled pork	**Mõo ob/mõo yang**	หมูอบ/หมูย่าง
Roast suckling pig	**Louk-mõo yang**	ลูกหมูย่าง
Squid salad	**Yam pla-muek**	ยำปลาหมึก
Satay (beef)	**Satay neua**	สะเต๊ะเนื้อ
Satay (pork/ chicken)	**Satay mõo/kai**	สะเต๊ะหมู/ไก่
Sauteed frog legs	**Khã-kob phad**	ขากบผัด
Shark's fins soup	**Soup hõu-shalãrm**	ซุปหูฉลาม

EATING AND DRINKING

Steamed fish with Chinese pickled plums	**Pla-nueng kab kiam-buai**	ปลานึ่งกับเกี้ยมบ๊วย
Stir-fried squid with oyster sauce	**Pla-muek phad narm-manh hõi**	ปลาหมึกผัดน้ำมันหอย
Stuffed pig leg	**Khã-mõo sawd sai**	ขาหมูสอดไส้
Sweet-sour spare-ribs	**Si-khrong mõo phad priao-wãan**	ซี่โครงหมูผัดเปรี้ยวหวาน
Tomyam pig legs	**Khã-mõo tomyam**	ขาหมูต้มยำ
Yam pla-thu	**Yam pla-thu**	ยำปลาทู

Small Eating Foodstalls

For the selective diner in all categories of interest from gourmet to average hungry visitor, Bangkok offers an interesting eating opportunity matched by few cities of the world. Restaurants range from elegant and luxurious to delightful small eating foodstalls and back-street establishments which serve quick lunches and dinners. You can experience the thrill of watching your meals cooked right in front of you at these stalls and you can have a bowl of noodle soup as cheap as one US dollar or dine on very exotic dishes. Many épicures maintain that the food is better than at some of Bangkok's chic air-conditioned restaurants. In any event these foodstalls have become such a part of the Bangkok scene that anyone who has been here will tell you that a Bangkok tour is incomplete without a leisurely eating at one of the stalls. It's the "in" thing to do.

EATING AND DRINKING

Although some stalls open for the lunch-time crowds, most of these stall-chefs are content to cook their hearts-out for the dinner and late supper customers. Not only is a meal at the stalls tasty and cheap, but on the same menu are literally thousands of dishes—many of which are seldom served in Bangkok's plusher restaurants. Specialities that are well worth a try are:

Egg noodles laced with crabmeat, roasted pork and vegetables	**Bah-mee haeng**	บะหมี่แห้ง
Crisp-fried noodles with chicken and gravy topping	**Bah-mee na kai**	บะหมี่หน้าไก่
Egg noodles soup	**Bah-mee narm**	บะหมี่น้ำ
Egg noodles with boiled meat	**Bah-mee neua toon**	บะหมี่เนื้อตุ๋น
Soft porridge cooked in chicken stock with chunks of chicken or minced pork, shredded ginger and spring onions	**Choke kai/Choke mõo**	โจ๊กไก่/โจ๊กหมู

Spicy fish or prawns in a banana leaf cup with coconut cream, egg and vegetables, steamed in a large aluminium steamer	**Haw-mok pla/ Haw-mok koung**	ห่อหมกปลา/ห่อหมกกุ้ง
Fried oysters in egg batter.	**Hŏi thawd**	หอยทอด
Deep fried/grilled chicken, highly seasoned .	**Kai thawd/Kai yang**	ไก่ทอด/ไก่ย่าง
This best known dish is cooked at the table on either an electric heater, a small gas stove or a traditional charcoal stove. Thin slices of beef, squids, prawns, meat balls, vegetables,	**Kantasuki**	แคนต้าสุกี้

and transparent noodles are cooked in a sauce and then dipped in raw eggs before eating

Steamed shrimp dumplings	**Khanŏm-cheep khão**	ขนมจีบขาว
Steamed minced pork wrapped in a thin paste A Dim Sum.	**Khanŏm-cheep lẽuang**	ขนมจีบเหลือง
Spicy fish gravy served with soft rice vermicelli, peasprouts, basil leaves and chillies	**Khanŏm-chine narm-ya**	ขนมจีนน้ำยา
White rice delicately cooked with chicken stock, onions and garlic, served with preserved ginger	**Khao-manh kai hãilãm**	ข้าวมันไก่ไหหลำ

and slices of chicken.		
Glutinous rice wrapped in banana leaves.	**Khao-nĭao ping**	ข้าวเหนียวปิ้ง
Glutinous rice with curry topping.	**Khao-nĭao na kari**	ข้าวเหนียวหน้ากะหรี่
Glutinous rice with barbecued pork.	**Khao-nĭao na mŏo-daeng**	ข้าวเหนียวหน้าหมูแดง
Curry poured sizzling hot on plate of rice.	**Khao raad-na kaeng**	ข้าวราดหน้าแกง
Rice pillau or saffron rice cooked in ghee and coconut milk, served with braised chicken or beef, an Islamic favourite	**Khao-mok kai/ neua**	ข้าวหมกไก่/เนื้อ
Rice topped with fried chicken, bamboo shoots or mushrooms in gravy	**Khao na kai**	ข้าวหน้าไก่

EATING AND DRINKING

Rice mixed with fish paste, dried prawns and egg, served with cucumber, spring onions and sliced lemon	**Khao khluk kapih**	ข้าวคลุกกะปิ
Rice mixed with fish or prawn paste and then fried with pork (slightly sweetened) or lobster, served with cucumber, spring onions and sliced lemon	**Khao phad kapih**	ข้าวผัดกะปิ
Small dish-shaped cake made of rice flour and coconut cream	**Khanõm- khrok**	ขนมครก
Steamed batter with a sweet filling.	**Khao-kriab paak maw**	ข้าวเกรียบปากหม้อ
A north-eastern relish composed of sliced green	**Khao-nĩao, somtam**	ข้าวเหนียวส้มตำ

papaya, pounded
dried shrimp and
toasted rice,
flavoured with
fish sauce, chil-
lies and brown
sugar, served
with steamed
glutinous rice

Boiled rice with pork, fish or prawns	**Khao-tom mõo/ pla/koung**	ข้าวต้มหมู/ปลา/กุ้ง
Wan-thanh or Chinese ravioli soup	**Kiao narm**	เกี๊ยวน้ำ
Fried flat rice noodles laced with pork and vegetables in gravy sauce	**Kwaitĩao raad-na**	ก๋วยเตี๋ยวราดหน้า
A clear beef soup with rice noodles and boiled meat	**Kwaitĩao neua peui**	ก๋วยเตี๋ยวเนื้อเปื่อย
Fried rice noodles topped with a thick stew of	**Kwaitĩao neua-sab**	ก๋วยเตี๋ยวเนื้อสับ

minced pork or meat		
Boiled duck with flat rice noodles served in soup'	**Kwaitĩao ped**	ก๋วยเตี๋ยวเป็ด
Fried rice noodles with egg, peasprouts, onion grass, dried prawns and chillies	**Kwaitĩao phad Thai**	ก๋วยเตี๋ยวผัดไทย
Deep-fried long strip dough	**Pa thong kõ**	ปาท่องโก๋
A crisp, deep fried spring roll stuffed with pork, bamboo shoots, beancurd cheese, peasprouts, served with sweetened sauce	**Poh-piah thawd**	เปาะเปี๊ยะทอด
A barbecue in which small pieces of pork, chicken or beef are marinated for	**Satay mõo/ kai or neua**	สะเต๊ะหมู/ไก่หรือเนื้อ

several hours, skewered and barbecued over a charcoal fire, served with cucumber, onion and sauce made from coconut cream, peanuts, spices and a little chilli		
A doughy bun stuffed with bar-becued or minced pork and steamed. A Dim Sum.	**Salapaow mõo sab/Salapaow mõo-daeng**	ซาลาเปาหมูสับ ซาลาเปาหมูแดง
Crisp fried nood-les with topping	**Senh-mee thawd krob raad-na**	เส้นหมี่ทอดกรอบ ราดหน้า
Spicy soup strongly flavoured with lemon grass, kaffir leaves, lime juice and chillies. It is made from	**Tomyam koung/ kai/mõo/pla**	ต้มยำกุ้ง/ไก่/หมู/ปลา

EATING AND DRINKING

shrimp or
lobster, chicken,
pork, fish or
fish-head.

The most surprising aspect about eating in Thailand is that first
class food need not be expensive. There are some excellent restaurants and eating houses which offer good food at little more
than prices charged at hawker stalls. However, it should be pointed
out that Thais take great pride in the cleanliness of their food
stalls, and the law makes provision for operators maintaining high
standards of hygiene. It helps make eating a pleasure at the stalls.

EATING AND DRINKING

Thailand's Coffee Shops

The coffee shop is the social symbol of equality between men and women in modern Thailand. Coffee is often merely the excuse for inexpensive and varied recreation. In the landscape of leisure, the coffee shop occupies a region fringed on the business conference room on one extreme and the nightclub on the other. Cheerful waitresses deliver coffee, cakes and sandwiches on request—or tea, beer, whiskey and food if required. Whether for a semi-private business conference, or a break from office routine, the appointment usually is: "Meet me at the such-and-such coffee shop." This will be a quiet room with comfortable seats around small tables where a cup of coffee costs 20 or 25 Baht each — an ideal rendezvous.

List of Drinks

Aerated water	Narm att-lom	น้ำอัดลม
Beer (light)	Beer khão	เบียร์ขาว
Beer (dark/stout)	Beerdamh/ stout	เบียร์ดำ สเตาท์
Brandy (French/ Thai)	Barandi (Farangset/Thai)	บรั่นดีฝรั่งเศส/ไทย
Chocolate (hot/ cold)	Koko (ronn/ yenh)	โกโก้ร้อน/เย็น
Coconut water	Narm maphrao onn	น้ำมะพร้าวอ่อน
Coffee (hot black)	Kafae damh ronn	กาแฟดำร้อน
Coffee (hot white)	Kafae ronn sai-nom	กาแฟร้อนใส่นม

EATING AND DRINKING

Coffee (cold black)	**Kafae damh yenh**	กาแฟดำเย็น
Coffee (cold white)	**Kafae yenh sai-nom**	กาแฟเย็นใส่นม
Coffee expresso	**Kafae expresso**	กาแฟเอ็กซ์เพรสโซ
Ice (crushed)	**Narm-khãeng konn**	น้ำแข็งก้อน
Ice (with syrup)	**Narm-khãeng sai narm-wãan**	น้ำแข็งใส่น้ำหวาน
Juice (orange)	**Narm-som/Narm-som khan**	น้ำส้ม/น้ำส้มคั้น
Juice (lemon)	**Narm manao**	น้ำมะนาว
Juice (palm)	**Narm-tarn sod**	น้ำตาลสด
Juice (pineapple)	**Narm sapparot khan**	น้ำสับปะรดคั้น
Milk (fresh cow)	**Nom-wua sod**	นมวัวสด
Milk (sweetened condensed)	**Nom-khon wãan**	นมข้นหวาน
Milk (UHT)	**Nom-sod UHT**	นมสดยูเอสที
Mineral water	**Narm rae**	น้ำแร่
Soda / Soda water	**Soda/Narm soda**	โซดา/น้ำโซดา
Sugarcane water	**Narm oi-khan**	น้ำอ้อยคั้น
Tea (hot black)	**Sha damh ronn**	ชาดำร้อน
Tea (hot white)	**Sha ronn sai-nom**	ชาร้อนใส่นม
Tea (cold black)	**Sha damh yenh**	ชาดำเย็น
Tea (cold white)	**Sha yenh sai-nom**	ชาเย็นใส่นม
Tea (Chinese)	**Sha chine**	ชาจีน

EATING AND DRINKING

Water (plain)	Narm	น้ำ
Water (previously boiled)	Narm souk	น้ำสุก
Water (hot boiling)	Narm ronn	น้ำร้อน
Water (iced / cold)	Narm yenh	น้ำเย็น
Thai whisky (Mekhong/ Saeng-Som)	Thai whisky (Mekhong/ Sãeng-Sõm)	ไทยวิสกี้ (แม่โขง แสงโสม)
Wine	Laow a-ngun	เหล้าองุ่น

General Conversation

Can you recommend a good restaurant, nothing too expensive?	Khun rouchak raan a-hãrn di rakha mai-phaeng mãi?	คุณรู้จักร้านอาหารดี ราคาไม่แพงไหม
Could we have a private room?	Khun mi hong-diao phiset mãi?	คุณมีห้องเดี่ยวพิเศษไหม
We want a large table.	Raow tongkarn toh yai.	เราต้องการโต๊ะใหญ่
I want a table for two.	Phõm tongkarn toh sãmrap sõng khon.	ผมต้องการโต๊ะสำหรับ สองคน
I want to eat something right now.	Phõm tongkarn tharn a-rai sak yang dĩao-ni.	ผมต้องการทานอะไร สักอย่างเดี๋ยวนี้

EATING AND DRINKING

I am hungry.	Phŏm hĩew.	ผมหิว
Anything will do.	Tham a-rai kaw-dai.	ทำอะไรก็ได้
Do you have a menu in English?	Banshi a-hǎrn bhasǎ Angkrit mi mãi?	บัญชีอาหารภาษาอังกฤษ มีไหม
What do you recommend?	Chah tham a-rai hai tharn?	จะทำอะไรให้ทาน
My wife is accustomed to Chinese food.	Phanraya-phom shob a-harn chine.	ภรรยาผมชอบอาหารจีน
Where is the waitress?	Dek-rap-shai pai nai?	เด็กรับใช้ไปไหน
Please switch on the fan.	Karuna perd phad-lom.	กรุณาเปิดพัดลม
I am fearfully thirsty.	Phŏm kra-hǎi narm maak.	ผมกระหายน้ำมาก
Please let me have......	Phŏm khaw......	ผมขอ......
– something refreshing	– arai yen-yen duem	– อะไรเย็นๆ ดื่ม
– whisky and soda	– whisky lae soda	– วิสกี้และโซดา
– French brandy	– Barandi farangset	– บรั่นดีฝรั่งเศส
– Thai whisky	– Thai Whisky	– วิสกี้ไทย
– Beer / Stout	– Beer/Beer damh	– เบียร์/เบียร์ดำ

EATING AND DRINKING

– some crushed ice	– narm-khãeng konn	– น้ำแข็งก้อน
I like to eat grilled chicken.	Phõm shob tharn kai-yang.	ผมชอบทานไก่ย่าง
I am very fond of eating hot food.	Phõm shob tharn a-hãrn phed-phed.	ผมชอบทานอาหารเผ็ดๆ
I'd like to eat Indian chicken curry.	Phõm yaak tharn kari-kai khaek.	ผมอยากทานกะหรี่ไก่ แขก
I will take some fish.	Phõm chah rab-pratharn plã.	ผมจะรับประทานปลา
I like fish very much.	Phõm shob pla maak.	ผมชอบปลามาก
Could I have......?	Khun mi...... mai?	คุณมี......ไหม
– European type sausages	– Sai-krawk farang	– ไส้กรอกฝรั่ง
– fried potatoes	– manh-farang thawd krob	– มันฝรั่งทอดกรอบ
– roasted ground-nuts	– thua-lisõng khua	– ถั่วลิสงคั่ว
– fried chicken	– kai thawd	– ไก่ทอด
– fried rice	– khao-phad	– ข้าวผัด
– chicken on rice	– khao na-kai	– ข้าวหน้าไก่
– Thai fish curry	– kaeng-phed pla	– แกงเผ็ดปลา
– stuffed omelet	– khai sawd-sai	– ไข่สอดไส้

89

EATING AND DRINKING

– prawns fried sweet sour	– koung phad priao wãan	กุ้งผัดเปรี้ยวหวาน
– prawn tomyam	– tomyam koung	ต้มยำกุ้ง
– Chinese vegetable soup	– kaeng-chued phak	แกงจืดผัก
– chicken fried with basil leaves	– kai phad kaphraow	ไก่ผัดกะเพรา
– plain rice	– khao plao	ข้าวเปล่า
Please let me have......	Phõm khãw......	ผมขอ......
– a pair of chopsticks	– takiab nueng khou	ตะเกียบหนึ่งคู่
– fork/spoon/ knife	– somm/shonn/ meed	ส้อม/ช้อน/มีด
– paper napkins	– kradad shed-paak	กระดาษเช็ดปาก
– extra plate	– chaan	จาน
– a glass/a cup	– thuai-kaew/ thuai sha	ถ้วยแก้ว/ถ้วยชา
– some toothpicks	– mai-chim-fanh	ไม้จิ้มฟัน
– salt and pepper	– kleua lae phrikthai	เกลือและพริกไทย
– tomato ketchup	– sauce makheua thesh	ซ้อสมะเขือเทศ
– Thai fish sauce	– narm pla	น้ำปลา
– Chinese sauce	– narm si-iew	น้ำซีอิ๊ว
– chilli vinegar	– phrik narm-som	พริกน้ำส้ม

EATING AND DRINKING

– Worcestershire sauce	– sauce angkrit	– ซ้อสอังกฤษ/ซ้อสฝรั่ง
I would like to have......	Phŏm khăw......	ผมขอ......
– hot black coffee	– kafae damh ronn	– กาแฟดำร้อน
– hot coffee with milk	– kafae ronn sai nom	– กาแฟร้อนใส่นม
– cold black coffee/tea	– owe-liang/ sha-damh yenh	– โอเลี้ยง/ชาดำเย็น
Put in two spoons of sugar.	Sai narm-tarn sŏng shonn.	ใส่น้ำตาลสองช้อน
I will put the sugar in myself.	Phŏm sai narm-tarn eng.	ผมใส่น้ำตาลเอง
No milk. No sugar.	Mai sai nom. Mai sai nam-tam.	ไม่ใส่นม ไม่ใส่น้ำตาล
Bring me another cup of coffee/ tea.	Aow kafae/Sha ik thuai.	เอากาแฟ/ชาอีกถ้วย
Give me the same.	Hai phŏm yang diao kanh.	ให้ผมอย่างเดียวกัน
Do you have......?	Khun mi...... mãi?	คุณมี......ไหม
– coconut ice cream	– ice-cream maphrao	– ไอศกรีมมะพร้าว
– orange squash	– narm-som khanh	– น้ำส้มคั้น
– coconut water	– namm maphrao onn	– น้ำมะพร้าวอ่อน

91

EATING AND DRINKING

– sugarcane water	– narm oi	– น้ำอ้อย
– Chinese tea	– sha chine	– ชาจีน
– Thai cakes	– khanom Thai	– ขนมไทย
– desserts	– khõng wãan	– ของหวาน
– filter-tip cigarettes	– buri kon krong	– บุหรี่ก้นกรอง
– cigarettes without filters	– buri thammada	– บุหรี่ธรรมดา
– box of matches	– mai khide fai	– ไม้ขีดไฟ
– an ash-tray	– thi khia buri	– ที่เขี่ยบุหรี่
– chilled towels	– pha yen	– ผ้าเย็น
Do you have any fruit?	Khun mi pholamai mãi?	คุณมีผลไม้ไหม
– Tangerine oranges	– Som khiao wãan	– ส้มเขียวหวาน
– Pumelo	– Som oh	– ส้มโอ
– Pineapple	– Sapparot	– สับปะรด
– Custard apple	– Noi-na	– น้อยหน่า
– Fragrant banana	– Kluai hõmm	– กล้วยหอม
– Papaya	– Malakaw	– มะละกอ
– Mangosteen	– Mang-khoud	– มังคุด
– Mangoes	– Ma-muang	– มะม่วง
– Watermelon	– Taeng Mo	– แตงโม
– Sapodilla	– Lamoud	– ละมุด
Where is the toilet, please?	Hong-suam/ Hong-narm you nãi?	ห้องส้วมห้องน้ำอยู่ไหน

EATING AND DRINKING

Do you want some more rice?	**Khun tongkarn khao ik mãi?**	คุณต้องการข้าวอีกไหม
Nothing more, thank you.	**Mai aow a-rai ik, Khob khun.**	ไม่เอาอะไรอีก, ขอบคุณ
How much all together?	**Thang-mod ruam kanh thaorai?**	ทั้งหมดรวมกันเท่าไร
Here is something for you.	**Ni sãmrab khun.**	นี่สำหรับคุณ
The food was tasty.	**Ahãm aroi di.**	อาหารอร่อยดี

Complaints

Please call the Manager/ Proprietor.	**Khãw phob Phu-chad-karn/ Thowkae.**	ขอพบผู้จัดการ/เถ้าแก่
Your food was very hot!	**A-hãm khun phed chang!**	อาหารคุณเผ็ดจัง
This is not fresh.	**Ni mai sod.**	นี่ไม่สด
This is too fat.	**Ni manh maak.**	นี่มันมาก
This is too sweet.	**Ni wãan maak.**	นี่หวานมาก
This is too salty.	**Ni khem maak.**	นี่เค็มมาก
This is not well cooked.	**Ni yang mai souk.**	นี่ยังไม่สุก
This curry is too hot.	**Kaeng ni phed maak.**	แกงนี้เผ็ดมาก

93

EATING AND DRINKING

This fork is dirty.	Somm sok-ka-prok.	ส้อมสกปรก
The spoon is not clean.	Shonn shed mai sa-ard.	ช้อนเช็ดไม่สะอาด
I didn't order this.	Chaan ni phõm mai dai sang.	จานนี้ผมไม่ได้สั่ง
Can I change this?	Phõm khãw plian dai mai?	ผมขอเปลี่ยนได้ไหม
The service is too slow.	Borikarn sha maak.	บริการช้ามาก
It is very noisy here.	Thi-ni nuak-hõo.	ที่นี่หนวกหู

Paying the Bill

Give me the bill, please.	Phõm khãw bill.	ผมขอบิล
Is the service charge included?	Kha borikarn ruam duai rũe-plao?	ค่าบริการรวมด้วยหรือเปล่า
You have charged too much for this.	Rai-karn ni khun khid phaeng kern pai.	รายการนี้คุณคิดแพงเกินไป
We did not have this.	Rai-karn ni mai dai hai ma.	รายการนี้ไม่ได้ให้มา
I know that. I am not blaming you.	Phõm saab. Phõm mai wa a-rai khun.	ผมทราบ ผมไม่ว่าอะไรคุณ

EATING AND DRINKING

There is a mistake in the bill.	**Rai-karn yang mai thouk tong.**	รายการยังไม่ถูกต้อง
Check it, please.	**Proad truat sĩa mai.**	โปรดตรวจเสียใหม่
I will not pay this.	**Rai karn ni phõm mai chaai.**	รายการนี้ผมไม่จ่าย
That's not what I ordered.	**Phõm mai dai sang yang ni.**	ผมไม่ได้สั่งอย่างนี้
Do you accept travellers' cheques?	**Khun rab cheques dern-thang mãi?**	คุณรับเช็คเดินทางไหม
Will you change this sum, and give me Thai baht?	**Khaw laek penh ngoen Thai dai mãi?**	ขอแลกเป็นเงินไทยได้ไหม
That was a very good meal.	**A-hãrn a-roi di.**	อาหารอร่อยดี
We'll come again next time.	**O-kas na raow chah ma ik.**	โอกาสหน้าเราจะมาอีก

MARKETING

Marketing

Market Produce and Glossary of Local Names

The following lists include meats and poultry, fishes, vegetables and fruits, groceries, currystuffs, etc. Each product is listed under its English name, also under its Thai name.

Meats and Poultry

Bacon	Mõo-bekon	หมูเบคอน
Bone	Kradouk	กระดูก
Brains	Samõng	สมอง
Breast	Na-ok	หน้าอก
Broiler chicken	Kai-shamlae	ไก่ชำแหละ
Calves' feet	Khã louk-wua	ขาลูกวัว
Capon	Kai tonn	ไก่ตอน
Chicken wings	Peek-kai	ปีกไก่
Chicken thighs	Nong-kai	น่องไก่
Chuck	Neua-lai	เนื้อไหล่
Dried beef	Neua haeng	เนื้อแห้ง
Duck/duckling	Ped/Louk-ped	เป็ด/ลูกเป็ด
Fillet or tenderloin	Sãn-nai	สันใน
Flare fat	Manh-pleow	มันเปลว
Fore shank	Neua-khã na	เนื้อขาหน้า
Giblets	Khreuang-nai	เครื่องใน

Ground beef	Neua bod	เนื้อบด
Heart	Hũa-chai	หัวใจ
Hind shank	Neua-khã lãng	เนื้อขาหลัง
Kidneys	Tai	ไต
Lard	Manh-moo chiao	มันหมูเจียว
Leg	Khã	ขา
Liver	Tab	ตับ
Loin strip	Neua-sãnh nawk	เนื้อสันนอก
Meat	Neua	เนื้อ
Meat scraps	Sesh-neua	เศษเนื้อ
Minced pork	Mõo-sab	หมูสับ
Mutton	Phaeh	แพะ
Ox tail	Hãang-wua	หางวัว
Ox tongue	Lin-wua	ลิ้นวัว
Pig's trotters	Khã-mõo	ขาหมู
Pork belly	Mõo sãnm-shanh	หมูสามชั้น
Pork lard	Manh-pleow	มันเปลว
Pork fillet	Sãnh-nai moo	สันในหมู
Pork lean	Neua-mõo tit-manh	เนื้อหมูติดมัน
Pork skin	Nang mõo	หนังหมู
Pullet	Kai noum / Kai são	ไก่หนุ่ม/ไก่สาว
Ribs	Si-khrong	ซี่โครง
Round of beef	Neua ta-phoke	เนื้อตะโพก
Rump	Neua kon-kob	เนื้อก้นกบ
Shank	Neua na-khaeng	เนื้อหน้าแข้ง

MARKETING

Short loin	Neua-sãnh tit sikhrong	เนื้อสันติดซี่โครง
Shoulder fillet	Neua-lai	เนื้อไหล่
Sirloin	Neua-san ok	เนื้อสันอก
Spare ribs	Si-khrong onn	ซี่โครงอ่อน
Standing ribs	Sãn-nawk tit sikhrong	สันนอกติดซี่โครง
Suckling pig	Louk-mõo yang	ลูกหมูย่าง
Suet	Manh-khãeng	มันแข็ง
Stew meat	Neua satu	เนื้อสตู
Sweetbread	Tab onn	ตับอ่อน
T-bone	Sãn tit-kradouk	สันติดกระดูก
Tongue	Lin	ลิ้น
Turkey	Kai-nguang	ไก่งวง
Veal	Neua louk-wua	เนื้อลูกวัว

Fishes

Anabus	Pla-mãw Thai	ปลาหมอไทย
Bass	Pla kaphong	ปลากะพง
Barracuda	Pla narm dork-mai	ปลาน้ำดอกไม้
Butter catfish	Pla neua-onn	ปลาเนื้ออ่อน
Butter fish	Pla charamed	ปลาจะละเม็ด
Catfish	Pladuk daan	ปลาดุกด้าน
Catlocarpio	Pla kraho	ปลากะโห้
Clarias macrocephalus	Pladuk oui	ปลาดุกอุย

98

Chinese carp	Pla lin-hue	ปลาลิ้นฮื้อ
Chirocentrus dorab	Pla darb-lao	ปลาดาบเลา
Cuttlefish	Pla-muek	ปลาหมึก
Cybium	Pla ln-see	ปลาอินทรี
Dangila	Pla taphian-saai	ปลาตะเพียนทราย
Dorosoma chacunda	Pla khoke	ปลาโคก
Eel (swamp)	Pla lāi	ปลาไหล
Featherback	Pla kraai	ปลากราย
Flathead gudgeon (goby)	Pla boo	ปลาบู่
Flatfish (florender)	Pla ta-diao	ปลาตาเดียว
Gar fish	Pla krathung-hĕow	ปลากระทุงเหว
Giant gouramy	Pla raed	ปลาแรด
Giant herring	Pla taleuak	ปลาตาเหลือก
Giant seaperch	Pla kaphong khāo	ปลากะพงขาว
Gizzard shad	Pla takoke	ปลาตะโกก
Grouper	Pla karang daeng	ปลากะรังแดง
Helostoma temminncki	Pla bai-tarn	ปลาใบตาล
Hilsa	Pla taloum-phuk	ปลาตะลุมพุก
Jewfish	Pla chuad	ปลาจวด
Kingfish (black banded)	Pla sām-lee	ปลาสำลี
Labeobarbus	Pla wien	ปลาเวียน
Lares calcarifer	Kaphong narm-chued	กะพงน้ำจืด
Ladyfish	Pla krabork	ปลากระบอก
Lizard fish	Pla tuk-kae	ปลาตุ๊กแก

MARKETING

Mackerel (rake gilled)	Pla-thu	ปลาทู
Milky whitefish	Pla nuan-chand	ปลานวลจันทร์
Notopterus	Pla chalard	ปลาฉลาด
Ophicephalus striatus	Pla shado	ปลาชะโด
Oriental sole, a flounder	Pla lin-mā	ปลาลิ้นหมา
Rachycentron	Pla shonn tha-lé	ปลาช่อนทะเล
Rastrelliger	Pla lang	ปลาลัง
Red snapper	Pla kaphong daeng	ปลากะพงแดง
Ribbon fish	Pla darb-ngoen	ปลาดาบเงิน
Sardinella melanura	Pla lāng-khīao	ปลาหลังเขียว
Scad (*cavalla*)	Pla si-kun	ปลาสิกุน
Serpenthead fish	Pla shonn	ปลาช่อน
Shark	Pla shalārm	ปลาฉลาม
Sphyraena	Pla dork-sark	ปลาดอกสาก
Spotted catfish	Pla kod	ปลากด
Squid	Pla-muek lek	ปลาหมึกเล็ก
Striped bass	Pla kaphong laai	ปลากะพงลาย
Tassel fish	Pla kuraow	ปลากุเลา
Thai goramy	Pla salid	ปลาสลิด
Tilapia	Pla-māw thesh	ปลาหมอเทศ
Tilapia nilotica	Pla nil	ปลานิล
Tuna	Pla hāng-khāeng	ปลาทางแข็ง
Tunny	Pla owe	ปลาโอ
Wallago	Pla khow	ปลาเค้า

| Whitefish (milky) | Pla bai khanŭn | ปลาใบขนุน |

Mollusks and Crustaceans

Abalone	Hŏi-khong thalé	หอยโข่งทะเล
Blue-legged lobsters	Koung karm-kram	กุ้งก้ามกราม
Clams	Hŏi-karb	หอยกาบ
Clams (sea)	Hŏi talab	หอยตลับ
Cockles (ark shell)	Hŏi khraeng	หอยแครง
Crab	Poo	ปู
Crab (horse)	Poo-thalé	ปูทะเล
Crab (purse)	Poo ma	ปูม้า
Donax foba	Hŏi-siab	หอยเสียบ
Modiola (horse mussels)	Hŏi kaphong	หอยกะพง
Penaeus (tiger prawns)	Koung shae-buai	กุ้งแชบ้วย
Metaphenaeus	Koung takard	กุ้งตะกาด
Ostrea edulis	Hŏi nang rom	หอยนางรม
Prawns (pink)	Koung o-khak	กุ้งโอค้ก
Sea mussels	Hŏi malaeng-phu	หอยแมลงภู่
Shrimp	Koung nang	กุ้งนาง
Trepang	Pling tha-lé	ปลิงทะเล
Vermetus sp.	Hŏi lawd	หอยหลอด
Vivipara doliaris	Hŏi khŏm	หอยขม

MARKETING

Vegetables

Ash-pumpkin	Fak khĩao	ฟักเขียว
Asparagus	Naw-mai farang	หน่อไม้ฝรั่ง
Bamboo shoot	Naw-mai Thai	หน่อไม้ไทย
Basil	Kaphrao	กะเพรา
Bay leaves	Bai krawaan	ใบกระวาน
Beans	Thua	ถั่ว
Beansprouts	Thua-ngork hua-yai	ถั่วงอกหัวใหญ่
Beetroot	Phak-kard daeng	ผักกาดแดง
Bell pepper	Phrik yuak	พริกหยวก
Bird chillies	Phrik khee-noo	พริกขี้หนู
Bitter melon	Ma-rah	มะระ
Black beans	Thua-damh	ถั่วดำ
Bonavista beans	Thua-paeb	ถั่วแปบ
Bottle gourd	Narm-taow	น้ำเต้า
Brinjal (green)	Makhẽua khĩao	มะเขือเขียว
Brinjal (aubergines)	Makhẽua muang	มะเขือม่วง
Cabbage	Kalampli	กะหล่ำปลี
Carrot	Khaerot	แครอท
Cassava	Manh-sãm-palãng	มันสำปะหลัง
Cauliflower	Dork kalam	ดอกกะหล่ำ
Celery	Khuen-shai	คื่นไฉ
Chai-sim	Phak-kwangtung	ผักกวางตุ้ง
Chick pea	Thua khaek	ถั่วแขก

Chillies (green)	Phrik cheefa khĭao	พริกชี้ฟ้าเขียว
Chillies (red)	Phrik cheefa daeng	พริกชี้ฟ้าแดง
Chinese kale	Phak khana	ผักคะน้า
Chinese mustard	Phak-kard khĭao	ผักกาดเขียว
Chinese parsley	Phak-shee	ผักชี
Chinese white cabbage	Phak-kard khăo	ผักกาดขาว
Chinese radish (Parsnip)	Shai-thaow	ไข้เท้า
Cucumber	Taeng-kwa	แตงกวา
Garlic	Krathiam	กระเทียม
Gherkin	Taeng-nŏo	แตงหนู
Gourd	Buab	บวบ
Green gram	Thua khĭao	ถั่วเขียว
Groundnuts	Thua-lisong	ถั่วลิสง
Haricot beans	Thua farangset	ถั่วฝรั่งเศส
Horse radish	Ma-roum	มะรุม
Kohl-Rabi	Kalam-pom	กะหล่ำปม
Lady's fingers	Krachiap khăo	กระเจี๊ยบขาว
Leek	Krathiam farang	กระเทียมฝรั่ง
Lettuce	Phak-kard hŏmm	ผักกาดหอม
Lima beans	Thua fak-yao	ถั่วฝักยาว
Loofah (angled)	Buab liam	บวบเหลี่ยม
Mint leaves	Bai sāra-nae	ใบสาระแหน่
Neptunia reracea	Phak ka-shet	ผักกะเฉด
Okra	Krachiap monn	กระเจี๊ยบมอญ

MARKETING

Onion grass	Kui-shai	กุยช่าย
Onions large/small	Hõmm yai/hõmm lek	หอมใหญ่/หอมเล็ก
Peasprouts	Thua-ngork hua lek	ถั่วงอกหัวเล็ก
Pigeon peas	Thua-raeh	ถั่วแระ
Pig weed	Phak-khõm	ผักขม
Potato	Manh farang	มันฝรั่ง
Pueraria phaseoloides	Thua khat-shu	ถั่วคัดฉุ
Pumpkin	Fak-thong	ฟักทอง
Radish	Phak-kard hua nõo	ผักกาดหัวหนู
Rice beans	Thua daeng	ถั่วแดง
Roselle	Krachiap daeng	กระเจี๊ยบแดง
Snake gourd	Buab ngoo	บวบงู
Soya beans	Thua lẽuang	ถั่วเหลือง
Sponge gourd	Buab hõmm	บวบหอม
Spring onions	Tonh hõmm	ต้นหอม
Sugar pea	Thua lan-tow	ถั่วลันเตา
Sword or Jack beans	Thua phra	ถั่วพร้า
Sweet basil	Bai maeng-lak	ใบแมงลัก
Sweet corn	Khao-phode wãan	ข้าวโพดหวาน
Sweet potato	Man-thesh	มันเทศ
Taro	Pheuak	เผือก
Tomato	Makhẽua-thesh	มะเขือเทศ
Water convolvulus	Phak-boung	ผักบุ้ง
Water cress	Phaeng-phuai	แพงพวย

104

Winged beans	**Thua-phoo**	ถั่วพู
Yam	**Pheuak hŭa-lek**	เผือกหัวเล็ก
Yam bean	**Manh-kaew**	มันแกว
Yellow beans	**Thua thong**	ถั่วทอง

Fruits

For tropical fruit Thailand offers a vast choice which surely can suit every taste. Mangoes, pineapples, mangosteen, bananas, jackfruits, custard apples, rambutans, dragon's eyes and of course the king of all fruits, the durian. The following list of fruits must suffice to introduce some of them to the reader.

Bael	**Ma-toom**	มะตูม
Banana (fragrant)	**Kluai-hŏmm**	กล้วยหอม
Bitter orange	**Som-kliang**	ส้มเกลี้ยง
Breadfruit	**Sã-ke**	สาเก
Bullock's heart	**Noi-noang**	น้อยโหน่ง
Cantaloup	**Taeng-laai**	แตงลาย
Carambola	**Mafeuang**	มะเฟือง
Cashew nuts	**Manuang hĭmapharn**	มะม่วงหิมพานต์
Coconut	**Ma-phrao**	มะพร้าว
Custard apple	**Noi-na**	น้อยหน่า
Durian	**Thurian**	ทุเรียน
Elephant apple	**Ma-kwid**	มะขวิด
Garcinia schomburgkiana	**Madan**	มะดัน

105

MARKETING

English	Thai (romanized)	Thai
Guava	**Farang**	ฝรั่ง
Jambu ayer	**Shomphu khĭao**	ชมพู่เขียว
Jackfruit	**Khanoun/Champa-dak**	ขนุน/จัมปาดะ
Lady's fingers bananas	**Kluai leb-mue-nang**	กล้วยเล็บมือนาง
Langsat	**Langsad**	ลางสาด
Limes (*Cilrus auranti folia*)	**Manao lek**	มะนาวเล็ก
Longan berry	**Ma-fai**	มะไฟ
Lychee	**Linchee**	ลิ้นจี่
Loongan (dragon's eyes)	**Lamyai**	ลำไย
Mandarin orange	**Som-chine**	ส้มจีน
Mango	**Ma-muang**	มะม่วง
Manila tamarind	**Makhărm-thesh**	มะขามเทศ
Mangosteen	**Mang-khud**	มังคุด
Marian plum	**Ma-prang**	มะปราง
Musk melon	**Taeng-thai**	แตงไทย
Neck orange	**Som-chouk**	ส้มจุก
Nipa fruit (palm fruit)	**Louk-chark**	ลูกจาก
Omblic, myrobalan	**Makhărm-pomm**	มะขามป้อม
Papaya	**Malakaw**	มะละกอ
Persimmon	**Louk-phlab**	ลูกพลับ
Phyllanthus distichus	**Mayom**	มะยม
Pineapple	**Sapparot**	สับปะรด

Pomegranate	Thab-thim	ทับทิม
Pumelo	Som-oh	ส้มโอ
(Shaddock)		
Rambutan	Ngoh	เงาะ
Roseapple	Shomphu narm-dorkmai	ชมพู่น้ำดอกไม้
Santol	Krathorn	กะท้อน
Sapodilla (Chiku)	Lamoud	ละมุด
Solamum ferox	Ma-uek	มะอึก
Soursop	Thurian-thesh	ทุเรียนเทศ
Tamarind	Ma-khãrm thai	มะขามไทย
Tangerine orange	Som-khĩao-wãan	ส้มเขียวหวาน
Watermelon	Taeng-mo	แตงโม
Crab-apple	Phud-sa	พุทรา

Curry-stuffs

Asafoetida	Mahã-hing	มหาหิงส์
Cardamom	Krawaan	กระวาน
Cinnamon	Ob-sheui	อบเชย
Cloves	Karn-phlu	กานพลู
Coriander seeds	Maled phak-shee	เมล็ดผักชี
Coriander roots	Raak phak-shee	รากผักชี
Cumin seeds	Maled yira	เมล็ดยี่หร่า
Curry powder	Phõng kari	ผงกะหรี่
Dried red chillies	Phrik-haeng	พริกแห้ง
Galanga	Kha	ข่า

MARKETING

Ginger (green)	**Khĭng sod**	ขิงสด
Ginger (dried)	**Khĭng haeng**	ขิงแห้ง
Kaffir limes	**Ma-krood**	มะกรูด
Kaffir leaves	**Bai ma-krood**	ใบมะกรูด
Kaempheria pandurata	**Kra-shaai**	กระชาย
Lemon grass	**Ta-khrai**	ตะไคร้
Licorice	**Cha-ém**	ชะเอม
Mace	**Dorkchand-thesh**	ดอกจันทร์เทศ
Nutmeg	**Louk-chand thesh**	ลูกจันทร์เทศ
Onions (large)	**Hŏmm yai**	หอมใหญ่
Paprika	**Phrik-daeng ponh**	พริกแดงป่น
Pepper	**Phrik-thai**	พริกไทย
Saffron	**Ya-faranh**	หญ้าฝรั่น
Star anise	**Poai-kak**	โป๊ยกั้ก
Turmeric	**Khamin**	ขมิ้น
Zingiber	**Kathue**	กะทือ
Zedoary	**Praw-homm**	เปราะหอม

Groceries

Agar agar	**Woon or Sărai tha-lé**	วุ้นหรือสาหร่ายทะเล
Baking powder	**Phŏng-fu**	ผงฟู
Bread	**Khanŏm-pang**	ขนมปัง
Biscuits	**Khanŏm-pang krobb**	ขนมปังกรอบ

Bread-crumbs	**Khanōm-pang ponh**	ขนมปังป่น
Butter	**Neui**	เนย
Cheese	**Neui-khāeng**	เนยแข็ง
Chilli sauce	**Sauce-phrik**	ซ้อสพริก
Coffee (ground)	**Kafae bod/phŏng**	กาแฟบด/ผง
Coffee (instant)	**Kafae sāmret**	กาแฟสำเร็จ
Coffee (seeds)	**Kafae maled/med**	กาแฟเม็ด
Flour (Rice)	**Paeng khao-chao**	แป้งข้าวเจ้า
Flour (Sago)	**Paeng sākhu**	แป้งสาคู
Flour (Wheat)	**Paeng sālee**	แป้งสาลี
Flour (Tapioca)	**Paeng manh**	แป้งมัน
Flour (Glutinous Rice)	**Paeng khao-nĩao**	แป้งข้าวเหนียว
Ghee	**Neui India/Neui khaek**	เนยอินเดีย/เนยแขก
Margarine	**Neui thiam**	เนยเทียม
Milk (Sweetened condensed)	**Nom-khon-wãan**	นมข้นหวาน
Milk (powdered)	**Nom phŏng**	นมผง
Milk (UHT)	**Nom-sod UHT**	นมสดยูเอชที
Noodles (Rice)	**Sen kwai-tĩao**	เส้นก๋วยเตี๋ยว
Noodles (Egg)	**Sen-mee**	เส้นหมี่
Noodles (Yellow egg)	**Sen-mee lẽuang**	เส้นหมี่เหลือง
Noodles (Flat rice)	**Kwaitĩao sen-yai**	ก๋วยเตี๋ยวเส้นใหญ่

MARKETING

Noodles (Narrow rice)	**Kwaitĩao sen-lek**	ก๋วยเตี๋ยวเส้นเล็ก
Red stained wheat vermicelli	**Mee-sua**	มี่สั้ว
Rice vermicelli	**Sen khanõm-chine**	เส้นขนมจีน
Rice (white)	**Khaosãrn khão**	ข้าวสารขาว
Rice (white glutinous)	**Khao-nĩao khão**	ข้าวเหนียวขาว
Rice (black glutinous)	**Khaonĩao damh**	ข้าวเหนียวดำ
Rice (fragrant)	**Khao hõmm**	ข้าวหอม
Salt	**Kleua**	เกลือ
Soy sauce (Red)	**Si-iew-khão**	ซีอิ๊วขาว
Soy sauce (Black)	**Si-iew-damh**	ซีอิ๊วดำ
Sugar (White crystal)	**Narm-tarn saai khão**	น้ำตาลทรายขาว
Sugar (Palm)	**Narm-tarn puek**	น้ำตาลปึก
Oil (Vegetable)	**Narm-manh phued**	น้ำมันพืช
Oil (Salad)	**Narm-manh salad**	น้ำมันสลัด
Oil (Groundnut)	**Narm-manh thua**	น้ำมันถั่ว
Oil (Coconut)	**Narm-manh maphrao**	น้ำมันมะพร้าว
Tea (Leaves)	**Bai-sha**	ใบชา
Tea (Instant)	**Sha sãmret**	ชาสำเร็จ
Tea (Chinese)	**Sha-chine**	ชาจีน

Miscellaneous

Bean-curd cheese (white)	**Taohu khão**	เต้าหู้ขาว
Bean-curd cheese (yellow)	**Taohu lĕuang**	เต้าหู้เหลือง
Black fermented beans	**Tao-see**	เต้าซี
Baking powder	**Phõng-fu**	ผงฟู
Chinese mush-rooms	**Hed-hõmm chine**	เห็ดหอมจีน
Chinese pickled cherries	**Kiam-buai**	เกี้ยมบ๊วย
Chinese fermented beans	**Tao-chiao**	เต้าเจี้ยว
Chinese sausages	**Koun-shiang**	กุนเชียง
Continental style sausages	**Sai-krawk farang**	ไส้กรอกฝรั่ง
Dried mussels	**Hõi haeng**	หอยแห้ง
Dried & salted fish	**Pla-khem**	ปลาเค็ม
Dried & salted scaled shrimps	**Koung haeng**	กุ้งแห้ง
Dried tiny shrimps	**Koung fõi haeng**	กุ้งฝอยแห้ง
Dried tamarind	**Makhãrm piak haeng**	มะขามเปียกแห้ง
Fish roe (dried & salted)	**Khai-pla taak haeng**	ไข่ปลาตากแห้ง

111

MARKETING

Fish paste/Shrimp paste	**Kapih pla/Kapih koung**	กะปิปลา/กะปิกุ้ง
Fried chilli paste	**Narm-phrik phão**	น้ำพริกเผา
Fish sauce	**Narm-pla**	น้ำปลา
Fruit juices	**Narm phõla-mai**	น้ำผลไม้
Gourmet powder	**Phõng shu rot**	ผงชูรส
Oyster sauce	**Narm hõi/Narm-manh hõi**	น้ำหอย/น้ำมันหอย
Pickled fish	**Pla-ra**	ปลาร้า
Preserved radish	**Shai-po**	ไชโป๊
Pickled turnip	**Kong-shai**	กงฉ่าย
Pickled cabbage	**Tang-shai**	ตั้งฉ่าย
Prawn crackers	**Khao-kriab koung**	ข้าวเกรียบกุ้ง
Ready mixed curry-stuffs	**Khreuang-kaeng sãmret**	เครื่องแกงสำเร็จ
Rice vinegar	**Narm-som sãai-shu**	น้ำส้มสายชู
Smoked dried fish	**Pla yang**	ปลาย่าง
Soft bean cheese	**Taohu yee**	เต้าหู้ยี้
Sweet dried beancurd skin	**Taohu phaen**	เต้าหู้แผ่น
Transparent green bean vermicelli	**Tang-hoon**	ตั้งฮุ่น
Thin rice vermicelli	**Sen-mee khão (mai-fãnh)**	เส้นหมี่ขาว (ไหมฝั่น)
Tomato ketchup	**Sauce makhẽua thesh**	ซ้อสมะเขือเทศ

112

| Woody ear fungus | Hed hõu-nõo | เห็ดหูหนู |

General Conversation

Sawadi Thowkay!	Sawadi thaokae!	สวัสดีเก้าแก่
How is the business today?	Wan-ni khãai di mãi?	วันนี้ขายดีไหม
What do you need to buy?	Khun tongkarn sue a-rai?	คุณต้องการซื้ออะไร
We have some nice tangerine oranges from Bangmod.	Raow mi som Bangmod louk ngarm-ngarm.	เรามีส้มบางมดลูกงามๆ
The oranges are in season now.	Khana-ni penh na som khĩao-wãan.	ขณะนี้เป็นหน้า ส้มเขียวหวาน
They're 15 Baht a kilo. How many kilos do you want?	Rakha kilo-lah sib-ha Baht. Khun tongkarn ki kilo?	ราคากิโลละ 15 บาท คุณต้องการกี่กิโล
I want some "ok-rong" mangoes.	Phõm tong-karn ma-muang "ok-rong."	ผมต้องการมะม่วง "อกร่อง"
They look green.	Dou yang-dip.	ดูยังดิบ
Have you some ripe ones?	Souk laew mi-mai?	สุกแล้วมีไหม
These are not ripe.	Ni yang mai souk.	นี่ยังไม่สุก
These are ripe, but have spoiled spots in them.	Ni souk tae mi chud naow-sia.	นี้สุกแต่มีจุดเน่าเสีย

MARKETING

I want some fragrant bananas.	Phõm yaak-dai kluai hõmm.	ผมอยากได้กล้วยหอม
How do you sell them?	Khãai yang rai?	ขายอย่างไร
How much a bunch?	Wẽe-lah thao rai?	หวีละเท่าไร
Do you need anything else in the fruit line?	Phõla-mai uen mai tongkarn bang rũe?	ผลไม้อื่นไม่ต้องการบ้างหรือ
I want some rambutans.	Phõm tongkarn louk ngawh.	ผมต้องการลูกเงาะ
Have you any big and sweet ones?	Louk toh-toh, wãan-wãan, mi mãi?	ลูกโตๆ หวานๆ มีไหม
But these are too small. I want bigger rambutans.	Ni lek pai. Phõm tongkarn louk yai-yai.	นี่เล็กไป ผมต้องการลูกใหญ่ๆ
I want 2 kilos of those "long-kong" fruits.	Phõm khãw "long-kong" song kilos.	ผมขอ "ลองกอง" 2 กิโล
Are these from Surash? Sweet or sour?	Long-kong chaak Surash shai mãi? Wãan rũe priao?	ลองกองจากสุราษฎร์ ใช่ไหมหวานหรือเปรี้ยว
Green grapes are cheap now.	A-ngoon kamlang thouk.	อง่นกำลังถูก

114

Nakhorn Jaisri pumelos are sweet and juicy.	Som-Oh Na-khorn Jaisri wãan-shamh.	ส้มโอนครชัยศรีหวานฉ่ำ
This one is the finest.	Louk-ni di thi-sut.	ลูกนี้ดีที่สุด
These are fixed prices.	Rakha khaad tua.	ราคาขาดตัว
Prices can be reduced.	Rakha yang lod dai ik.	ราคายังลดได้อีก
How much are they altogether?	Thang-mod ruam-kanh thaorai?	ทั้งหมดรวมกันเท่าไร
I want a nice piece of round steak.	Phom tongkarn neua-sãnh sa-phoke.	ผมต้องการ เนื้อสันสะโพก
One kilo ground beef.	Neua-bod nueng kilo.	เนื้อวัวบดหนึ่งกิโล
What ingredients shall I use in making Tomyam koung?	Tham tomyam koung tong sai a-rai bang?	ทำต้มยำกุ้งต้องใส่อะไร บ้าง
This piece of pork is nice.	Mõo shin-ni sũai di.	หมูชิ้นนี้สวยดี
How do you sell it?	Khãai yang rai? Aow thao-rai?	ขายอย่างไร เอาเท่าไร
Isn't it very dear?	Mai phaeng pai rue?	ไม่แพงไปหรือ

SHOPPING

Products Made in Thailand

The products listed below are being exported regularly from Thailand to many parts of the world.

Aluminium products	**Phlit-phand aluminium**	ผลิตภัณฑ์อะลูมิเนียม
Animal food	**A-hãrn satt**	อาหารสัตว์
Anklets	**Kamlai thao**	กำไลเท้า
Antennae & TV boosters	**Sãi-akas vithayu lae TV**	สายอากาศวิทยุและทีวี
Antiques & Decorative Arts	**Khreuang laai-khram lae Borarn-watthu**	เครื่องลายครามและ โบราณวัตถุ
Aquarium fish	**Pla Tou**	ปลาตู้
Artcraft furniture	**Khreuang-reuan baeb sĩlpa**	เครื่องเรือนแบบศิลปะ
Artificial flowers	**Dawkmai thiam**	ดอกไม้เทียม
Baby goods	**Sinkha sãmrap dek**	สินค้าสำหรับเด็ก
Bags (shopping)	**Thõung plastic/ kradad**	ถุงพลาสติก/กระดาษ
Ball pens	**Pak-ka louk-luen**	ปากกาลูกลื่น
Bamboo products	**Phlit-phand chaak mai-phai**	ผลิตภัณฑ์จากไม้ไผ่
Basket ware	**Kraboung-takra**	กระบุง ตะกร้า

116

Bathroom equipment	Upakorn hong-narm	อุปกรณ์ห้องน้ำ
Batik sarong	Sarong patek	โสร่งปาเต๊ะ
Beauty & Health products	Sĩnkha songsĕrm khwam ngarm	สินค้าส่งเสริมความงาม
Belts (silver/gold)	Khĕmkhad ngoen/thong	เข็มขัดทอง/เงิน
Blankets & Bedsheets	Pha-hom nonn/pha pou thi-nonn	ผ้าห่มนอน/ผ้าปูที่นอน
Blouses	Seua sattri	เสื้อสตรีแขนสั้น
Bolsters; Pillows	Mõnn-khang; Mõnn nõun	หมอนข้าง หมอนหนุน
Books on Thailand	Nãngsue reuang meuang-thai	หนังสือเรื่องเมืองไทย
Bracelets	Soi khaw mue	สร้อยข้อมือ
Brassières & Underwears	Seua yok-song; Seua shan-nai	เสื้อยกทรง เสื้อชั้นใน
Bronze & Brass products	Sĩnkha thong lẽuang/thong sãmrit	สินค้าทำด้วยทองเหลือง และทองสำริด
Buckles (silver/gold)	Hũa khĕm-khad (ngoen/thong)	หัวเข็มขัด (เงิน/ทอง)
Buttons (silver/gold)	Doum-seua (ngoen/thong)	ดุมเสื้อ (เงิน/ทอง)
Bicycles	Rot chak-krayarn	รถจักรยาน
Canned food-stuffs	A-hãrn krapong	อาหารกระป๋อง

SHOPPING

Canned sardines	Pla sardine krapong	ปลาซาร์ดีนกระป๋อง
Canned fruit juices	Narm phõla-mai krapong	น้ำผลไม้กระป๋อง
Car batteries	Battery rot-yont	แบตเตอรี่รถยนต์
Carpets & Rugs	Phrom/Phrom shed thao	พรม/พรมเช็ดเท้า
Carved wood products	Phlit-phand mai kaeh-salak	ผลิตภัณฑ์ไม้แกะสลัก
Ceramics	Khreuang-panh din-phãow	เครื่องปั้นดินเผา
Chains (silver/gold)	Soi (ngoen/thong)	สร้อยทอง/สร้อยเงิน
Children & Infant garments	Seua dek	เสื้อเด็ก
Cigarette cases/ Cigar boxes	Klong cigarettes/ cigars	กล่องซิกาแร็ต/ซิการ์
Cigarette lighters	Khreuang choud buri	เครื่องจุดบุหรี่
Coffee & Tea sets	Shoud kafae/narm sha	ชุดกาแฟ/น้ำชา
Confectionery	Khanom wãan	ขนมหวาน
Cooking oil (vegetable)	Narm-manh phued	น้ำมันพืช
Cosmetics & Toiletries	Khreuang sãm-ang	เครื่องสำอาง

118

Costume jewelry	Sĭng-pradab petch phloi	สิ่งประดับเพชรพลอย
Cotton and Cotton products	Sĭnkha pha lae faai	สินค้าผ้าและผ้าฝ้าย
Cuff-links (silver/gold)	Doum-shirt (ngoen/thong)	ดุมเชิ้ต (ทอง/เงิน)
Curtains (window)	Pha-marn	ผ้าม่าน
Cushions	Plawk-mŏnn	ปลอกหมอน
Cutlery	Khreuang tat a-harn	เครื่องตัดอาหาร
Deck chairs	Kao-ee dard-fa	เก้าอี้ดาดฟ้า
Dentifrices & Toothpowder	Ya-sĕe-fanh	ยาสีฟัน
Diamonds & Pearls	Petch lae khai-mouk	เพชรและไข่มุก
Drapery fabrics	Pha buh kao-ee	ผ้าบุเก้าอี้
Dresses (ready made)	Seua-pha sămret-roup	เสื้อผ้าสำเร็จรูป
Earrings	Toum-hŏo	ตุ้มหู
Electric appliances	Khreuang-shai fai-fa	เครื่องใช้ไฟฟ้า
Fancy kites	Waow mi luad-lai	ว่าวมีลวดลาย
Fashion wigs	Wig phŏm	วิกผม
Feather fans	Phad khŏn-nok	พัดขนนก
Fishing equipment	Upakorn tok pla	อุปกรณ์ตกปลา
Fish mobiles	Pla taphian bai-larn	ปลาตะเพียนใบลาน

119

SHOPPING

Flowers (freshly cut)	Dawk-mai sod	ดอกไม้สด
Flowers (artificial)	Dawk-mai thiam	ดอกไม้เทียม
Flower vases	Chae-kanh dawk-mai	แจกันดอกไม้
Folding chairs	Kao-ee phab	เก้าอี้พับ
Frozen foods	A-harn shae-khaeng	อาหารแช่แข็ง
Fruits (fresh)	Phõlamai sod	ผลไม้สด
Fruits (preserved and dried)	Phõlamai dong/ taak haeng	ผลไม้ดองและตากแห้ง
Fruit juices	Narm phõlamai	น้ำผลไม้
Food seasoning	Phõng shu-rot	ผงชูรส
Footwear (leather)	Rong-thao nãng	รองเท้าหนัง
Fruit trays	Thard phõlamai	ถาดผลไม้
Furniture (knocked down)	Furniture thawd dai	เฟอร์นิเจอร์ถอดได้
Garments (ready made)	Seua-pha sãmret roup	เสื้อผ้าสำเร็จรูป
Gems	Anya-mani	อัญมณี
Gifts & Souvenirs	Khõng khwãn	ของขวัญ
Glassware	Khreuang kaew	เครื่องแก้ว
Gloves (rubber)	Thõung-mue yang	ถุงมือยาง
Golf equipment	Upakorn lenh golf	อุปกรณ์เล่นกอล์ฟ
Hair ornaments	Khreuang pradab-phõm	เครื่องประดับผม
Hair curlers	Lawd muan-phõm	หลอดม้วนผม

120

Hair pieces	Poi-phõm	ปอยผม
Hair pins	Khem pak-phõm	เข็มปักผม
Handbags & purses	Krapao thũe	กระเป๋าถือ
Handmade jewellery	Khreuang petch phloi	เครื่องเพชรพลอย
Hats & caps	Muak lae muak caps	หมวกและหมวกแก๊ป
Hillcraft products	Phlit-phand shao khõw	ผลิตภัณฑ์ชาวเขา
Hot water bottles	Kratik narm-ronn	กระติกน้ำร้อน
Household wares	Khreuang shai nai reuan	เครื่องใช้ในเรือน
Ice buckets	Thang narm khãeng	ถังน้ำแข็ง
Insect killer	Ya kha malaeng	ยาฆ่าแมลง
Ironing board	Kradarn reed pha	กระดานรีดผ้า
Ivory carvings	Nga-shang salak	งาช้างสลัก
Kitchen utensils	Khreuang shai nai krua	เครื่องใช้ในครัว
Knitted goods	Phlit-phand thak duai mue	ผลิตภัณฑ์ถักด้วยมือ
Lacquer wares	Khreuang khẽrn	เครื่องเขิน
Lamp shades	Poh-takiang	โป๊ะตะเกียง
Leather goods	Sinkha nãng	สินค้าหนัง
Mudmee silk fabric	Phrae Mudmee	แพรมัดหมี่
Mattresses (spring)	Thi-nonn spring	ที่นอนสปริง
Medicinal herbs	Samũn-phrai	สมุนไพร

SHOPPING

Melamine ware	Phashana Melamine	ภาชนะเมลามีน
Mirrors & glasses	Khreuang kaew; Krachok ngaow	เครื่องแก้วและกระจกเงา
Musical instruments	Khreuang don-tri	เครื่องดนตรี
Mosquito coils	Ya lai yung	ยาไล่ยุง
Napkin rings	Huang pha shed-mue	ห่วงผ้าเช็ดมือ
Napkins (paper)	Kradas shed-paak	กระดาษเช็ดปาก
Necklaces	Soi khaw	สร้อยคอ
Niello silverware	Khreuang-thõm ngoen	เครื่องถมเงิน
Night dresses	Seua nonn	เสื้อนอน
Office furniture	Furniture sãmnak-ngarn	เฟอร์นิเจอร์สำนักงาน
Office sundries	Khreuang-shai sãmnak-ngarn	เครื่องใช้เบ็ดเตล็ด สำนักงาน
Orchids	Kluai-maai	กล้วยไม้
Paintings	Pharb khĩan sĩ narm/Narm-manh	ภาพเขียนสีน้ำหรือ น้ำมัน
Pewter ware	Phlitphand lohah phasom dibuk	ผลิตภัณฑ์โลหะผสม ดีบุก
Pharmaceutical products	Phlit-phand ya raksã roke	ผลิตภัณฑ์ยารักษาโรค
Photo albums	Album pharb	อัลบั้มภาพ
Picture frames	Krobb-roup	กรอบรูป

Pillows, Pillow cases	Mõnn, plawk-mõnn	หมอน, ปลอกหมอน
Plastic goods	Sĩnkha plastic	สินค้าพลาสติก
Pottery & Porcelain vases	Maw/Hai	หม้อไห
Powder compacts	Talab paeng	ตลับแป้ง
Precious/semiprecious stones	Petch-phloi	เพชรพลอย
Provisions	Phlit-phand a-hãrn	ผลิตภัณฑ์อาหาร
Radio & Television	Vithayu lae TV	วิทยุและทีวี
Rattan furniture	Phlit-phand wãai	ผลิตภัณฑ์หวาย
Reptile skin goods	Sĩnkha nãng-sat leui-khlaan	สินค้าทำจากหนังสัตว์เลื้อยคลาน
Rings	Wãen	แหวน
Rubber products	Phlit-phand yang	ผลิตภัณฑ์ยาง
Shell products	Phlit-phand pleuak hõi	ผลิตภัณฑ์เปลือกหอย
Shoes (leather & canvas)	Rongthao nãng/ pha bai	รองเท้าหนังและผ้าใบ
Silk and cotton made up goods	Phlit phand pha-faai lae phrae	ผลิตภัณฑ์ผ้าฝ้ายและแพร
Silk dresses	Seua-shoud phrae	เสื้อชุดแพร
Silk sarongs & silk trousers	Sarong mãi/ kangkeng phrae	โสร่งไหม/กางเกงแพร
Silverware	Sĩnkha khreuang ngoen	สินค้าเครื่องเงิน

SHOPPING

Slippers	Rongthao taeh/ sonh-tia	รองเท้าแตะ/ส้นเตี้ย
Soaps & Detergents	Sabu lae phõng sak-fawk	สบู่และผงซักฟอก
Sound Tapes	Tape banthuek sĩang	เทปบันทึกเสียง
Spectacles, Sunglasses	Waenta kanh- daed	แว่นตากันแดด
Sports Goods	Sĩnkha khreuang lenh kila	สินค้าเครื่องเล่นกีฬา
Sport Shoes	Rong-thao kila	รองเท้ากีฬา
Sportwear & Accessories	Shoud lenh kila	ชุดเล่นกีฬา
Stainless Steel cutlery	Khreuang tat- ahãrn stainless	เครื่องตัดอาหาร สเตนเลส
Stationery goods	Khreuang khĩan	เครื่องเขียน
Suitcases	Krapão dern thang	กระเป๋าเดินทาง
Swimwear	Shoud waai-narm	ชุดว่ายน้ำ
Table cloth	Pha pou toh	ผ้าปูโต๊ะ
Tiffin carriers	Pin-toh	ปิ่นโต
Thai dolls and toys	Touk-krata Thai	ตุ๊กตาไทย
Thai embroidery goods	Sĩnkha thak	สินค้าถัก
Thai silk goods	Phlit phand mãi thai	ผลิตภัณฑ์ไหมไทย
Toilet paper, facial tissue	Kradad shamrah/ shed-na	กระดาษชำระ/เช็ดหน้า

124

Towels (bath)	**Pha shed tua**	ผ้าเช็ดตัว
Trays	**Thard**	ถาด
Umbrellas (Chiengmai)	**Rom shiang-mai**	ร่มเชียงใหม่
Wall paints	**Sĕe tha barn**	สีทาบ้าน
Vanity cases	**Klong khreuang sãm-ang**	กล่องเครื่องสำอาง
Video tapes	**Tape Video**	เทปวิดีโอ
Walking sticks	**Mai thao; Mai thũe**	ไม้เท้า, ไม้ถือ
Woodenware	**Phlit-phand chaak maai**	ผลิตภัณฑ์จากไม้
Working gloves	**Thõung-mue tham ngarn**	ถุงมือทำงาน
Works of art	**Ngarn sĩlpa**	งานศิลป์

General Conversation

Here are some expressions which will be useful to you when you are out shopping.

I want to go shopping.	**Phõm tongkarn pai sue khõng.**	ผมต้องการไปซื้อของ
Where's the main shopping area?	**Soon karn-kha mi thi-nãi?**	ศูนย์การค้ามีที่ไหน
Where do you like to shop?	**Sue thi-nai di?**	ซื้อที่ไหนดี

SHOPPING

I like to shop at......	Phõm shob sue khõng thi......	ผมชอบซื้อของที่......
– a department store	– hang sanpha-sĩnkha	– ห้างสรรพสินค้า
– a supermarket	– supermarket	– ซูเปอร์มาเก็ต
– a Trade Centre	– Sõon karn-kha	– ศูนย์การค้า
– a Week-end Market	– Talat Nat	– ตลาดนัด
– a Four-Corners Market	– Talat Si-Moum Meuang	– ตลาดสี่มุมเมือง
– Shopping Arcades	– Raan-kha arcades	– ร้านค้าอาเขต
How does one get there?	Pai dai yang-rai?	ไปได้อย่างไร
Take a taxi or go by bus.	Khuen taxi rũe rot prachamthang	ขึ้นแท็กซี่หรือ รถประจำทาง
Where can I find......?	......you thi nãi?	......อยู่ที่ไหน
– an antique shop	– raan khãi khong borarn	– ร้านขายของโบราณ
– a barber's shop	– raan taeng-phõm shaai	– ร้านแต่งผมชาย
– a beauty salon	– raan sẽrm-suai	– ร้านเสริมสวย
– a book store	– raan nãng-sũe	– ร้านหนังสือ
– a cake shop	– raan khanõm	– ร้านขนม
– a children's and toy shop	– raan seua-pha dek lae tuk-krata	– ร้านเสื้อผ้าเด็ก และตุ๊กตา

126

– a coffee & tea shop	– raan narm-sha kafae	– ร้านน้ำชากาแฟ
– a cosmetics shop	– **raan khreuang sǎm-ang**	– ร้านเครื่องสำอาง
– a costume jewelry shop	– **raan sǐnkha pradab-kaai**	– ร้านสินค้าประดับกาย
– a custom tailor shop	– **raan tat-seua kang-keng**	– ร้านตัดเสื้อกางเกง
– a doctor's office	– **raan mǎw**	– ร้านหมอ
– a dress-maker's shop	– **raan shang-seua yǐng**	– ร้านช่างเสื้อหญิง
– a drug store	– **raan khǎai ya**	– ร้านขายยา
– a duty-free shop	– **raan sǐnkha plawd phasǐ**	– ร้านสินค้าปลอดภาษี
– a filling station	– **sathǎrn borikarn narm-manh**	– สถานบริการน้ำมัน
– a flower shop	– **raan khǎi dawk-mai**	– ร้านขายดอกไม้
– a food shop, eating shop	– **raan a hǎrn**	– ร้านอาหาร
– a fruit shop	– **raan phǒla-mai**	– ร้านผลไม้
– a furniture shop	– **raan furniture**	– ร้านเฟอร์นิเจอร์
– a gift shop	– **raan khǒng thi-raluek**	– ร้านของที่ระลึก
– a grocer's shop	– **raan khǎi-khǒng sham**	– ร้านขายของชำ

127

SHOPPING

– an interior decorator	– shang tob-taeng phai-nai	– ช่างตกแต่งภายใน
– a jeweller's shop	– raan khreuang petch thong	– ร้านเครื่องเพชรทอง
– a laundry	– raan sak-reed	– ร้านซักรีด
– a leather goods shop	– raan sĭnkha khreuang-nãng	– ร้านสินค้าเครื่องหนัง
– a noodle shop	– raan kwaitĩao bah-mee	– ร้านก๋วยเตี๋ยวบะหมี่
– an optical shop	– raan waen-ta	– ร้านแว่นตา
– a photographic supply shop	– raan chamnai u-pakorn thaai-roup	– ร้านจำหน่ายอุปกรณ์ถ่ายรูป
– a record tape/ video tape shop	– raan khaai tape/ video tape	– ร้านเทป/วิดีโอเทป
– a shoemaker's shop	– raan rong-thao	– ร้านรองเท้า
– a sporting goods shop	– raan khreuang ki-la	– ร้านเครื่องกีฬา
– a stationer's shop	– raan khreuang khĩan	– ร้านเครื่องเขียน
– a sundries shop	– raan sĭnkha betta-let	– ร้านสินค้าเบ็ดเตล็ด
– a Thai silk shop	– raan pha-mãi thai	– ร้านผ้าไหมไทย
– a watch-repair shop	– raan somm nalika	– ร้านซ่อมนาฬิกา

128

I'd like to buy......	Phõm tongkarn sue......	ผมต้องการซื้อ......
– an attache case	– krapãow ekka-sãrn.	– กระเป๋าเอกสาร
– a watchstrap	– sãai nalika	– สายนาฬิกา
I'm just looking around.	Phõm khãw shom sĩnkha	ผมขอชมสินค้า
Do you sell......?	Mi......khãai mãi?	มี......ขายไหม
– Mudmee silk fabric	– phrae Mudmee	– แพรมัดหมี่
– artificial flowers	– dawk-mai pradit	– ดอกไม้ประดิษฐ์
– Thai dolls	– tukkrata Thai	– ตุ๊กตาไทย
– Thai greeting cards	– bat oai-phorn Thai	– บัตรอวยพรไทย
– leather belts	– khemkhat nãng	– เข็มขัดหนัง
– Thai umbrellas	– rom Thai	– ร่มไทย
– Chinese silk trousers	– kang-keng phrae chine	– กางเกงแพรจีน
– batik sarongs	– sarong patek	– โสร่งปาเต๊ะ
Where's the shoe department?	Pha-naek rong-thao you thi-nãi?	แผนกรองเท้าอยู่ที่ไหน
I would like to see some leather shoes.	Khãw shom rong-thao nãng.	ขอชมรองเท้าหนัง
– round toes	– baeb hũa klom	– แบบหัวกลม
– square toes	– baeb hũa liam	– แบบหัวเหลี่ยม
– pointed toes	– baeb hũa-lãem	– แบบหัวแหลม

SHOPPING

They are a bit tight/ loose.	Khap pai/lŭam pai.	คับไป/หลวมไป
I can't get them on.	Phŏm suam mai-dai.	ผมสวมไม่ได้
Can you show me the one in the show case?	Khăw dou thi you nai tou-show?	ขอดูที่อยู่ในตู้โชว์
Can you show me some more?	Mi hai shom ik măi?	มีให้ชมอีกไหม
Do you have Thai silk sarongs?	Pha-sin măi Thai mi măi?	ผ้าซิ่นไหมไทยมีไหม
Have you got it in……?	Khun mi……măi?	คุณมี……ไหม
– black	– sĭ damh	– สีดำ
– blue	– sĭ narm-ngoen	– สีน้ำเงิน
– brown	– sĭ narm tam	– สีน้ำตาล
– cream	– sĭ cream	– สีครีม
– green	– sĭ khĭao	– สีเขียว
– grey	– sĭ thaow	– สีเทา
– orange	– sĭ som	– สีส้ม
– pink	– sĭ shom-phu	– สีชมพู
– purple	– sĭ muang	– สีม่วง
– red	– sĭ daeng	– สีแดง
– white	– sĭ khăo	– สีขาว
– yellow	– sĭ lĕuang	– สีเหลือง
I don't like this colour.	Phŏm mai-shob sĭ ni.	ผมไม่ชอบสีนี้

130

I prefer it in blue/ black/green.	Phŏm shob sĭ narm-ngoen/ damh/khĭao.	ผมชอบสีน้ำเงิน/ดำ/ เขียว
I want	Phŏm tong-karn......	ผมต้องการ......
– a larger one	– yai kwa nid-noi	– ใหญ่กว่านิดหน่อย
– a smaller one	– lek kwa nid-noi	– เล็กกว่านิดหน่อย
– a cheaper one	– thook-kwa nid-noi	– ถูกกว่านิดหน่อย
– a better quality	– shanid di-kwa nid-noi	– ชนิดดีกว่านิดหน่อย
It's too expensive.	Phaeng pai.	แพงไป
It's too big/too small.	Yai maak/lek maak.	ใหญ่มาก/เล็กมาก
It's too dark/too light.	Sĭ khem maak pai/ sĭ onn maak pai.	สีเข้มมากไป/ สีอ่อนมากไป
I am looking for ready-to-wear dresses.	Phŏm khăw shom seua-pha sămret roup.	ผมขอชมเสื้อผ้าสำเร็จรูป
Do you have it in stripes?	Yang penh-laai mi măi?	อย่างเป็นลายมีไหม
Have you anything bigger/smaller?	Yai-kwa mi-măi/ lek-kwa mi-măi?	ใหญ่กว่ามีไหม/ เล็กกว่ามีไหม
The sleeves are too wide/narrow.	Khăen kwang pai/ khaen khaeb pai.	แขนกว้างไป/แขนแคบไป
The dress is too short/long.	Seua sanh maak pai/ yao maak pai.	เสื้อสั้นมากไป/ ยาวมากไป

SHOPPING

I prefer a darker/ lighter colour.	Phõm shob sĩ khem/sĩ on-onn.	ผมชอบสีเข้ม/สีอ่อนๆ
I don't like this colour.	Phõm mai shob sĩ ni.	ผมไม่ชอบสีนี้
Red doesn't suit me.	Sĩ daeng mai moh sãmrap phõm.	สีแดงไม่เหมาะสำหรับผม
I want something to match this.	Phõm tongkarn sĩ thi khow kap shout ni.	ผมต้องการสีที่เข้ากับ ชุดนี้
It does not fit me.	Mai phaw-di kap tua.	ไม่พอดีกับตัว
It is too tight.	Khap maak pai.	คับมากไป
Have you any good trousers?	Kang-keng di-di mi mãi?	กางเกงดีๆ มีไหม
The style is all right, but the size is wrong.	Roup song di, tae khanard tong kae.	รูปทรงดีแต่ขนาด ต้องแก้
May I try this on?	Phõm khãw long dai mai?	ผมขอลองได้ไหม
I am afraid, it is a bit too small.	Phõm wa lek pai.	ผมว่าเล็กไป
It looks very nice, but the price is too high.	Sũai-di, tae ra-kha phaeng.	สวยดีแต่ราคาแพง
Have you any-thing better than this?	Thi di kwa-ni mi mãi?	ที่ดีกว่านี้มีไหม

This style is not popular.	Style ni mai ni-yom kanh laew.	สไตล์นี้ไม่นิยมกันแล้ว
I'd like to buy a skirt.	Phõm tong-karn sue kaprong.	ผมต้องการซื้อกระโปรง
The skirt is too long.	Kaprong-ni yao.	กระโปรงนี้ยาว
It must be altered.	Tong kae.	ต้องแก้
When can you have it ready?	Meua-rai chah kae set?	เมื่อไรจะแก้เสร็จ
Is that the cheapest you have ?	Ni rakha thouk thi-sut shai mãi?	นี่ราคาถูกที่สุด ใช่ไหม
I will take this one......	Phõm sue......	ผมซื้อ......
Do you accept......	Khun rap......	คุณรับ......ไหม
– Traveller's Cheques	– Sheck dern-thang	– เช็คเดินทาง
– Credit Cards	– Credit Cards	– เครดิต การ์ด
– Personal cheques	– Sheck suan buk-khon	– เช็คส่วนบุคคล
Will you wrap it, please?	Karuna haw hai duai dai-mãi?	กรุณาห่อให้ด้วยได้ไหม
Send it to the hotel.	Song khõng hai-phõm thi rong-raem.	ส่งของให้ผมที่โรงแรม
I will take it with me.	Phõm chah aow-pai eng.	ผมจะเอาไปเอง

133

SHOPPING

| I will pay cash. | **Phŏm chah chaai-sod.** | ผมจะจ่ายสด |
| I would like to have a receipt. | **Karuna tham bai-rap hai phŏm.** | กรุณาทำใบรับให้ผม |

Buying Thai Jewellery

See the matchless collection of diamonds, sapphires, rubies, emeralds, jade, cultured pearls, precious stones and costume jewellery of timeless beauty — from rings and bracelets to chains and lockets and from brooches and pendants to necklaces and earrings. They come in all shapes and sizes, in exclusive designs, and set in precious stones at prices that are far more reasonable here than anywhere else in the world. If you're looking for unusual exotic jewellery, Bangkok is where you'll find it, and especially those who really care for quality and a lifetime guarantee.

One word of advice though. Make your purchases only from a reputable firm. Insist on a certificate of authenticity. And never buy from a peddlar — no matter how fantastic the bargain offered is.

General Conversation

| I want a small present for my wife / daughter. | **Phŏm tongkarn khŏng-khwăn sămrab phan-raya / louk săo** | ผมต้องการของขวัญ สำหรับภรรยา/ลูกสาว |
| May I look at your...... | **Phŏm khăw shom......** | ผมขอชม...... |

134

– gold bracelets	– soi khaw-mue thongkham	– สร้อยข้อมือทองคำ
– earrings	– toum-hŏo	– ตุ้มหู
– gold chains	– soi-khaw thongkham	– สร้อยคอทองคำ
– armbands	– kamlai khăen	– กำไลแขน
What carat?	Ki karat?	กี่กะรัต
Do you sell......?	Khun mi khăai ......mai?	คุณมีขาย......ไหม
– engagement rings	– wăen manh	– แหวนหมั้น
– wedding rings	– wăaen mong-khon	– แหวนมงคล
– sapphire rings	– wăen nil sĭ narm-goen	– แหวนนิลสีน้ำเงิน
– princess rings	– wăen chao-yĭng	– แหวนเจ้าหญิง
– snake /naga rings with sapphires	– wăen ngou/waen nagh pradab nil	– แหวนงู/แหวนนาคประดับนิล
– puzzle rings	– wăen prisnã	– แหวนปริศนา
– gold enamelled rings	– wăen thongkham long-ya	– แหวนทองคำลงยา
– gold bangles	– kamlai-mue thong	– กำไลมือทอง
– brooches	– khĕm-klad	– เข็มกลัด
– silver belts	– khĕm-khad ngoen	– เข็มขัดเงิน
– armbands	– kamlai khăen	– กำไลแขน

SHOPPING

– anklets	– kamlai thao	– กำไลเท้า
– crown	– mong-kut	– มงกุฎ
– pins	– khẽm	– เข็ม
– the nine-gem stone ring containing different stones	– waen nobha-kaow:	– แหวนนพเก้า
• diamond	• petch	• เพชร
• ruby	• thab-thim	• ทับทิม
• emerald	• maw-rakot	• มรกต
• topaz	• bussara-kham	• บุษราคัม
• garnet	• komen	• โกเมน
• sapphires	• nil sī-khram	• นิลสีคราม
• moonstone	• phloi-khão	• พลอยขาว
• zircon	• phe-thaai	• เพทาย
• cat's eye	• petch ta-maew	• เพชรตาแมว
How do you sell them?	Khun khāai yang-rai?	คุณขายอย่างไร
What is that stone?	Nanh med a-rai?	นั่นเม็ดอะไร
Are they really Thai stones?	Penh khong hã-dai nai Thai rũe?	เป็นของหาได้ในไทยหรือ
I wish to buy......	Phõm tongkarn sue......	ผมต้องการซื้อ......
– silver/gold belts in bronze treated with silicone	– khemkhad ngoen/thawng sãmrit phasõm silicone	– เข็มขัดเงิน/ทองสำริด ผสมซิลิโคน

136

– bracelet made from diamond crystal	– kamlai-mue fãng petch	– กำไลมือฝังเพชร
– pendants made from 24k gold	– chee thong-kham yisib-si karat	– จี้ทองคำ 24 กะรัต
– pendants made of jade	– chee tham duai yok	– จี้ทำด้วยหยก
– cut and polished rubies & sapphires	– thab-thim lae nil tat chiara-nai laew	– ทับทิมและนิล ตัดเจียระไนแล้ว
– a diamond solitaire of 1k	– petch diao nueng karat	– เพชรเดี่ยวหนึ่งกะรัต
– earrings of diamonds and rubies set in 18k gold	– toumhoo petch pradab thab-thim thawng 18 karat	– ตุ้มหูเพชรประดับ ทับทิมทอง 18 กะรัต
– necklaces of pearls/diamonds	– soi-khaw mouk/ soi-khaw fãng petch	– สร้อยคอมุก/ สร้อยคอฝังเพชร
I see that Bangkok has a large assortment of jewellery.	Phõm hẽn Krunthep mi khreuang petch-phloi di-di maak maai.	ผมเห็นกรุงเทพฯ มี เครื่องเพชรพลอย ดีๆ มากมาย
Thai jewellery is	Khreuang petch-	เครื่องเพชรพลอยไทย

SHOPPING

popular in the United States.	phloi Thai kamlang pen-thi niyom nai America.	กำลังเป็นที่นิยมใน อเมริกา
Especially engraved jewellery.	Shaphaw yang-ying phuak mi laai kaeh-salak.	เฉพาะอย่างยิ่งพวก มีลายแกะสลัก
If your prices are right I will send a stock order.	Tha rakha mai phaeng phõm chah sang pai khaai.	ถ้าราคาไม่แพงผมจะ สั่งไปขาย
I am interested in the genuine sapphires and rubies in oval shapes.	Phõm yaak dai nil lae thabthim thae-thae roup khai.	ผมอยากได้นิลและทับทิม แท้ๆ รูปไข่
I wish to buy waen tabai, waen khaw-makharm and a variety of silver niello products.	Phõm yaakdai waen tabai, waen khaw makhãrm lae khreuang thõm na-na shanid.	ผมอยากได้แหวนตะไบ แหวนข้อมะขามและ เครื่องถมนานาชนิด
What discount do you allow on them?	Mi suan-lod thao-rai?	มีส่วนลดเท่าไร

138

Do you allow a term of credit?	Sue ngoen-phonn/ ngoen sheua dai mãi?	ซื้อเงินผ่อน/เงินเชื่อ ได้ไหม
I'll pay when you deliver the goods to the steam-ship company for shipment.	Phõm chah chaai ngoen meua sĩnkha thueng borisat reua.	ผมจะจ่ายเงินให้เมื่อ สินค้าถึงบริษัทเรือ

GOING ABOUT

Going about

Bangkok—a Profile

Bangkok, the capital of Thailand, is one of the fastest developing cities in Southeast Asia, also the commercial centre, port, seat of administration for a centralised system of government, and repository of the nation's historical and cultural heritage. Bangkok is also an internationally famous centre of recreational and cultural attractions: home of that most unique sport, kite-fighting, bull-fighting, sepak takraw, and the equally unique *Muay Thai* or Thai boxing, a city of bright new lights and of homes with shrines to house their guardian spirits. The temples and palaces of Bangkok stand like oasis of peace and quiet amid its hustle and bustle.

Bangkok lies at almost the exact epicentre from Washington D.C. and, as the largest city in Southeast Asia, is served by almost 45 airlines and more than 75 shipping lines. Bangkok's unique geographic position is the ideal gateway to Asia and Europe and an important regional distribution point for cargo to and from Australia, North America and the Middle East.

Bangkok Metropolitan today has a population of 5,535,048; the latest census shows that there are 2,802,867 men and 2,732,181 women. It is the second largest metropolis in Southeast Asia.

All over this city, on the newly-opened up outskirts as much as in the midtown areas, one is struck by the omnipresence of those most obvious signs of growth: tall glass and concrete structures, hotels or office blocks cocooned in spiderweb scaffoldings; pile drivers; concrete mixers, bulldozers— not to mention the blue-

140

jacketed labourers and artisans (women as well as men) who man the machines and swarm like busy ants over the city's numerous building sites: more houses, apartments, condominiums, hotels, factories, school-buildings, office blocks, government offices, police stations, petrol stations, hospitals, shopping centres, cultural centres, religious centres, etc. This is the physical scene, and it reflects the increasing activity, the faster pace of life in all its social, economic, cultural and personal aspects. Yet in the midst of this exhilarating change, traditional Bangkok still flourishes.

A walk down the streets of Bangkok will offer more in mystery and fascination than 1000 miles of western travel. Here are many things of beauty, and it is beauty coupled with the strange and the unique. The modern aspects of the city are in sharp contrast to centuries-old customs and practices. There is evidence on all sides of modern progress, yet the people have not lost their sense of proportion and retain old and tried practices which still fit best into their way of life.

Bangkok has developed as a commercial and industrial city, and today it forms the economic core of Thailand. Thai industry has gained world recognition for new products which it has designed and produced. Bangkok is known for its wide variety of light manufacturing companies plus numerous diversified trading firms. The standard of living of Bangkok people has been rising increasingly over the last few years and members of the new generations are becoming more westernized and taking more pride in their homes.

Bangkok is changing. Every year the city boasts a bigger and better skyline, as new buildings are constructed. Thailand's airports are expanding and the road systems are improving. Rather

GOING ABOUT

than clash with the squarish multi-story concrete and glass structures, Bangkok's 500 monasteries with their golden chedis, their spacious tree-shaded compounds, their sloping glittering roofs, seem to impart their own exotic gentleness and old-world charm to the other architectural style. The contrast is dramatic, not disharmonious. Indeed, more than ever before, Bangkok is looking like a deliberate meeting place of the old and the new, of East and West, of the time-honoured customs and the customs of the age of rising expectations. The achievements of Thai culture can be seen at their finest, be it the glittering spires of the Temple of the Dawn, the gilded splendour of the Grand Palace and the Temple of the Emerald Buddha, or the intricate subtlety of Thai music and dance. Tourists can spend hours roaming through the modern shopping centres, which sell everything from finest silver filigree to haute couture, or zip through the all-inclusive department stores. There are bargains to be had in small shops as well as big stores.

In Bangkok you can find more fun, more variety and more excitement packed into one cosmopolitan city than anywhere else on earth.

Some places of interest

English	Thai Version	Where located
Ananta Samakhom Throne Hall	Phra thi-nang Ananta Samakhom	Bangkok
Ancient City	Meuang Borarn	Bangkok

The Aquariums	Piphit-phand Satt-narm	Samud-prakarn
The Ayudhya National Museum	Piphit-phand sathãrn Chao Sãrm Phya	Ayudhya
Bang-Pa-In Summer Palace	Phra Rajawang Bang-Pa-In	Ayudhya
Bangsaen Marine Science Centre	Sõon Vithayasart Bangsãen	Bangsaen
Bangsai Royal Folk Arts and Craft Centre	Sõon Sĩlpa sheep phiset Bangsai	Bangkok
Bor Sang — the Umbrella Village	Baan Bor Sang	Chiangmai
Bridge on the River Kwai	Saphan Tha Makharm	Kanchanaburi
Buddha Sanctuary	Buddha Monthon	Nakhorn Pathom
Buddha Statue (World's Largest)	Phra Buddha Khodom Wat Phai Rong Wua	Suphanburi
Bhumibol Dam	Kheuan Bhumibol	Tak
Chiangmai Cultural Centre	Sõon Vathanatham Chiangmai	Chiangmai
Chiangmai National Museum	Piphit-phand Sathãrn Chiangmai	Chiangmai

143

GOING ABOUT

Chiangmai University	Mahã Vithayalai Chiangmai	Chiangmai
Chiangmai Zoo	Sũan Satt Chiangmai	Chiangmai
China Town	Sãmpheng	Bangkok
Chulalongkorn University	Chulalongkorn Mahã Vithayalai	Bangkok
Crocodile Farm & Zoo	Farm Chawra- khe	Samud Prakarn
Emerald Buddha	Phra Kaew Mawrakot	Bangkok
The Erawan Falls	Narm-Tok Erawan	Kanchanaburi
The Floating Market	Talad-narm Damnoem Saduak	Rajburi
The Giant Stupa	Phra Pathõm Chedi	Nakhorn Pathom
The Giant Swing	São Shing-sha	Bangkok
The Golden Buddha	Buddha-roup Thong-kham Wat Traimit	Bangkok
The Golden Mount	Phu-khão Thong Wat Sraket	Bangkok
The Grand Palace	Phra Boromaha Rajawang	Bangkok
The Hindu Temple	Wat Khaek Sĩlom	Bangkok

Jim Thompson's Thai House	Baan Jim Thompson	Bangkok
King Mongkut's Summer Palace	Khão Wang Petchburi	Petchburi
Marble Temple	Wat Benchama-bophit	Bangkok
The Monument of Our Glorious Death	Anusāwari Shai Samōraphum	Bangkok
The National Assembly	Sabha Phu-thaen Rassadorn	Bangkok
The National Library	Hŏr Samud Haeng Shart	Bangkok
The National Park and Game Sanctuary	Vana-Uthayarn Haeng Shart Khão Yai	Saraburi
National Museum	Piphit-phand Sathārn Haeng Shart	Bangkok
The National Theatre	Rong Lakhorn Haeng Shart	Bangkok
The Orchid & Flower Gardens	Suān Thonburi-rom	Thonburi
Phimai Stone Palace	Prasard Hĭn Phimai	Khorat
Palace of King Mongkut	Khão Wang, Petchburi	Petchburi

145

GOING ABOUT

Planetarium	Thong-fa Chamlong	Bangkok
Phra Pathom Golden Chedi	Phra Pathom Chedi	Nakhorn Pathom
Phra Rajawang Derm Throne Hall	Phra Rajawang Derm	Thonburi
Phra Samud Chedi	Phra Samud Chedi Paknam	Samud Prakarn
Phra Thart Phanom	Phra Thart Phanom	Nakhorn Phanom
Phu-kradueng National Park	Phu-Kradueng	Loei
Rama IX Garden	Sūan Lāang Raw Kao	Bangkok
Reclining Buddha	Phra Nonn Wat Pho	Bangkok
Rose Gardens Country Resort	Suan Sārm-phran	Bangkok
Royal Phuping Palace	Phra Tamnak Phuphing	Chiangmai
Salika Falls	Narm Tok Sālika	Nakhorn Nayok
Shell Museum	Piphit-phand Pleuak Hõi	Samud Prakarn
The Shrine of Holy Footprint	Phra Buddha-bart Saraburi	Saraburi

146

Sirikit Hydro-electric Dam	Kheuan Sirikit	Uttradith
Snake Farm	Sũan Ngoo Sathãrn Sãowabha	Bangkok
Spirit House of the City	Sarn-Chaophaw Lak Meuang	Bangkok
Standing Buddha	Phra Buddha Roup Wat Indra	Bangkok
Suan Phakkard Palace	Wang Sũan Phakkard	Bangkok
Temple of the Dawn	Wat Aroon Rajvararam	Bangkok
United Nations Organisation	Ong-karn Saha Prashashart	Bangkok
Zoological Gardens	Sũan Satt Dusit	Bangkok

Getting Around by Taxi

Hired car	Rot-shaow	รถเช่า
Where can I rent a car?	Chah shaow rot dai thi-nãi?	จะเช่ารถได้ที่ไหน
Please call a taxi for me.	Proad riak taxi.	โปรดเรียกแท็กซี่
I want to see the town.	Phõm tongkam thiao shom changwad.	ผมต้องการเที่ยวชม จังหวัด

147

GOING ABOUT

Do you know the city very well?	Khun rou-chak tua-changwad di mãi?	คุณรู้จักตัวจังหวัดดีไหม
What is your fare by the hour?	Shaow penh shua-mong khid thaorai?	เช่าเป็นชั่วโมงคิดเท่าไร
Show me everything that is interesting.	Pha phõm pai thouk sathãrn thi-thi na shom.	พาผมไปทุกสถานที่ที่น่าชม
Would you please drive more slowly?	Proad khab sha-sha?	โปรดขับช้าช้า
Where are you taking me?	Chah pha phõm pai thi-nãi?	จะพาผมไปที่ไหน
Where does this street lead to?	Thanõn-ni pai thang nãi?	ถนนนี้ไปออกทางไหน
What is the name of that road?	Thanõn-nanh thanõn a-rai?	ถนนนั้นชื่อถนนอะไร
What is the name of this place?	Thi-ni riak a-rai?	ที่นี่เรียกอะไร
What is that monument?	Nanh anu-sawari a-rai?	นั่นอนุสาวรีย์อะไร
What building is that?	Nanh akharn a-rai?	นั่นอาคารอะไร
Do you know where the public park is?	Sũan satharanah you klai mãi?	สวนสาธารณะอยู่ไกลไหม

148

GOING ABOUT

Drive on!	Khab-pai!	ขับไป ไม่ต้องหยุด!
Don't stop!	Mai-tong yout!	
Are the museums open today?	Wan-ni phiphit-phand sathãrn perd mãi?	วันนี้พิพิธภัณฑ์สถาน เปิดไหม
Shall we visit......?	Raow pai shom ...... di mãi?	เราไปชม......ดีไหม
– the Temple of the Emerald Buddha	– Bote Wat Phra Kaew	– โบสถ์วัดพระแก้ว
– the Grand Palace	– Phra Boromaha Rajawang	– พระบรมมหาราชวัง
– the Museums	– Phiphit-phand sathãrn	– พิพิธภัณฑ์สถาน
– the Ancient City	– Meuang boraan	– เมืองโบราณ
– the Crocodile Farm	– Farm Chawra-khé	– ฟาร์มจระเข้
What is the name of this temple ?	Wat ni riak wat a-rai?	วัดนี้เรียกวัดอะไร
Can we go in?	Raow khao-pai dai-mãi?	เราเข้าไปได้ไหม
Is it alright to take pictures?	Thaai pharb dai mãi?	ถ่ายภาพได้ไหม
How much is the admission charge?	Kha pharn thao-rai?	ค่าผ่านเท่าไร

149

GOING ABOUT

It's nearly six o'clock now.	Keuab hok-mong laew.	เกือบหกโมงแล้ว
Drive us to a good eating house.	Pha raow pai raan a-harn di-di.	พาเราไปร้านอาหารดีๆ
Let us go back to the hotel.	Klab pai rongraem.	กลับไปโรงแรม
How long have we kept you?	Shao-rot khun ki shua-mong laew?	เช่ารถคุณนานกี่ชั่วโมงแล้ว
How much do we have to pay you?	Tong chaai khun thaorai?	ต้องจ่ายคุณเท่าไร
We will give you 50 US dollars.	Raow hai khun ha-sib dollars American.	เราให้คุณห้าสิบดอลลาร์อเมริกัน

Travel by Bus or Coach

Do you have timetables and information about express bus services?	Khun mi rair-kam kamnod vela rot duan mãi?	คุณมีรายการและกำหนดเวลารถด่วนไหม
Where can I get a bus to Phuket?	Rot pracham-thang pai Phuket mi mãi?	รถประจำทางไปภูเก็ตมีไหม
Where is	......you thi nãi?	......อยู่ที่ไหน

150

– the bus stop	– Paai chawd-rot pracham thang	– ป้ายจอดรถประจำทาง
– the bus terminal	– Sathãni khõn-song	– สถานีขนส่ง
How many buses are there daily to Phuket?	Rot pai Phuket mi wan-lah ki-thiao?	รถไปภูเก็ตมีวันละกี่เที่ยว
How long does the journey take to Phuket?	Ki shua-mong thũeng Phuket?	กี่ชั่วโมงถึงภูเก็ต
When does the last bus leave?	Rot thiao sud-thai awk meua-rai?	รถเที่ยวสุดท้ายออกเมื่อไร
How much is the fare to Phuket?	Kha doai-sarn pai Phuket thao-rai?	ค่าโดยสารไปภูเก็ตเท่าไร
What number bus shall I take?	Phõm tong khuen-rot beur a-rai?	ผมต้องขึ้นรถเบอร์อะไร
When does the first bus leave?	Rot thiao-raek awk meua-rai?	รถเที่ยวแรกออกเมื่อไร
When is the next bus to Trang?	Rot paiTrang awk meua-rai?	รถไปตรังออกเมื่อไร
How long must I wait?	Tong khoi naan mãi?	ต้องคอยนานไหม
– 15 minutes	– sib-ha nathi	– สิบห้านาที
– 30 minutes	– sarm-sib nathi	– สามสิบนาที

151

GOING ABOUT

Please reserve a seat for me.	Phõm khãw chawng thi-nang nueng thi.	ผมขอจองที่นั่งหนึ่งที่
I should like to have......	Phõm khãw......	ผมขอ......
– a seat near the window	– thi-nang shid na-tang	– ที่นั่งชิดหน้าต่าง
– a seat in front next to driver	-thi-nang klai khon-khab	– ที่นั่งใกล้คนขับ
Are there any coaches to Surash?	Mi rot pai Surash mãi?	มีรถไปสุราษฎร์ไหม
Do the coaches leave often?	Mi rot awk boi-boi rũe?	มีรถออกบ่อยบ่อยหรือ
How much is the return fare to Surash?	Kha doai-sãrn pai-klap Surash thao-rai?	ค่าโดยสารไป-กลับ สุราษฎร์เท่าไร
Does the coach stop here?	Rot chawd thi-ni mãi?	รถจอดที่นี่ไหม
Can you help me with my suitcases?	Shuai yok krapaow dern-thang phom dai-mãi?	ช่วยยกกระเป๋าเดินทาง ผมได้ไหม
Conductor, I gave you a 500-Baht note.	Krapaow, phõm hai thanabat khun pai ha-roi Baht.	กระเป๋า ผมให้ธนบัตร คุณไปห้าร้อยบาท

You didn't give me the change.	Khun yang mai thonn ngoen hai phõm.	คุณยังไม่ทอนเงินให้ผม
I want to get off here.	Phõm tongkarn long thi-ni.	ผมต้องการลงที่นี่
I want to get off at the next bus-stop.	Phõm chah long thi paai-na.	ผมจะลงที่ป้ายหน้า
I want my baggage, please.	Khãw krapãow hai phõm.	ขอกระเป๋าให้ผม

Travelling by Tricycle; Motor Tricycle (Touk-Touk)

Tricycle/Motor tricycle	Sãm-lor/Sãmlor Khreuang (Touk-Touk)	สามล้อ/สามล้อเครื่อง (ตุ๊ก-ตุ๊ก)
Microbus	Rot-bus lek	รถบัสเล็ก
What's the charge......?	Khid yang-rai......?	คิดอย่างไร......
– per hour	– shua-mong lah	– ชั่วโมงละ
– per day	– wanh-lah	– วันละ
Drive me to the office of......	Pai song thi sãmnak-ngarn......	ไปส่งที่สำนักงาน......
How much do you charge?	Khid thao-rai?	คิดเท่าไร

153

GOING ABOUT

I want to go to this address.	Tongkarn pai thi-ni.	ต้องการไปที่นี่
Do you know where the place is?	Rou mãi you thi-nãi?	รู้ไหมอยู่ที่ไหน
I am in a hurry.	Shan tong reep pai.	ฉันต้องรีบไป
Do you understand?	Khun khao-chai mãi?	คุณเข้าใจไหม
Are you sure?	Nae-chai rũe?/ Nae rũe?	แน่ใจหรือ?/แน่หรือ
Please speak slowly.	Karuna phoud sha-sha.	กรุณาพูดช้า-ช้า
Are we near the Police Station?	Keuab thueng Sathani Tamruat rue-yang?	เกือบถึงสถานีตำรวจ หรือยัง
Where is the W.C./bathroom?	Thi-nai mi hong-suam/hong-narm?	ที่ไหนมีห้องส้วม/ห้องน้ำ
Stop in front of that shop.	Yout thi na raan nanh.	หยุดที่หน้าร้านนั้น
Wait for me here!	Khoi thi-ni!	คอยที่นี่!
Let's go!	Pai kan therd!	ไปกันเถิด
What street is this?	Ni thanõn a-rai?	นี่ถนนอะไร
I wish to buy some Thai silk.	Shãn tongkam sue pha-mãi Thai.	ฉันต้องการซื้อผ้าไหมไทย

154

Stop at the next corner.	Yout thi hũa thanõn-none.	หยุดที่หัวถนนโน่น!
Where are you going?	Chah pai nãi?	จะไปไหน
I don't understand.	Mai khao-chai/Mai rou wa phoud reuang a-rai.	ไม่เข้าใจ ไม่รู้ว่าพูดเรื่องอะไร
Will you wait?	Chah khoi mãi?	จะคอยไหม
Please go straight.	Trong pai.	ตรงไป
Turn to the left/ right.	Liao-saai/ Liao khwa.	เลี้ยวซ้าย/เลี้ยวขวา
I have had a very good time.	Pai-thiao sanuk di.	ไปเที่ยวสนุกดี
Thank you.	Khob-chai maak.	ขอบใจมาก
Where do you live?	Khun you thi-nãi?	คุณอยู่ที่ไหน
Hope to see you again!	Khong mi okas phob kanh ik!	คงจะมีโอกาสพบกันอีก
Keep the change!	Keb wai!	เก็บไว้!

Travelling by River Boat

| I/We would like to go sightseeing by boat. | Phõm/Raow tongkarn pai thasana-chorn thang reua. | ผม/เรา ต้องการไปทัศนาจร ทางเรือ |

155

GOING ABOUT

What are the main points of interest?	Mi a-rai na-dou, na-shom bang?	มีอะไรน่าดู น่าชมบ้าง
We want to have a day-long boat excursion.	Raow tongkarn thiao thang reua talawd wanh.	เราต้องการเที่ยวทางเรือ ตลอดวัน
We would like to have a sampan ride by moon-light in the klong and the river.	Raow yaak nang reua khow klong lae menam vela deuan-ngai.	เราอยากนั่งเรือเข้าไปใน คลองและแม่น้ำเวลา เดือนหงาย
We would like to see a green water-way crowded with sampans.	Raow yaak henh thang-narm thi mi reua pai-ma maak.	เราอยากเห็นทางน้ำที่มี เรือไปมามาก
With stops to see the lives of the klong people, the floating houses, the floating restaurants, and the monastery close up.	Tongkarn yout shom shivit shao klong, shom reuan-phae, shom phatakharn phae, wat-wa a-rarm, nai rayah klai.	ต้องการหยุดชมชีวิต ชาวคลอง, ชมเรือนแพ ชมภัตตาคารแพ และ วัดวาอารามในระยะ ใกล้

We are interested in the main shopping area, and the river craft plying their trade.	Raow tongkarn shom boriven kha-khāi sīnkha, lae reua-phae thi kha-khai klang narm.	เราต้องการชมบริเวณ ค้าขายสินค้า และ เรือนแพที่ค้าขาย กลางน้ำ
We want to remain there some hours and then return.	Raow tongkarn yout thinanh narn laai shuamong laew klab.	เราต้องการหยุดที่นั่นนาน หลายชั่วโมงแล้วกลับ
We would like to see the water sport and the dinghy racing.	Raow yaak henh kila thang narm lae karn khaeng reua yao.	เราอยากเห็นกีฬาทางน้ำ และการแข่งเรือยาว
Where can we get ……?	Chah ha…… dai thi-nai?	จะหา……ได้ที่ไหน
– a motor boat	– reua-yont	– เรือยนต์
– a cabin cruiser	– reua mi cabin	– เรือยนต์มีเคบิน
– a walla walla (water taxi)	– reua hang-yao lit-khreuang	– เรือหางยาวติดเครื่อง
– a rowing boat	– reua phaai	– เรือพาย
– a sampan	– reua sampan	– เรือสำปั้น
What do you charge……?	Khun khid kha borikarn yang-rai?	คุณคิดค่าบริการอย่างไร

157

GOING ABOUT

– per person	– penh raai hũa	– เป็นรายหัว
– per trip	– penh thiao	– เป็นเที่ยว
– per hour	– penh shua-mong	– เป็นชั่วโมง
How much does the tour cost?	Khid mãow thang-mod aow thao-rai?	คิดเหมาทั้งหมดเอาเท่าไร
Have you any English-speaking guides?	Khun mi khon rou bhasã angkrit penh laam mãi?	คุณมีคนรู้ภาษาอังกฤษเป็นล่ามไหม
Can you help me?	Khun chah shuai phõm dai mãi?	คุณจะช่วยผมได้ไหม
When can you be of service to us?	Meua-rai khun chah borikarn dai?	เมื่อไรคุณจะบริการได้
How about going to that famous shrine?	Pha pai dou sathãrn-thi saksit dai mãi?	พาไปดูสถานที่ศักดิ์สิทธิ์ได้ไหม
Are there many crocodiles around here?	Boriven ni mi chawrakhe maak mai?	บริเวณนี้มีจระเข้มากไหม
What is the Thai name for "crocodile'?'	"Crocodile" bhasã Thai riak a-rai?	"ครอกโคไดล์" ภาษาไทยเรียกอะไร
Stop here a moment.	Yout thi-ni khru-nueng.	หยุดที่นี่ครู่หนึ่ง

I want to buy something for my people at home.	Phõm tongkarn sue khõng-khwãn pai faak khon thi baan.	ผมต้องการซื้อของขวัญไปฝากคนที่บ้าน
Will you wrap them up for me?	Karuna haw hai-noi dai mãi?	กรุณาห่อให้หน่อยได้ไหม
Have you got a box/a carrier bag?	Khun mi klong-kradad/mi thõung mãi?	คุณมีกล่องกระดาษ/มีถุงไหม
Let's go to a floating restaurant.	Pai tharn a-harn thi phatakharn reuan-phae.	ไปทานอาหารที่ภัตตาคารเรือนแพ
Would you like to have a glass of beer?	Duem beer sak-kaew di-mãi?	ดื่มเบียร์สักแก้วดีไหม
We have spent a very pleasant day.	Wan-ni thiao sanuk di.	วันนี้เที่ยวสนุกดี

159

RAIL TRAVEL

A Journey by Railway

Classification of Trains

International Express Trains	**Rot-duan phaan khet**	รถด่วนผ่านเขต
Internal Express Trains	**Rot-duan**	รถด่วน
Long Distance Rapid Trains	**Rot-réow**	รถเร็ว
Local Passenger Trains	**Rot-thammada**	รถธรรมดา
Mixed Trains	**Rot-ruam**	รถรวม
Diesel Rail-car	**Rot diesel rang**	รถดีเซลราง
The State Railway of Thailand	**Karn Rotfai Thai**	การรถไฟไทย
The Malayan Railway	**Rotfai Malayu**	รถไฟมลายู
The Northern Line	**Rot-fai Saai Nẽua**	รถไฟสายเหนือ
The North-eastern Line	**Rot-fai Saai Tawan-Awk Shiang nẽua**	รถไฟสายตะวันออกเฉียงเหนือ
The Eastern Line	**Rot-fai Saai Tawan-Awk**	รถไฟสายตะวันออก
The Southern Line	**Rot-fai Saai Taai**	รถไฟสายใต้

From Hotel to the Railway Station

Taxi, take me to the Railway Station.	Taxi, pha-phõm pai Sathãni Rot-fai.	แท็กซี่ พาผมไป สถานีรถไฟ
What is your fare?	Kha-doai-sãrn thaorai?	ค่าโดยสารเท่าไหร่
I will give you 150 Baht.	Phõm hai roi hasib Baht.	ผมให้ร้อยห้าสิบบาท
There are three of us and there is our luggage.	Raow mi sãrm-khon, nanh krapaow dern-thang khong raow.	เรามีสามคน นั่นกระเป๋า เดินทางของเรา
What is the time now?	Dĩao-ni ki mong laew?	เดี๋ยวนี้กี่โมงแล้ว
I want to go by the 16:10 train to Butterworth.	Phõm tong-karn chap rot sib-hok nalika sib nathi pai Butterworth.	ผมต้องการจับรถ สิบหก นาฬิกาสิบนาทีไป บัตเตอร์เวอร์ธ
We haven't got much time to spare.	Vela mi noi.	เวลามีน้อย
Go as quickly as possible, or we shall miss the train.	Pai reow noi, dĩao chah mai thanh rot.	ไปเร็วหน่อย เดี๋ยวจะไม่ ทันรถ

RAIL TRAVEL

| Please drive carefully. | Karuna khab rawang-rawang noi. | กรุณาขับระวังระวังหน่อย |
| Where is the railway station ? | Sathani rot-fai you nai? | สถานีรถไฟอยู่ไหน |

At the Railway Inquiry Office

Where is the Inquiry Office?	Phanaek sobb-thãrm you thi nai?	แผนกสอบถามอยู่ที่ไหน
At what time does it open?	Ki mong chah perd tham-ngam?	กี่โมงจะเปิดทำงาน
At what time will the Express train from Butterworth arrive?	Ki-mong Rot-duan Butterworth chah ma thũeng?	กี่โมงรถด่วน บัตเตอร์เวอร์ธจะมาถึง
At what time will the train arrive at Chiangmai?	Ki-mong rot chah thũeng Sathani Chiangmai?	กี่โมงรถจะถึงสถานี เชียงใหม่
At what time will the rapid train leave for Haadyai?	Ki-mong Rot-réow chah awk-pai Haadyai?	กี่โมงรถเร็วจะออกไป หาดใหญ่
From which platform?	Rot awk-chaak shan-shala darn nai?	รถออกจากชานชาลา ด้านไหน

162

Is that a train for Sungei Golok?	Nanh rot pai Sungẽi Golok shai-mãi?	นั่นรถไปสุไหง โก-ลค ใช่ไหม
Is it a through train to Nakhorn?	Rot-ni trong pai Nakhom rũe?	รถนี้ตรงไปนครๆ หรือ
No, you have to change the train at Khão Chumthong.	Mai, khun tong plian rot thi Khão Chumtong.	ไม่-คุณต้องเปลี่ยนรถ ที่เขาชุมทอง
Does the train stop at Hua Hin?	Rot yout thi Sathãni Hũa Hĩn mãi?	รถหยุดที่สถานีหัวหินไหม
Yes, Hua Hin is a compulsory stop.	Shai, rot yout thi Sathãni Hũa Hĩn.	ใช่-รถหยุดที่สถานีหัวหิน
Can I break the trip at Haadyai?	Phõm chah yout thiao Haadyai dai mãi?	ผมจะหยุดเที่ยวหาดใหญ่ ได้ไหม

Where is......?

The Advance Booking Office	Thi chawng-tũa luang na	ที่จองตั๋วล่วงหน้า
Ticket Office	Hong chamnai tũa	ห้องจำหน่ายตั๋ว
The Station Master	Nai Sathãni	นายสถานี
The Railway Inquiry Office	Phanaek sobb-thãrm	แผนกสอบถาม

163

RAIL TRAVEL

The Railway Parcels Office	Phanaek rab-song phasadu	แผนกรับส่งพัสดุ
The Cloak Room	Hong faak khŏng	ห้องฝากของ
The Passenger Waiting Room	Hong phak phu-doai-sărn	ห้องพักผู้โดยสาร
The Departure Platform	Shan shala rot awk	ชานชาลารถออก
The Arrival Platform	Shan shala rot khow	ชานชาลารถเข้า
The Restaurant	Phatakharn	ภัตตาคาร
The Lavatory	Hong Sukha	ห้องสุขา
The Sleeping car	Rot nonn	รถนอน
The Buffet Car	Rot sabiang	รถเสบียง
The Third Class Sleeperette Coach	Rot nang-nonn Shan-sărm	รถนั่ง-นอนชั้นสาม
The Luggage Van	Rot săm-pha-rah	รถสัมภาระ
The Post Office Van	Rot praisani	รถไปรษณีย์
The First Class Air-pressurised Cabin	Rot shan-nueng prab-akas	รถชั้นหนึ่งปรับอากาศ
Berth in 2nd Class Coach	Thi nonn bonh rot shan-song	ที่นอนบนรถชั้นสอง
The Refreshment Stall	Raan chamnai khreuang duem	ร้านจำหน่ายเครื่องดื่ม
The Station Book Stall	Raan chamnai năngsŭe	ร้านจำหน่ายหนังสือ

Tickets

Ticket Office	**Hong chamnaai tũa**	ห้องจำหน่ายตั๋ว
Tickets	**Tũa**	ตั๋ว
Ticket Collector	**Phanak-ngarn kep tũa**	พนักงานเก็บตั๋ว
Fares	**Kha doai-sãrn**	ค่าโดยสาร
Reserved Seats	**Thi-nang sãm-rong**	ที่นั่งสำรอง
Sleeping Berths	**Thi-nonn**	ที่นอน
I want......	**Phõm tong-karn......**	ผมต้องการ......
– Single	**– Tũa pai thiao-diao**	– ตั๋วไปเที่ยวเดียว
– Return	**– Tũa pai-klab**	– ตั๋วไปกลับ
– First Class ticket	**– Tũa shan-thi-nueng**	– ตั๋วชั้นที่หนึ่ง
– Second Class ticket	**– Tũa shan-thi-sõng**	– ตั๋วชั้นที่สอง
– Third Class ticket	**– Tũa shan-thi-sãrm**	– ตั๋วชั้นที่สาม
– First Class air-conditioned cabin	**– Rot-air shan-thi-nueng**	– รถแอร์ชั้นที่หนึ่ง
– First Class air-pressurised cabin	**– Rot prab-akas shan-thi-nueng**	– รถปรับอากาศชั้นที่หนึ่ง

RAIL TRAVEL

– Berth in 2nd Class coach	– Thi-nonn bonh rot shan-sŏng	– ที่นอนบนรถชั้นสอง
– Upper Berth	– Thi-nonn bonh	– ที่นอนบน
– Lower Berth	– Thi-nonn lang	– ที่นอนล่าง
– Platform Ticket	– Tua shan-shala	– ตั๋วชานชาลา
How much is the fare to Chiangmai?	Kha doai-sãrn pai Chiang-mai thao-rai?	ค่าโดยสารไปเชียงใหม่ เท่าไหร่
How much is the fare for a child?	–Dek sĩa kha-doai-sarn thao-rai?	– เด็กเสียค่าโดยสาร เท่าไหร่
She is under 12 years.	A-yu tam kwa sibsŏng.	อายุต่ำกว่าสิบสอง
She is 13 years.	A-yu sib-sãrm.	อายุสิบสาม
Does the ticket include Supplementary Charge?	Tũa ruam kha-thamniam duai rũe-plao?	ตั๋วรวมค่าธรรมเนียมด้วย หรือเปล่า
I want to change my journey to Haadyai.	Phõm khãw plian dern-thang pai Haadyai.	ผมขอเปลี่ยนเดินทางไป หาดใหญ่
I want to break my journey here.	Phõm khãw long thi-ni.	ผมขอลงที่นี่
I will leave Haadyai on......	Phõm chah awk chaak Haad-yai wan-thi......	ผมจะออกจากหาดใหญ่ วันที่......
Please endorse my tickets.	Karuna salak-lãng tũa hai phõm.	กรุณาสลักหลังตั๋วให้ผม

With the Porters

I need a porter.	Phõm tong-karn khon yok khõng.	ผมต้องการคนยกของ
Porter, here is my luggage.	Ni krapaow dern-thang khõng phõm.	นี่กระเป๋าเดินทางของผม
Help me get this luggage down.	Shuai phõm yok long.	ช่วยผมยกลง
I want to take a train to Lampang.	Phõm chah khuen rot pai Lampang.	ผมจะขึ้นรถไปลำปาง
I booked the seat on......	Phõm sãmrong thi-nang wai bonh......	ผมสำรองที่นั่ง ไว้บน......
– First Class Coach	– rot shan-thi nueng	– รถชั้นที่หนึ่ง
– Second Class Coach	– rot shan-thi sõng	– รถชั้นที่สอง
– Third Class (Economy) Coach	– rot shan-thi sãrm	– รถชั้นที่สาม
The number of my reserved seat is 32.	Mãai-lek sãmrong thi sãrm-sib sõng.	หมายเลขสำรองที่ สามสิบสอง
My seat is near the window.	Thi-nang rim na-tang.	ที่นั่งริมหน้าต่าง
When will the train leave?	Meua rai rot chah awk?	เมื่อไรรถจะออก

167

RAIL TRAVEL

These are my suitcases.	Laow-ni penh kra pãow dern-thang phõm.	เหล่านี้เป็นกระเป๋า เดินทางผม
Have you got everything?	Khun dai kra-pãow ma khrob laew rũe?	คุณได้กระเป๋ามาครบแล้ว หรือ
I will take the small bag with me.	Phõm chah thũe kra-pãow bai-lek.	ผมจะถือกระเป๋าใบเล็ก
Wait for me here.	Khoi phõm thi ni.	คอยผมที่นี่
I will get my tickets first.	Phõm chah pai sue tũa.	ผมจะไปซื้อตั๋ว
Meet me at the Mail Coach.	Phob-phõm thi na Rot Prai-sani.	พบผมที่หน้ารถไปรษณีย์
You can go now.	Khun pai dai.	คุณไปได้
Here is something for you	Ni sãmrab khun tharn kafae.	นี่สำหรับคุณทานกาแฟ

In Train — With Railway Officials

I am travelling to Kuala Lumpur.	Phõm pai Kuala Lumpur.	ผมไปกัวลาลัมเปอร์
Have I to change trains anywhere on the way?	Phõm tong plian rot thi-nãi?	ผมต้องเปลี่ยนรถที่ไหน
Yes, change at Butterworth.	Tong plian thi Buttereworth.	ต้องเปลี่ยนที่ บัทเตอร์เวอร์ธ

How long will the train stop there?	Rot chawd naan mãi?	รถจอดนานไหม
When shall we arrive at the border?	Meuarai chah thũeng shaai-daen?	เมื่อไรจะถึงชายแดน
Does the train stop here long enough to give us time to dine?	Rot chawd naan phaw ha a-rai tharn mãi?	รถจอดนานพอหาอะไรทานไหม
Do the Immigration officials come into the train?	Phanak-ngarn khow meuang chah truad bonh rot rũe?	พนักงานเข้าเมืองจะตรวจบนรถหรือ
Have we to get out for the Customs examination?	Raow tong aow sing-khõng pai hai phasĩ truad mãi?	เราต้องเอาสิ่งของไปให้ภาษีตรวจไหม
Will you please tell us when to get ready?	Proad chaeng hai saab pheua triam-tua?	โปรดแจ้งให้ทราบเพื่อเตรียมตัว
Where is the luggage examined?	Truad kra-paõw-dern-thang thi nãi?	ตรวจกระเป๋าเดินทางที่ไหน
Will the train stop at Jaiya?	Rot chah yout thi sathãni Jaiya mãi?	รถจะหยุดที่สถานีไชยาไหม
I have got onto the wrong train.	Phõm khuen rot phid khabuan.	ผมขึ้นรถผิดขบวน

RAIL TRAVEL

I have missed the train.	Phom tok rot.	ผมตกรถ
Is there any other train this evening?	Yen ni mi rot khabuan uen pai mãi?	เย็นนี้มีรถขบวนอื่นไป ไหม
Would you find a seat for me, please?	Proad hã thi-nang hai phõm?	โปรดหาที่นั่งให้ผม
Thank you very much.	Khob khun maak.	ขอบคุณมาก

In Train — With Other Passengers

Is this seat occupied?	Thi ni mi khon laew rũe-yang?	ที่นี่มีคนแล้วหรือยัง
No, it is free.	Yang mai mi.	ยังไม่มี
Yes, it is occupied.	Mi laew.	มีแล้ว
This is my seat.	Ni penh thi-nang phõm.	นี่เป็นที่นั่งผม
Won't you change seats with me?	Plian thi-nang kab phõm mai?	เปลี่ยนที่นั่งกับผมไหม
Do you smoke?	Khun soub-buri mãi?	คุณสูบบุหรี่ไหม
Thanks, I don't smoke.	Khob-khun, phõm mai soub.	ขอบคุณ ผมไม่สูบ
I do smoke, but I don't have any matches.	Phom soub, tae mai mi mai khide-fai.	ผมสูบ แต่ไม่มีไม้ขีดไฟ

170

Have you got a light, please?	Khaw phõm choud buri?	ขอผมจุดบุหรี่
Do you mind if I smoke?	Rangkiat mãi tha phõm soub buri?	รังเกียจไหมถ้าผมสูบบุหรี่
May I turn on/turn off the fan?	Phõm perd/ pid phad-lom dai mãi?	ผมเปิด/ปิดพัดลมได้ไหม
May I open the window?	Khãw perd na-tang dai mãi?	ขอเปิดหน้าต่างได้ไหม
Shall I shut the window?	Khãw pid na-tang dai mãi?	ขอปิดหน้าต่างได้ไหม
Please close the door.	Karuna pid pra-tou.	กรุณาปิดประตู
Where are you going?	Khun chah pai nãi?	คุณจะไปไหน
I want to go to Prachuab.	Phõm chah pai Prachuab.	ผมจะไปประจวบ
Where will you get off?	Khun chah long thi-nãi?	คุณจะไปที่ไหน
I will get off at the next station.	Phõm chah long thi sathãni na.	ผมจะลงที่สถานีหน้า
I will get off at Hua Hin.	Phõm chah long thi sathãni Hũa Hĩn.	ผมจะลงที่สถานีหัวหิน
Is this train late?	Rot ni khong sĩa vela?	รถนี้คงเสียเวลา

171

RAIL TRAVEL

What is the name of this station?	Thi ni riak sa-thāni a-rai?	ที่นี่เรียกสถานีอะไร
How long do we stop here?	Rot chah yout thi-ni naan thao-rai?	รถจะหยุดที่นี้นานเท่าไร
Would you please look after my seat for a while?	Karuna doo thi-nang hai phõm khru nueng?	กรุณาดูที่นั่งให้ผมครู่หนึ่ง
Do you want to read this book?	Khun tongkarn arn nãng-sũe ni mãi?	คุณต้องการอ่านหนังสือนี้ไหม
I want to go to the lavatory.	Phõm chah pai hong sukhã.	ผมจะไปห้องสุขา
I want to eat in the Dining Car.	Phõm chah pai tharn a-harn thi rot-sabiang.	ผมจะไปทานอาหารที่รถเสบียง

In the Dining Car

Are you the Dining Car attendant?	Phanak-ngarn Rot-sabiang shai-mãi?	พนักงานรถเสบียงใช่ไหม
Please let me have ……	Phõm khãw……	ผมขอ……
– Mekhong and soda	– Mekhõng lae soda	– แม่โขงและโซดา
– a small bottle of Singha beer	– Beer Sĩngh nueng khuad-lek	– เบียร์สิงห์หนึ่งขวดเล็ก

172

– a bottle of stout	– **Beer damh nueng khuad**	– เบียร์ดำหนึ่งขวด
– a bottle of Coca Cola	– **Coca-Cola nueng khuad**	– โคคา-โคล่าหนึ่งขวด
– a glass of cold water	– **Narm yenh-yenh**	– น้ำเย็นเย็น
– crushed ice	– **Narm-khãeng konn**	– น้ำแข็งก้อน
– a plate of curry & rice	– **Khao raad kaeng**	– ข้าวราดแกง
– a plate of fried rice	– **Khao phad**	– ข้าวผัด
– a plate of steak on rice	– **Khao raad-na sa-teck**	– ข้าวราดหน้าสเต็ก
– a plate of fried beehoon	– **Sen-mi Khão phad**	– เส้นหมี่ขาวผัด
– a plate of ham sandwiches	– **Sandwiches mõu-haem**	– แซนด์วิชหมูแฮม
– a plate of sausages and eggs	– **Khai-dao sai-krawk**	– ไข่ดาวไส้กรอก
– a plain omelet	– **Khai-chiao**	– ไข่เจียว
– a bowl of Chinese vegetable soup	– **Kaeng-chued phak**	– แกงจืดผัก
– a bowl of prawn Tomyam	– **Tom-yam koung**	– ต้มยำกุ้ง

173

RAIL TRAVEL

– a plate of plain rice	– Khao-Plao	– ข้าวเปล่า
– Two toasts with butter/no butter	– Khanõm-pang-ping tha-neui/ mai tha-neui	– ขนมปังปิ้งทาเนย/ ไม่ทาเนย
– a glass of lime juice with ice	– Narm-som khanh	– น้ำส้มคั้น
– a glass of cold black coffee/tea	– Kafae/Sha damh-yenh	– กาแฟ/ชาดำเย็น
– a glass of cold white coffee/tea	– Kafae/Sha yenh sai-nom	– กาแฟ/ชาเย็นใส่นม
– a cup of hot black coffee/tea	– Kafae/Sha damh-ronn	– กาแฟ/ชาดำร้อน
– a cup of white hot coffee	– Kafae ronn sai-nom	– กาแฟร้อนใส่นม
I take strong coffee.	Phõm khaw kafae kae-kae.	ผมขอกาแฟแก่ๆ
I don't want milk and sugar.	Mai-sai nom lae narm-tarn.	ไม่ใส่นมและน้ำตาล
Do you sell imported cigarettes?	Mi buri-nawk khaai mãi?	มีบุหรี่นอกขายไหม
Do you sell matches?	Mi mai khide-fai mãi?	มีไม้ขีดไฟไหม
How much altogether?	Thang-mod thao-rai?	ทั้งหมดเท่าไร
Keep the change.	Keb wai.	เก็บไว้

On Arrival by Train During Short Stay at Station

What station is this?	**Thi ni sathãni a-rai?**	ที่นี่สถานีอะไร
How long does the train stop here?	**Rot yout naan thao-rai?**	รถหยุดนานเท่าไร
Does the train stop here long enough to give us time to eat?	**Rot yout naan phaw rap-pra-tharn a-harn set mãi?**	รถหยุดนานพอรับประทานอาหารเสร็จไหม
Where is the Refreshment Room?	**Hong chamnai a-hãrn khreuang duem you nai?**	ห้องจำหน่ายอาหารเครื่องดื่มอยู่ไหน
Is the train late?	**Rot-khong sĩa-vela?**	รถคงเสียเวลา
When do we arrive at Surash Thani?	**Meuarai raow chah thũeng Surash Thani?**	เมื่อไรเราจะถึงสุราษฎร์ธานี
I am going on to Haadyai tomorrow on the 10:38 train.	**Phõm chah pai Haadyai phrung-ni sib na-lika sãrm-sib paed.**	ผมจะไปหาดใหญ่พรุ่งนี้สิบนาฬิกาสามสิบแปด
Is there a micro-bus from here to the town?	**Rot bus lek chaak ni pai nai meuang mi mãi?**	รถบัสเล็กจากนี้ไปในเมืองมีไหม

175

RAIL TRAVEL

| I want to look around the town. | **Phõm tong-karn thiao shom changwad.** | ผมต้องการเที่ยวชม จังหวัด |

From Station to Hotel

Is there a hotel nearby?	**Thi klai-klai ni mi rongraem mãi?**	ที่ใกล้ใกล้นี้มีโรงแรมไหม
Drive me to the Wang Tai Hotel.	**Pha phõm pai thi rongraem Wang Tai.**	พาผมไปที่โรงแรมวังใต้
Do you know where the hotel is?	**Khun rou mãi rongraem you thi-nãi?**	คุณรู้ไหมโรงแรมอยู่ ที่ไหน
Load the luggage, please.	**Karuna shuai yok khõng.**	กรุณาช่วยยกของ
Is there room for everything?	**Mi thi-waang phaw mãi?**	มีที่ว่างพอไหม
Put these parcels/ suit-cases next to you in the taxi.	**Shuai aow haw/ krapãow laow-ni pai waang nai rot.**	ช่วยเอาห่อ/กระเป๋าเหล่านี้ ไปวางในรถ
We have alto-gether six pieces.	**Thang-mod mi hok shin.**	ทั้งหมดมีหกชิ้น
I will take the small parcels.	**Phõm aow haw lek pai.**	ผมเอาห่อเล็กไป

176

There are two suitcases, two bags, and two valises.	Mi krapaõw dern-thang yai sõng bai, thõung sõng thõung, kra-pãow-lek sõng bai.	มีกระเป๋าเดินทางใหญ่ สองใบ, ถุงสองถุง, กระเป๋าเล็กสองใบ
Drive carefully, please.	Karuna khap rawang-rawang noi.	กรุณาขับระวังระวังหน่อย
Please help me take these things down.	Shuai yok khong-ni long.	ช่วยยกของนี้ลง
Please watch my suitcases for a while.	Shuai dou kra-pãow hai phõm khru nueng.	ช่วยดูกระเป๋าให้ผม ครู่หนึ่ง
How much must I pay you?	Phõm tong chaai khun thao-rai?	ผมต้องจ่ายคุณเท่าไร
Keep the change.	Khun keb wai.	คุณเก็บไว้

LIVING

Living in Thailand

Renting an Apartment

I understand you have an apartment for rent.	Phõm saab-wa thanh mi hong-phak hai shaow.	ผมทราบว่าท่านมีห้องพักให้เช่า
What floor is it on?	You shanh nãi khrap?	อยู่ชั้นไหนครับ
Do you have an automatic elevator which operates twenty-four hours a day?	Mi lift attanomat shai-dai talawd yisibsi shua-mong mai khrap?	มีลิฟต์อัตโนมัติใช้ได้ตลอดยี่สิบสี่ชั่วโมงไหมครับ
Do you have car-parking facilities?	Mi thi chawd-rot mãi?	มีที่จอดรถไหม
How much does the apartment rent for?	Thanh khid kha-shaow yang-rai?	ท่านคิดค่าเช่าอย่างไร
Where is the entrance hall, the kitchen, and the living room?	Khow hong-thõng hong khrua laa hong nang-lenh thang nai?	เข้าห้องโถง ห้องครัว และห้องนั่งเล่นทางไหน
May I see the other room?	Phõm khãw shom hong thad-pai?	ผมขอชมห้องถัดไป

What about decorating?	Chah tha-sĭ tob-taeng hai duai mãi?	จะทาสีตกแต่งให้ด้วยไหม
I suppose you repaint/white-wash the apartment when someone moves in?	Phõm-wa thanh khong tha-sĭ hai konn mi khrai khow you shaimãi?	ผมว่าท่านคงทาสีให้ก่อนมีใครเข้าอยู่ใช้ไหม
On a two-year lease we will paint the whole apartment in whatever colours you want.	Tha tham-sãnya shaow sõng-pi chah tha-si hai mai sĭ arai kaw dai.	ถ้าทำสัญญาเช่าสองปีจะทาสีให้ใหม่-สีอะไรก็ได้
On a one-year lease, there is no redecorating.	Shaow nueng-pi mai-mi karn tha-sĭ tob-taeng a-rai thang-sin.	เช่าหนึ่งปีไม่มีการทาสีตบแต่งอะไรทั้งสิ้น
We might white-wash the walls, but nothing else.	Tae ach tha-sĭ phanang hai mai.	แต่อาจทาสีผนังให้ใหม่
May I see the bedroom, the bathroom?	Khãw shom hong-nonn, hong-narm hong suam.	ขอชมห้องนอน ห้องน้ำ ห้องส้วม
The bedroom is quite small.	Hong nonn lek pai.	ห้องนอนเล็กไป

LIVING

Do you like to sing?	Khun khong shob rong-phleng?	คุณคงชอบร้องเพลง
Play loud hi-fi records or cassette tapes, radios, or TV?	Perd phaen-siang, perd tapes dang-dang, perd vithayu rue TV dang-dang?	เปิดแผ่นเสียง เปิดเทป ดังๆ เปิดวิทยุ หรือ ทีวีดังๆ
We like to keep the place absolutely quiet.	Raow mai prasõng hai-mi sĩang rob-kuan baan-klai reuan-khiang.	เราไม่ประสงค์ให้มีเสียง รบกวนบ้านใกล้เรือน เคียง
I like a quiet place myself.	Phõm penh khon shob ngiap-ngiap you laew.	ผมเป็นคนชอบเงียบๆ อยู่แล้ว
If I decide to take the apartment, how soon could I move in?	Tha phõm tok-long chai shaow phõm chah khow ma you dai tang tae meua-rai?	ถ้าผมตกลงใจเช่า ผมจะเข้ามาอยู่ได้ ตั้งแต่เมื่อไร
It would take about a week or ten days to paint the whole thing.	Karn tha-sĩ hong, tong shai vela pramarn nueng a-thit rũe sib wanh.	การทาสีห้องต้องใช้เวลา ประมาณหนึ่งอาทิตย์ หรือสิบวัน

180

Assuming of course that you signed a two-year lease.	Phõm khid-wa khun khong tham sãnya shaow song pi.	ผมคิดว่าคุณคงทำสัญญา เช่าสองปี
I'd want my wife to see the apartment first.	Phõm khãw prueksã phan-raya lae hai khõw ma shom hong konn tatsĩn chai.	ผมขอปรึกษาภรรยาและ ให้เขามาชมห้องก่อน ตัดสินใจ
Perhaps I can come back with her sometime late this afternoon.	Bang-thi phõm chah ma kap theu yenh wan-ni.	บางทีผมจะมากับเธอเย็น วันนี้

Engaging a Servant

Come in! Who are you?	Nanh khrai? Khow ma dai!	นั่นใคร เข้ามาได้
What do you want?	Tong-karn a-rai?	ต้องการอะไร
Are you hunting for a job?	Maung-hã ngarn thamh rũe?	มองหางานทำหรือ
What's your name, please?	Khun shue a-rai?	คุณชื่ออะไร
What do you do for a living?	Tham-ma hã-kin a-rai?	ทำมาหากินอะไร

181

LIVING

Are you from up country?	Ma chaak tang-changwad rŭe?	มาจากต่างจังหวัดหรือ
Where do you live now?	Diao-ni phak thi-nǎi?	เดี๋ยวนี้พักที่ไหน
Where have you worked before and how long?	Tae-konn tham ngarn a-rai? Tham-ma narn thao-rai?	แต่ก่อนทำงานอะไร ทำมานานเท่าไร
What work experience do you have?	Mi khwam-rou, khwam sham-narn a-rai?	มีความรู้ ความชำนาญ อะไร
What did your work consist of exactly?	Ngam-sǎmkhan thi kheui tham penh ngarn a-rai?	งานสำคัญที่เคยทำเป็น งานอะไร
The job we have is somewhat similar.	Ngarn thi raow chah hai thamh kaw khlai-khlai kanh.	งานที่เราจะให้ทำก็คล้ายๆ กัน
What are your likes and dislikes?	Ngarn a-rai thi khun shob lae mai-shob?	งานอะไรที่คุณชอบและ ไม่ชอบ
Can you show me testimonials?	Mi bai rap-rong mai?	ใบรับรองมีไหม
Can you scrub, polish, sweep the floors and clean the toilets?	Khun thǒu-phuen, khad lae kwaad phuen dai mai?	คุณถูพื้น ขัดและกวาด พื้นได้ไหม

Can you clean up the yard, cut the grass, wash windows, wash the car?	Khun kwaad sanārm-ya, tat ya, shed natang, lang rot dai mai?	คุณกวาดสนามหน้า ตัดหญ้า เช็ดหน้าต่าง ล้างรถยนต์ ได้ไหม
Can you do some housework, cook Thai food, help in the kitchen?	Thamh ngarn-baan, tham a-hām Thai, penh louk-mue mae-khrua dai māi?	ทำงานบ้าน ทำอาหารไทย เป็นลูกมือในครัวได้ ไหม
What salary do you want?	Tong-karn ngoen-deuan thaorai?	ต้องการเงินเดือนเท่าไร
Do you prefer monthly salary or weekly wages?	Tongkarn chaai penh deuan rūe pen a-thit?	ต้องการจ่ายเป็นเดือน หรือเป็นอาทิตย์
I shall employ you and your salary will be 2500 baht a month.	Phŏm chah hai ngoen-deuan, deuan-lah song phan- ha-roi Baht.	ผมจะให้เงินเดือน เดือนละสองพันห้าร้อย บาท
Can you furnish me with 2 letters of reference?	Hã bai rap-rong chaak sãwng buk-khon ma duai dai-māi?	หาใบรับรองจากสอง บุคคลมาด้วยได้ไหม
When could you start working?	Chah rerm tham-ngarn dai tae meua-rai?	จะเริ่มทำงานได้แต่เมื่อไร

LIVING

I like people who are neat and clean in dress and personal habits.	Phõm tongkarn khon taeng-tua sa-ard riab-roi.	ผมต้องการคนสะอาด แต่งตัวเรียบร้อย
Don't call up your girl friends during working hours.	Ya sia-vela phoud-khui kap phuyĭng nai vela ngarn.	อย่าเสียเวลาพูดคุยกับ ผู้หญิงในเวลางาน

At a Barber Shop

Please give me a haircut.	Phõm tongkarn tat phõm.	ผมต้องการตัดผม
I'm in a terrible hurry.	Proad reng-mue phõm tong reep-pai.	โปรดเร่งมือ, ผมต้องรีบไป
Cut it short/very short.	Tat hai sanh /sanh maak-maak.	ตัดให้สั้น/สั้นมากๆ
Leave it long.	Ploi yao.	ปล่อยยาว
A little shorter here.	Trong-ni sanh nid-noi.	ตรงนี้สั้นนิดหน่อย
Don't cut it too short......	Ya hai sanh maak......	อย่าให้สั้นมาก......
– at the back	– thi darn-lãng	– ที่ด้านหลัง
– in front	– thi khang-na	– ที่ข้างหน้า
– at the sides	– thi darn-khang	– ที่ด้านข้าง

184

– on top	– thi tonn-bonh	– ที่ตอนบน
Don't cut any off the top.	Khang-bonh mai-tong tat.	ข้างบนไม่ต้องตัด
Cut a little more……	Karuna tat-awk ik……	กรุณาตัดออกอีก……
– off the neck	– thi tonh khaw	– ที่ต้นคอ
– off the sides	– thi darn khang	– ที่ด้านข้าง
– off the top	– thi tonn-bonh	– ที่ตอนบน
Don't take too much……	Ya tat hai sanh maak……	อย่าตัดให้สั้นมาก
– off the top	– thi khang-bonh	– ที่ข้างบน
– off the sides	– thi darn khang	– ที่ด้านข้าง
Please give me a mirror.	Khaw krachok-song.	ขอกระจกส่อง
You already cut too much off the back.	Khun tat khang-lãng awk maak pai.	คุณตัดข้างหลังออกมากไป
When you cut it short, I can't comb it.	Khun tat sanh maak, phõm wẽe mai dai.	คุณตัดสั้นมากผมหวีไม่ได้
Would you trim……?	Proad khlib……?	โปรดขลิบ……
– the moustache	– nuad awk	– หนวดออก
– the beard	– khrao awk	– เคราออก
I'd like to have ……	Karuna……	กรุณา……
– a shave	– kone	– โกน

185

LIVING

– a scalp massage	– nuad nãng si-sah	– นวดหนังศีรษะ
– my hair tinted	– yomm-phõm	– ย้อมผม
– an eyewash	– laang ta	– ล้างตา
I would like a shampoo and set.	Karuna sah-phõm lae set phõm.	กรุณาสระผมและเซ็ทผม
I don't want any oil or cosmetic.	Ya sai narm-manh rũe khreuang sãm-ang.	อย่าใส่น้ำมันหรือเครื่องสำอาง
A little brilliantine.	Sai cream narm-manh nid-noi	ใส่ครีมน้ำมันนิดหน่อย

At a Hairdresser and Beauty Salon

Can you recommend a good beauty parlour/hairdresser?	Sathãrn taeng-phõm/taeng-na di-di mi thi-nãi?	สถานแต่งผม/แต่งหน้าดีๆ มีที่ไหน
Can I make an appointment for sometime on Thursday?	Shãn khãw-chawng vela wanh pharuehat chah dai mãi?	ฉันขอจองเวลาวันพฤหัสจะได้ไหม
I want to have my hair permanently waved.	Shãn tongkarn dad-phõm baeb thãvorn.	ฉันต้องการตัดผมแบบถาวร

186

Please select a style to suit my face.	Proad ha baeb-phõm thi moh kab bai-na.	โปรดหาแบบผมที่เหมาะ กับใบหน้า
My hair is very long. I think you will have to cut my hair first.	Phõm shãn yao. Khid-wa Khun tong tat hai sanh konn.	ผมฉันยาว คิดว่าคุณต้อง ตัดให้สั้นก่อน
Give my hair a trim.	Proad lem awk sĩa bang.	โปรดเล็มออกเสียบ้าง
After that a wet shampoo.	Laew chueng sah duai shampoo.	แล้วจึงสระด้วยแชมพู
I would like to have......	Shãn tongkarn	ฉันต้องการ......
– a bleach	– kad sĩ phõm	– กัดสีผม
– a blow dry	– pow-haeng duai praeng	– เป่าแห้งด้วยแปรง
– a blow wave	– pow chab lawn	– เป่าจับลอน
– a colour rinse	– khleuab-sĩ phõm/ kroke phõm	– เคลือบสีผม/โกรกผม
– a complete re-style	– wée mai/plian-song phõm mai	– หวีใหม่/เปลี่ยนทรงผม ใหม่
– a demi-wave	– dad yang onn	– ดัดอย่างอ่อน
– a dye/dark rinse	– yomm-phõm/ yomm hai khem kwa derm	– ย้อมผม/ย้อมให้เข้ม กว่าเดิม
– a face-pack	– phawk-na duai mask	– พอกหน้าด้วยมาสก์

187

LIVING

– a facial and skin pack	– nuad-na lae phawk mask	– นวดหน้าและพอกมาสก์
– a form cutting	– tat hai khow roup	– ตัดให้เข้ารูป
– the finger waves	– chab lawn piak	– จับลอนเปียก
– a frizzy style	– song-phõm yik-yãwng	– ทรงผมหยิกหยอง
– my hair in a bun	– klao-phõm penh muai-klom	– เกล้าผมเป็นมวยกลม
– hair curls	– dad-phõm baeb lawn yik	– ดัดผมแบบลอนหยิก
– hair styling	– taeng song-phõm	– แต่งทรงผม
– a razor-cut	– tat-phõm duai meed-kone	– ตัดผมด้วยมีดโกน
– a re-comb	– wee phõm hai khow roup	– หวีผมให้เข้ารูป
– a page-boy style	– phõm song-mode/song bob	– ผมทรงโม้ด/ทรงบ๊อบ
– a poodle-cut	– tat-phõm song poodle	– ตัดผมทรงพุดเดิล
– a scissor-cut	– tat-phõm duai kan-krai	– ตัดผมด้วยกรรไกร
– style support perm	– dad-phõm hai you tua	– ตัดผมให้อยู่ตัว
– a tint	– taem si phõm	– แต้มสีผม

188

– a touch up	– yomm term thi khone phõm	– ย้อมเติมที่โคนผม
– with bangs	– tham-phõm prok na-phark	– ทำผมปรกหน้าผาก
– with ringlets	– tham-phõm penh khord	– ทำผมเป็นขอด
– with a fringe (long/short)	– song phõm ma (yao/sanh)	– ทรงผมม้า (ยาว/สั้น)
– to set the waves a little looser	– set phõm hai yik-saluai	– เซ็ทผมให้หยิกสลวย
I'd like......	Shãn tongkarn	ฉันต้องการ......
– the same colour	– sĭ diao kanh	– สีเดียวกัน
– a darker colour	– sĭ khem-khem	– สีเข้มๆ
– a lighter colour	– sĭ on-onn	– สีอ่อนๆ
– auburn/blond	– sĭ narm-tarn daeng/si blond	– สีน้ำตาลแดง/สีบลอนด์
– brunette	– sĭ phĭew-nãng	– สีผิวหนัง
Would you put this hair-piece/ wig on for me?	Sũam wig hai duai dai-mãi?	สวมวิกให้ด้วยได้ไหม

At the Cosmetics and Toiletries Shop

I would like to buy......	Phõm tong karn sue......	ผมต้องการซื้อ......

LIVING

– acne cream	– cream raksã sĩew fa	– ครีมรักษาสิวฝ้า
– after shave lotion	– nam-hõmm lãng kone nuad	– น้ำหอมหลังโกนหนวด
– antiseptic cream	– cream kha sheua	– ครีมฆ่าเชื้อ
– astringent cream	– cream sa-mãrn phĩew	– ครีมสมานผิว
– baby powder	– paeng roai-tua dek	– แป้งโรยตัวเด็ก
– bath essence	– nam-hõmm phasõm narm abb	– น้ำหอมผสมน้ำอาบ
– bath oil	– narm-mann shalom tua	– น้ำมันชโลมตัว
– bleaching cream	– cream lawk-na	– ครีมลอกหน้า
– brilliantine	– narm-manh sai phõm	– น้ำมันใส่ผม
– calamine	– ya kae-phod phuen-khan	– ยาแก้ผดผื่นคัน
– cleansing cream	– cream shamrah lang bai na	– ครีมชำระล้างใบหน้า
– conditioning lotion	– narm-ya bam-rung phĩew	– น้ำยาบำรุงผิว
– cold cream	– cream lang na	– ครีมล้างหน้า
– complexion milk	– narm-nom khad phĩew	– น้ำนมขัดผิว

190

– cuticle remover	– ya tham kwam sa-ard khob-leb	– ยาทำความสะอาดขอบเล็บ
– deodorant	– ya kamchad klin-tua	– ยากำจัดกลิ่นตัว
– deodorant spray	– spray sheed kamchad klin tua	– สเปรย์ฉีดกำจัดกลิ่นตัว
– dental cream	– ya sĭ fanh	– ยาสีฟัน
– dry shampoo	– shampoo sah phŏm haeng	– แชมพูสระผมแห้ง
– eye brow pencil	– din-săw khĭan khiew	– ดินสอเขียนคิ้ว
– eye darkener	– sĭ tha khŏn-ta/ khiew	– สีทาขนตา/คิ้ว
– eye shadow	– cream tha pleuak ta	– ครีมทาเปลือกตา
– face powder	– paeng phad na	– แป้งผัดหน้า
– face pack	– paeng phawk na	– แป้งพอกหน้า
– feminine syringe	– soub lang shong-klawd	– สูบล้างช่องคลอด
– foundation cream	– cream rong phuen	– ครีมรองพื้น
– hair bleach preparation	– ya kat-sĕe phŏm	– ยากัดสีผม
– hair restorer tonic	– shampoo kanh rang-khae	– แชมพูกันรังแค
– hair colour restorer	– ya yomm-phŏm	– ยาย้อมผม

LIVING

– hair brush	– praeng praeng-phõm	– แปรง แปรงผม
– hair cream	– cream sai phõm	– ครีมใส่ผม
– hand cream	– cream tha mue	– ครีมทามือ
– hair dye	– ya yomm phõm	– ยาย้อมผม
– hair lacquer	– lacker khleuap phõm	– แล็กเกอร์เคลือบผม
– hair pommade	– cream taeng phõm	– ครีมแต่งผม
– hair remover	– ya kamchad phõm/khõn	– ยากำจัดผม/ขน
– hair scalp condition cream	– cream bam-rung nãng sĩ-sah	– ครีมบำรุงหนังศีรษะ
– hair tonic	– ya bamrung sen phõm	– ยาบำรุงเส้นผม
– hair setting lotion	– narm-hõmm set phõm	– น้ำหอมเซทผม
– hair spray	– spray sheed phõm	– สเปรย์ฉีดผม
– hair tint	– sĩ taem phõm	– สีแต้มผม
– hormone cream	– cream phasom hormone	– ครีมผสมฮอร์โมน
– lip pencil	– din-sãw waad khob paak	– ดินสอวาดขอบปาก
– lipstick	– lipstick	– ลิปสติก
– liquid shampoo	– shampoo narm	– แชมพูน้ำ
– manicure set	– shoud tham leb	– ชุดทำเล็บ

– mascara	– si tha khõn-ta	– สีทาขนตา
– medicated soap	– sabu ya	– สบู่ยา
– moisturising cream	– cream bam-rung phĩew	– ครีมบำรุงผิว
– moisturising lotion	– narm-hõmm bamrung phĩew	– น้ำหอมบำรุงผิว
– mouth wash	– ya buan paak	– ยาบ้วนปาก
– nail brush	– praeng khad leb	– แปรงขัดเล็บ
– nail enamel	– ya tha leb	– ยาทาเล็บ
– nail file	– tabai leb	– ตะไบเล็บ
– nail polish	– ya khad leb	– ยาขัดเล็บ
– nail lacquer	– narm-manh tha leb	– น้ำมันทาเล็บ
– nail varnish remover	– ya laang leb	– ยาล้างเล็บ
– nail cream	– cream tha leb	– ครีมทาเล็บ
– nail scissor	– kan-krai tat leb	– กรรไกรตัดเล็บ
– perfume/lotion	– narm ob/narm hõmm	– น้ำอบ/น้ำหอม
– permanent wave curler	– lawd muan phõm	– หลอดม้วนผม
– powder compact	– paeng talab	– แป้งตลับ
– pumice stone	– hin khat	– หินขัด
– razor & razor blades	– meed lae bai meed-kone	– มีดและใบมีดโกน
– rouge cream	– cream tha kaem	– ครีมทาแก้ม
– rouge	– sĩ tha kaem	– สีทาแก้ม

LIVING

– shampoo oil/cream	– shampoo narm manh/cream	– แชมพูน้ำมัน/ครีม
– skin cream	– cream lang phĩew	– ครีมล้างผิว
– shaving brush	– praeng-praeng nuad	– แปรง-แปรงหนวด
– shaving cream	– cream kone nuad	– ครีมโกนหนวด
– sanitary napkins	– pha a-namai	– ผ้าอนามัย
– sponge	– fawng narm	– ฟองน้ำ
– spray perfume	– narm-ob spray	– น้ำอบสเปรย์
– sunning cream	– cream kae phit-daed	– ครีมแก้พิษแดด
– sun-glasses	– waenta kanh daed	– แว่นตากันแดด
– talcum powder	– foun roai-tua	– ฝุ่นโรยตัว
– toothbrush	– praeng sĩ fanh	– แปรงสีฟัน
– toilet soap	– sabu thũ tua	– สบู่ถูตัว
– vitamin hair tonic	– vitamin rak-sã-sen phõm	– วิตามินรักษาเส้นผม
– vitamin cream	– cream vitamin	– ครีมวิตามิน

At a Camera Shop

I want to buy......	Phõm tong-karn sue......	ผมต้องการซื้อ......

194

– an inexpensive camera	– klong thaai-pharb rakha yaow	– กล้องถ่ายภาพราคาเยา
– a fully automatic camera	– klong thaai shanid attano-mat	– กล้องถ่ายชนิดอัตโนมัติ
– an auto focus camera	– klong-thaai ruam-sãeng attanomat	– กล้องถ่ายรวมแสงอัตโนมัติ
– a pocket camera	– klong-thaai baeb kra-pãow	– กล้องถ่ายแบบกระเป๋า
– a cine camera	– klong-thaai pharbhayont	– กล้องถ่ายภาพยนตร์
– binoculars	– klong song thang-klai	– กล้องส่องทางไกล
Show me that one in the window, please.	Khãw shom klong thi waang nai tou-show.	ขอชมกล้องที่วางในตู้โชว์
I'd like......	Phõm yaak dai......	ผมอยากได้......
– colour negative films	– film sẽe	– ฟิล์มสี
+ GA 135	+ GA roi samsib-ha	+ ร้อยสามสิบห้า
+ CP 126	+ CP roi yisib hok	+ ร้อยยี่สิบหก
– black & white films	– film khão-damh	– ฟิล์มขาวดำ

195

LIVING

+ 135-36	+ roi samsib-ha	+ ร้อยสามสิบท้า
+ 120	+ roi yisib	+ ร้อยยี่สิบ
– movie films	– film pharbha-yont	– ฟิล์มภาพยนตร์
+ Super 8	+ super paed	+ ซูเปอร์แปด
– Reversal Roll Films	– film klab-see	ฟิล์มกลับสี
Do you have......?	Khun mi mãi......?	คุณมีไหม......
– camera lenses	– lens klong	– เลนส์กล้อง
– camera accessories	– upakorn a-lai	– อุปกรณ์กล้อง
– view-finders	– khreuang hã ra-yah	– เครื่องหาระยะ
– electro flash gun	– fire flash	– ไฟแฟลช
– exposure meter	– meter wat sãeng	– มิเตอร์วัดแสง
– filters	– krachok krong sãeng	– กระจกกรองแสง
– tripod	– sãrm-khã	– สามขา
How much do you charge for......?	Khun khid rakha yang-rai......?	คุณคิดราคาอย่างไร
– enlarging	– khayãi pharb	– ขยายภาพ
– developing	– lang film	– ล้างฟิล์ม
– printing	– add pharb	– อัดภาพ
Will you print this roll?	Khun shuai add pharb film muan ni hai dai mãi?	คุณช่วยอัดภาพฟิล์มม้วนนี้ให้ได้ไหม

I want two prints of each negative.	Phõm tong-karn pharb-lah sõng phaen.	ผมต้องการภาพละสอง แผ่น
Will you enlarge this?	Khayãai pharb-ni hai dai mãi?	ขยายภาพนี้ให้ได้ไหม
When will it be ready?	Meua-rai chah set?	เมื่อไรจะเสร็จ

At the Drugstore

I want......	Phõm tong-karn......	ผมต้องการ......
– something for a cold	– ya kae what	– ยาแก้หวัด
– a cough & sore throat	– ya kae aye lae cheb-khaw	– ยาแก้ไอและเจ็บคอ
– a headache & fever	– ya kae khai lae puad sĩsah	– ยาแก้ไข้และปวดศีรษะ
– burns and scalds	– ya phlãe narm-ronn luak	– ยาแผลน้ำร้อนลวก
– a sunburn	– ya kae phit daed	– ยาแก้พิษแดด
– minor cuts	– ya baad-phlãe lek-noi	– ยาบาดแผลเล็กน้อย
– insect-bites	– ya kae malaeng kad toi	– ยาแก้แมลงกัดต่อย

LIVING

May I have......?	Phõm yaak dai......	ผมอยากได้......
– antacids & digestives	– ya lod-krot lae khleuap-phlãe kra-phaw a-hãrm.	– ยาลดกรดและเคลือบแผลกระเพาะอาหาร
– nerve tonic	– ya bamrung prasard	– ยาบำรุงประสาท
– eye drops/eye wash, lotion	– ya yawd ta/ya lang-ta	– ยาหยอดตา/ยาล้างตา
– mouthwash	– ya buan paak	– ยาบ้วนปาก
– cough syrup	– ya kae aye	– ยาแก้ไอ
– stomach pills	– ya kae puad-thong	– ยาแก้ปวดท้อง
– kidney pills	– ya raksã tai	– ยารักษาไต
– castor oil	– narm-manh la-houng	– น้ำมันละหุ่ง
– throat lozenges	– ya omm kae cheb-khaw	– ยาอมแก้เจ็บคอ
– cod liver oil	– narm-manh tab-pla	– น้ำมันตับปลา
– contraceptive pills	– ya khoum kam-nerd	– ยาคุมกำเนิด
– migraine remedies	– ya puad sisah, puad prasard	– ยาปวดศีรษะ, ปวดประสาท
– insect repellent cream	– cream lai yung	– ครีมไล่ยุง

198

– paracetamol	– ya kae puad paracetamol	– ยาพาราเซตามอล แก้ปวด
– vitamin complex	– vitamin ruam	– วิตามินรวม
– Mixt. Salol & Menthol	– ya thart Narm Khăo	– ยาธาตุน้ำขาว
– spiritus menthae pipperitae	– laow saranae	– เหล้าสะระแหน่
– spirit of ammonia aromatic	– yiao Oudh	– เยี่ยวอูฐ
– solution of mercuro-chrome	– ya daeng	– ยาแดง
– acriflavine solution	– ya lĕuang	– ยาเหลือง
– tincture iodine	– tincture iodine	– ทิงเจอร์ไอโอดีน
– embrocation	– ya tha kae puad	– ยาทาแก้ปวด
– analgesic balm	– ya maung	– ยาหม่อง
– gauze bandage	– pha phan-phlãe	– ผ้าพันแผล
– cotton wool	– săm-lee	– สำลี
– plasters	– plasters	– พลาสเตอร์
– menthol plasters	– plaster-ya banthao puad	– พลาสเตอร์ยา บรรเทาปวด
– eucalyptus oil	– narm-manh eucalyptus	– น้ำมันยูคาลิปตัส
– prickly heat powder	– paeng-hŏmm prickly heat	– แป้งหอมปริกลีฮีท
– denture cleaning powder	– ya lang-fanh plomm	– ยาล้างฟันปลอม

LIVING

| – earache drops | – ya yawd-hoo | – ยาหยอดหู |

Accidents and Illnesses

I don't feel good. I need a doctor.	Phõm mai sabaai. Phõm tong phob mãw.	ผมไม่สบาย ผมต้องพบหมอ
Send for a doctor, please.	Karuna riak mãw.	กรุณาเรียกหมอ
Is there a drugstore near here?	Thi klai-klai mi raan-khãai-ya mãi?	ที่ใกล้-ใกล้มีร้านขายยา ไหม
I want to go to a hospital/clinic.	Phõm tong pai rong phaya-bam/ clinic phaed.	ผมต้องไปโรงพยาบาล/ คลินิกแพทย์
Are you the doctor?	Khun-mãw shai mãi?	คุณหมอใช่ไหม
Would you have a look at......	Khun-mãw karuna truad......	คุณหมอ กรุณาตรวจ......
– my face	– bai-na phõm	– ใบหน้าผม
– my tonsils	– tom tonsil	– ต่อมทอมซิล
– my throat	– lamh-khaw	– ลำคอ
– this wound	– bard-phlãe	– บาดแผล
– this boil	– fẽe	– ฝี
– this rash	– phuen phuh- phong	– ผื่นพุพอง

200

– this swelling	– a-karn buam	– อาการบวม
I have a headache/ dizziness.	Phõm puad sĩ-sah/ mi a-karn mueng-ngong.	ผมปวดศีรษะ/ มีอาการมึนงง
I have an uncom-fortable feeling.	Phõm rou-suek mai sa-baai.	ผมรู้สึกไม่สบาย
I have caught a cold.	Phõm penh what.	ผมเป็นหวัด
I feel very sick.	Phõm mai sa-baai maak.	ผมไม่สบายมาก
I have pains in all my bones and joints.	Phõm puad meui thang tua, kradouk lae khaw-taw.	ผมปวดเมื่อยทั้งตัว, กระดูกและข้อต่อ
I have a sore throat.	Phõm cheb khaw.	ผมเจ็บคอ
I have been vomiting.	Phõm mi ar-chian.	ผมมีอาเจียน
I cough frequently.	Phõm aye boi-khrang.	ผมไอบ่อยครั้ง
I don't sleep well.	Phõm nonn mai-lab.	ผมนอนไม่หลับ
I suffer from indigestion.	A-hãrn mai yoi.	อาหารไม่ย่อย
I am suffering from constipation.	Thong phouk.	ท้องผูก

LIVING

I have diarrhoea and gripping pains in the abdomen.	Thong dern lae puad thong.	ท้องเดินและปวดท้อง
I have been shivering all night long.	Phõm não sanh talawd khuen.	ผมหนาวสั่นตลอดคืน
I have pains in my stomach.	Phõm puad thong.	ผมปวดท้อง
I have got a pain here.	Phõm puad trong-ni.	ผมปวดตรงนี้
I think I have broken......	Phõm khid-wa......	ผมคิดว่า......
– my arm/my leg	– khãen hak/ khã hak	– แขนหัก/ขาหัก
– my neck/collar bone	– khaw/kradouk hãi-pla-ra hak	– คอ/กระดูก ไหปลาร้าหัก
Are you the dentist?	Thanh penh mãw-fanh rũe?	ท่านเป็นหมอฟันหรือ
I have an acute toothache.	Phõm puad fanh maak.	ผมปวดฟันมาก
I want a tooth to be pulled out.	Proad thãwn fanh.	โปรดถอนฟัน

The Post & Telegraph Office

I want to post this letter.	Phõm tongkarn thing chodmãi ni.	ผมต้องการทิ้งจดหมายนี้
Where is the Post Office?	Thi-thamkarn Praisani you thi nãi?	ที่ทำการไปรษณีย์อยู่ที่ไหน
What is the postage on this letter......?	Tong tit stamp thao-rai sãmrap chod mãi ni?	ต้องติดแสตมป์เท่าไร สำหรับจดหมายนี้
– printed book	– nãngsũe lem ni	– หนังสือเล่มนี้
– post card	– post card	– บัตรโปสการ์ด
– by airmail	– thaang a-kas	– ทางอากาศ
– by surface mail	– thaang reua	– ทางเรือ
I want to register this letter.	Phõm tongkarn long thabian chodmãi ni.	ผมต้องการลงทะเบียนจดหมายนี้
I want to send this parcel to the United States.	Phõm tongkam song phasadu ni pai Amerika.	ผมต้องการส่งพัสดุนี้ไปอเมริกา
I want to send this......	Phõm tongkam song......	ผมต้องการส่ง......
– small packet	– phasadu yoi ni	– พัสดุย่อยนี้
– postcard	– praisani-bat ni	– ไปรษณียบัตรนี้
– printed matter	– sing-phim ni	– สิ่งพิมพ์นี้

LIVING

I want to send this package by…	Phõm tongkarn song haw ni pai thang…	ผมต้องการส่งห่อนี้ไปทาง
– express delivery	– praisani duan	– ไปรษณีย์ด่วน
– acknowledged delivery	– praisani tob-rab	– ไปรษณีย์ตอบรับ
– parcel post	– phasadu praisani	– พัสดุไปรษณีย์
I want to insure these goods.	Phõm tongkam aow prakanh.	ผมต้องการเอาประกัน
I want to buy……	Phõm khãw sue……	ผมขอซื้อ……
– five air letters	– chodmãi a-kas ha phaen	– จดหมายอากาศห้าแผ่น
– ten 2-Baht stamps	– stamps rakha sõng Baht sib duang	– แสตมป์ราคาสองบาท สิบดวง
– different stamps for a collection	– stamps keb wai dou-lenh	– แสตมป์เก็บไว้ดูเล่น
Where is the posting box?	Tou chodmãi you thi nãi?	ตู้จดหมายอยู่ที่ไหน
Where is the Poste Restante?	Praisani raw-chaai you thi nãi?	ไปรษณีย์รอจ่ายอยู่ที่ไหน
My name is Richard Ho from Singapore.	Phõm shue Richard Ho chaak Sĩngkhapo.	ผมชื่อ ริชาร์ด โฮ จากสิงคโปร์
Here is my passport.	Ni nãngsũe dern-thang phõm.	นี่หนังสือเดินทางผม

204

Is there any mail for me?	Mi chodmãi thũeng phõm mãi?	มีจดหมายถึงผมไหม
I want to send a Money Order.	Phõm tongkarn song thana-nat.	ผมต้องการส่งธนาณัติ
I want to cash this Money Order.	Phõm tongkarn rab thana-nat.	ผมต้องการรับธนาณัติ
I want to send a telegram.	Phõm tongkarn song thoralek.	ผมต้องการส่งโทรเลข
May I have a telegraphic form, please?	Karuna khãw baeb-form phõm nueng phaen.	กรุณาขอแบบฟอร์ม ผมหนึ่งแผ่น
How much is it per word?	Thoralek kham-lah thaorai?	โทรเลขคำละเท่าไร
When does the office close?	Meuarai thi-tham-karn chah pid?	เมื่อไรที่ทำการจะปิด
Telephone booth (Public Telephone)	Tou thorasab Sãtharanah	ตู้โทรศัพท์สาธารณะ
Telephone exchange	Shoum-sãai thorasab	ชุมสายโทรศัพท์
Telephone operator	Phanak-ngam thorasab	พนักงานโทรศัพท์
Telephone directory	Samud thorasab	สมุดโทรศัพท์
Where is the telephone booth?	Tou thorasab mi thi-nãi? you thi-nãi?	ตู้โทรศัพท์มีที่ไหน/ อยู่ที่ไหน
I would like to telephone.	Phõm tongkarn thorasab.	ผมต้องการโทรศัพท์

LIVING

May I use your telephone, please?	Karuna hai phõm shai thorasab dai mãi?	กรุณาให้ผมใช้โทรศัพท์ได้ไหม
Do you have a telephone directory?	Khun mi samud thorasab mãi?	คุณมีสมุดโทรศัพท์ไหม
What is your telephone number?	Thorasab khun beur a-rai?	โทรศัพท์คุณเบอร์อะไร
I cannot read Thai.	Phõm ann bhasã Thai mai-dai.	ผมอ่านภาษาไทยไม่ได้
Would you please help me find the number?	Proad hã beur thorasab hai phõm dai-mãi?	โปรดหาเบอร์โทรศัพท์ให้ผมได้ไหม
I want to pay for the call.	Phõm chah hai kha-borikarn.	ผมจะให้ค่าบริการ
Hello, I'd like to talk to Mr. Phongthip.	Hello, phõm khaw phoud kab Mr. Phongthip.	เฮลโล, ผมขอพูดกับมิสเตอร์พงศ์ทิพย์
This is Ali bin Karim speaking.	Ni phõm Ali bin karirn phoud.	นี่ผม อาลี บิน การิม พูด
Who's that speaking?	Nanh khrai phoud?	นั่นใครพูด
Speak a little louder, I can't hear you.	Phoud dang-dang Phõm mai-dai yin.	พูดดังๆ ผมไม่ได้ยิน
Please speak more slowly.	Karuna phoud sha-sha.	กรุณาพูดช้าๆ

206

Please hold the line.	Karuna ya waang hõu.	กรุณาอย่าวางหู
The line is engaged. Could I ring up again later?	Sãai mai waang. Phõm thoh ma mai ik dai mãi?	สายไม่ว่าง ผมโทรมาใหม่อีกได้ไหม
There's no answer.	Mai mi sĩang tobb.	ไม่มีเสียงตอบ
The phone is out of order.	Sãai sĩa.	สายเสีย
Operator, you gave me the wrong number.	Khun phanak-gnam, khun hai number phõm phid.	คุณพนักงาน คุณให้นัมเบอร์ผมผิด
Hello! This is Jack Anderson.	Hello! Ni Jack Anderson.	เฮลโหล นี่แจ๊คแอนเดอร์สัน
I want to speak to Khun Thawatchai.	Phõm tongkarn phoud kap Khun Thawatchai.	ผมต้องการพูดกับคุณ ธวัชชัย
He's out at the moment.	Dĩao-ni khão pai khang-nawk.	เดี๋ยวนี้ เขาไปข้างนอก
When will he be back?	Meuarai khão chah klab?	เมื่อไรเขาจะกลับ
Will you tell him I called?	Shuai bawk khão wa phõm thoh ma?	ช่วยบอกเขาว่าผมโทรมา
Would you ask him to call me?	Shuai bawk khão hai thoh ma hã phõm?	ช่วยบอกเขาให้โทรมาหาผม

LIVING

My telephone number is 5883655.	**Beur thorasab phõm 5883655.**	เบอร์โทรศัพท์ผม 5883655
I would like to make a long-distance call to Chiangmai.	**Phõm tongkarn thorasab thang-klai pai Chiangmai.**	ผมต้องการโทรศัพท์ทาง ไกลไปเชียงใหม่
I want to call number 235334.	**Phõm tongkarn riak beur 235334.**	ผมต้องการเรียกเบอร์ 235334
How much will you charge for a call?	**Attra phoud khid yang-rai?**	อัตราพูดคิดอย่างไร

Calling on a Friend

Will you show me which is Mr. Suraphong's house?	**Karuna shi baan thi khun Suraphong you?**	กรุณาชี้บ้านที่คุณสุรพงศ์ อยู่
Is this where Suraphong lives?	**Ni baan khun Suraphong shai mãi?**	นี่บ้านคุณสุรพงศ์ใช่ไหม
Is he at home?	**Khun Suraphong you mãi?**	คุณสุรพงศ์อยู่ไหม
How do you do, Mr. Suraphong?	**Khun Suraphong, sabaai di rũe?**	คุณสุรพงศ์สบายดีหรือ

I am Ishiyama from Tokyo and this is my wife Yukiko.	Phõm Ishiyama chaak Tokyo lae ni Yukiko, phan-raya phõm.	ผมอิชิยามาจากโตเกียว และนี่ยูกิโกะภรรยาผม
I'd like you to meet my friend, Mr. Arshad Othman from Singapore.	Phõm khãw nae namh pheuan Mr. Arshad Othman chaak Singkhapo.	ผมขอแนะนำเพื่อน มิสเตอร์อารชัด อ๊อทมัน จากสิงคโปร์
Delighted to meet you.	Yindi thi rouchak khun.	ยินดีที่รู้จักคุณ
Please come in. Let's sit down and have a chat.	Shern khang-nai, ma sõn-thana kanh.	เชิญข้างใน มาสนทนากัน
Would you like to drink something?	Khun duem a-rai mãi?	คุณดื่มอะไรไหม
What good wind brings you to Thailand ?	Lom a-rai phad-pha khun ma Prathesh Thai?	ลมอะไรพัดพาคุณมา ประเทศไทย
Is this your first visit to Thailand?	Ni penh khrang-raek thi khun ma Prathesh Thai shai-mãi?	นี่เป็นครั้งแรกที่คุณมา ประเทศไทยใช่ไหม
How long have you been here?	Khun ma thi-ni naan thaorai laew?	คุณมาที่นี่นานเท่าไรแล้ว

209

LIVING

We have been here a week.	Raow ma nueng sapda laew.	เรามาหนึ่งสัปดาห์แล้ว
At what hotel are you staying?	Khun phak rongraem nãi?	คุณพักโรงแรมไหน
Are you staying here long?	Chah phak you naan sak thaorai?	จะพักอยู่นานสักเท่าไร
Only four more days.	Phiang si wanh thao-nanh.	เพียงสี่วันเท่านั้น
How do you find Bangkok? A lot of fun?	Krungthep penh yang-rai? Sanuk mãi?	กรุงเทพฯ เป็นอย่างไร สนุกไหม
What kind of business are you in?	Khun tham thurakich a-rai?	คุณทำธุรกิจอะไร
I'm in the clothing business.	Phõm chamnaai seua-pha sãmret roup.	ผมจำหน่ายเสื้อผ้า สำเร็จรูป
I'm here on a business trip.	Phõm ma tham thura-kich thi-ni.	ผมมาทำธุรกิจที่นี่
Would you like a cigarette?	Soup buri mãi?	สูบบุหรี่ไหม
Have you got a light, please?	Khun mi mai khide-fai mãi?	คุณมีไม้ขีดไฟไหม
Will you have coffee?	Duem kafae mãi?	ดื่มกาแฟไหม
Are you free this evening?	Yenh-ni khun waang mãi?	เย็นนี้คุณว่างไหม

210

LIVING

Do stay for dinner with me.	Shern you rappratharn a-hãrn duai kanh.	เชิญอยู่รับประทานอาหาร ด้วยกัน
Would you like to go dancing?	Khun yaak pai tenh-ram mãi?	คุณอยากไปเต้นรำไหม
I know a good discotheque.	Phõm rou-chak disco nightclub thi di-di.	ผมรู้จัก ดิสโก้ ไนท์คลับ ที่ดีๆ
Are you doing anything tomorrow?	Phrung-ni khun chah tham a-rãi?	พรุ่งนี้คุณจะทำอะไร
Can you come round for dinner?	Phrung-ni tharn a-harn duai-kanh mãi?	พรุ่งนี้ทานอาหาร ด้วยกันไหม
Great, I'd love to come.	Visesh, phõm yin-di ma.	วิเศษ-ผมยินดีมา
It's very kind of you!	Khun chai-di chang!	คุณใจดีจัง
This is Thai food. I hope you like it.	Ni penh a-hãrn Thai. Khun khong shob.	นี่เป็นอาหารไทย คุณคงชอบ
Thank you for your nice dinner.	Khob-khun maak samrab a-hãrn rot visesh.	ขอบคุณมากสำหรับ อาหารรสวิเศษ
I have really enjoyed it.	Phõm tharn dai a-roi ching-ching.	ผมทานได้อร่อยจริงๆ

211

LIVING

It's getting late and I have to go now.	Duek laew, phõm tong khãw tua klab konn.	ดึกแล้ว ผมต้องขอตัวกลับก่อน
Thank you very much; it's been a wonderful evening.	Phõm khob-khun maak, khuen ni phõm mi khwam souk.	ผมขอบคุณมาก คืนนี้ผมมีความสุข

Emergencies

Thief! Stop thief!	Khamoai! Chab khamoai!	ขโมย! จับขโมย!
Hurry up. Call the police?	Reow. Riak tamruat!	เร็ว เรียกตำรวจ
Help me!	Shuai-duai!	ช่วยด้วย!
Look out!	Rawang!	ระวัง!
Stop! Stay where you are!	Yout! Ya khleuan-thi!	หยุด! อย่าเคลื่อนที่
Excuse me, could you help me?	Shuai-phõm noi dai mãi?	ช่วยผมหน่อยได้ไหม
Get a doctor quick!	Shuai riak mãw reow!	ช่วยเรียกหมอเร็ว!
I have been assaulted by two gunmen.	Phõm thouk song mue-puen tham-rai.	ผมถูกสองมือปืนทำร้าย
I have been held at gun-point.	Phõm thouk chi duai puen.	ผมถูกจี้ด้วยปืน

212

Last night a thief broke into my house.	Khamoai khow baan-phŏm meua-khuen ni.	ขโมยเข้าบ้านผมเมื่อคืนนี้
That man stole my money.	Khon nanh khamoai ngoen phŏm.	คนนั้นขโมยเงินผม
I have been robbed of everything.	Phŏm thouk khamoai kliang-tua.	ผมถูกขโมยเกลี้ยงตัว
What things were stolen?	Khamoai a-rai pai?	ขโมยอะไรไป
– My camera	– Klong thaai-roup	– กล้องถ่ายรูป
– My wrist-watch	– Nalika khaw-mue	– นาฬิกาข้อมือ
– Gold ornaments	– Khreuang petch-thawng	– เครื่องเพชรทอง
– My passport	– Nǎngsüe dern-thang	– หนังสือเดินทาง
– My traveller's cheques	– Cheques dern-thang	– เช็คเดินทาง
– My plane tickets	– Tǔa khreuang-bin	– ตั๋วเครื่องบิน
– 5,000 Baht in cash	– Ngoen sot ha-phan Baht	– เงินสดห้าพันบาท
– 500 U S dollars	– Ha-roi dollar American	– ห้าร้อยดอลลาร์ อเมริกัน

213

LIVING

– 500 Malaysian ringgit	– Ha-roi rĩan Malaysia	– ห้าร้อยเหรียญมาเลเซีย
– I have lost all my money.	– Ngoen phõm hãai mod.	– เงินผมหายหมด
Where was the crime committed?	Head kerd thi-nãi?	เหตุเกิดที่ไหน
It was committed only 200 metres from here.	Haang chaak-ni sõng-roi metres.	ห่างจากนี้สองร้อยเมตร
When did the police arrive on the scene?	Tamruat ma thũeng meua-rai?	ตำรวจมาถึงเมื่อไร
I don't know exactly what time it was.	Phom mai sab vela thi nae-nonn.	ผมไม่ทราบเวลาที่แน่นอน
At midnight I think.	Pramarn sõng-yarm hẽn cha-dai.	ประมาณสองยามเห็น จะได้
Police Headquarters	Kawng bansha-karn tamruat	กองบัญชาการตำรวจ
Police Station	Sathãni tamruat	สถานีตำรวจ
Policeman	Tamruat	ตำรวจ
Police Inspector	Sãravat tamruat	สารวัตรตำรวจ
Desk-Sargeant	Sib-vain	สิบเวร
Chief of Police	Phu kamkab	ผู้กำกับ
Country Police	Tamruat phu-thorn	ตำรวจภูธร

214

May I......?

May I know your name and address?	Phom khãw shue lae thi-you dai-mãi?	ผมขอชื่อและที่อยู่ได้ไหม
May I occupy this seat?	Phõm nang thi-ni dai mãi?	ผมนั่งที่นี่ได้ไหม
May I help you?	Phõm shuai dai mãi?	ผมช่วยได้ไหม
May I be excused?	Phõm khaw-tua dai mãi?	ผมขอตัวได้ไหม
May I use your phone?	Khãw shai thorasab dai mãi?	ขอใช้โทรศัพท์ได้ไหม
May I borrow your pen?	Yuem pak-ka khun dai mãi?	ยืมปากกาคุณได้ไหม
May I have this?	Ni phõm khãw dai mãi?	นี่ผมขอได้ไหม
May I look at your book?	Khãw phõm dou nãngsũe dai mãi?	ขอผมดูหนังสือได้ไหม
May I intro- duce......?	Phõm khãw naeh- nam......?	ผมขอแนะนำคุณ......
May I photograph here?	Khãw thaai-roup thi-ni dai mãi?	ขอถ่ายรูปที่นี่ได้ไหม
May I ask you something?	Khãw thãrm a-rai noi dai mãi?	ขอถามอะไรหน่อยได้ไหม

215

LIVING

May I kiss you?	**Khãw choub noi dai mãi?**	ขอจูบหน่อยได้ไหม
May I go inside?	**Khãw khow-pai khang-nai dai mãi?**	ขอเข้าไปข้างในได้ไหม
May I see the room?	**Khãw doo hong dai mãi?**	ขอดูห้องได้ไหม
May I sleep with you?	**Nonn duai-khon dai mãi?**	นอนด้วยคนได้ไหม
May I leave my things here for a while?	**Faak khõng wai sak-khrou dai mãi?**	ฝากของไว้สักครู่ได้ไหม
May I have a receipt?	**Tham bai-rap hai phõm dai mãi?**	ทำใบรับให้ผมได้ไหม
May I smoke?	**Phõm soub buri dai mãi?**	ผมสูบบุหรี่ได้ไหม
May I park my car here?	**Phõm khãw chawd rot thi-ni dai mãi?**	ผมขอจอดรถที่นี่ได้ไหม
May I borrow your newspaper?	**Yuem nãngsũe-phim dai mãi?**	ยืมหนังสือพิมพ์ได้ไหม
May I look at your picture?	**Phõm khãw shom pharb-thaai khun dai mãi?**	ผมขอชมภาพถ่ายคุณได้ไหม
May I use your lavatory?	**Khãw a-nuyart shai suam khun dai mãi?**	ขออนุญาตใช้ส้วมคุณได้ไหม

May I change this?	Phõm khãw plian dai mãi?	ผมขอเปลี่ยนได้ไหม
May I look around?	Phõm khãw dern shom dai mãi?	ผมขอเดินชมได้ไหม
May I switch on your radio/T.V.?	Phõm perd vithayu/ T.V. dai mai?	ผมเปิดวิทยุ/ทีวีได้ไหม
May I close the window?	Phõm pid na-tang dai mãi?	ผมปิดหน้าต่างได้ไหม
May I open the window?	Phõm perd na-tang dai mãi?	ผมเปิดหน้าต่างได้ไหม
May I switch on the light?	Phõm perd fai dai mãi?	ผมเปิดไฟได้ไหม
May I switch off the light?	Khãw pid fai dai mãi?	ขอปิดไฟได้ไหม
May I speak to......?	Khãw phõm phoud kab...... dai mãi?	ขอผมพูดกับคุณ...... ได้ไหม
May I go first?	Khãw phõm pai konn dai mãi?	ขอผมไปก่อนได้ไหม
May I join you?	Khãw ruam duai dai mãi?	ขอร่วมด้วยได้ไหม
May I have a glass of cold water?	Khãw narm yenh sak kaew dai mãi?	ขอน้ำเย็นสักแก้วได้ไหม
May I trouble you for a light?	Khãw rob-kuan mai khide-fai dai mãi?	ขอรบกวนไม้ขีดไฟ ได้ไหม

LIVING

May I have the bill?	Khãw bill dai mãi?	ขอบิลได้ไหม
May I give you a lift?	Hai phõm pai song dai-mãi?	ให้ผมไปส่งได้ไหม
May I pick you up this evening?	Phõm ma rab khun yen-ni dai mãi?	ผมมารับคุณเย็นนี้ได้ไหม
May I call on you again?	Khãw phob ik dai mãi?	ขอพบอีกได้ไหม
May I leave a message for him?	Khãw faak khao thũeng khõw dai mãi?	ขอฝากข่าวถึงเขาได้ไหม

Social Conversation

How are you?	Khun sabaai di rũe?	คุณสบายดีหรือ
I am quite well, thank you.	Phõm sabaai di, khob khun.	ผมสบายดี ขอบคุณ
I haven't seen you for a long time.	Mai dai phop kanh narn (thi-diao).	ไม่ได้พบกันนานทีเดียว
How is your family?	Khrob-khrua khun penh yang-rai?	ครอบครัวคุณเป็นอย่างไร
They are all fine, thanks.	Thouk-khon sabaai di, khob-khun.	ทุกคนสบายดี ขอบคุณ

218

May I introduce my friend, Miss Yvonne.	Khaw nae-namh pheuan-phõm Khun Yvonne.	ขอแนะนำเพื่อนผม คุณอีวอน
Her home is in Paris.	Baan theu you nai Paris.	บ้านเธออยู่ในปารีส
She wants to see your beautiful country.	Yvonne yaak-ma prathesh sũai-ngarm khõng khun.	อีวอนอยากมาประเทศ สวยงามของคุณ
She loves to speak Thai.	Theu sõn-chai phoud Thai.	เธอสนใจพูดไทย
She wishes to have Thai friends.	Theu tongkarn mi pheuan Thai.	เธอต้องการมีเพื่อนไทย
Do you speak French?	Khun phoud Farangset dai mãi?	คุณพูดฝรั่งเศสได้ไหม
No, I speak only English.	Mai, phõm phoud dai tae Angkrit.	ไม่-ผมพูดได้แต่อังกฤษ
Can you speak Chinese?	Khun phoud Chine dai mai?	คุณพูดจีนได้ไหม
Yes, a little Mandarin. But I can speak more Cantonese.	Phoud Chine Mandarin dai-tae bhasa Kwangtung dai maak kwa.	พูดจีนแมนดารินได้ แต่ภาษากวางตุ้งได้ มากกว่า
I want to learn Thai.	Phõm son-chai rian bhasã Thai.	ผมสนใจเรียนภาษาไทย

LIVING

Is the Thai language difficult?	Bhasā Thai yaak mãi?	ภาษาไทยยากไหม
No, Thai is not difficult and will be most useful in the future.	Bhasā Thai rian mai yaak lae chah mi prayote nai a-na-khot.	ภาษาไทยเรียนไม่ยาก และจะมีประโยชน์ ในอนาคต
It's good to know Thai.	Rou bhasa Thai wai di.	รู้ภาษาไทยไว้ดี
Can you tell me where the Railway Station is?	Karuna bawk-phom dai mãi pai Sathani Rot-fai thang nãi?	กรุณาบอกผมได้ไหม ไปสถานีรถไฟทางไหน
How do I get there?	Pai thũeng dai yang-rai?	ไปถึงได้อย่างไร
I want to go to this address.	Phõm tongkam pai thi-ni.	ผมต้องการไปที่นี่
How far is it from here?	Chaak ni pai ik klai mãi?	จากนี้ไปอีกไกลไหม
Where does this bus go?	Rot pracham-thang ni pai nãi?	รถประจำทางนี้ไปไหน
Does it go into the city?	Rot-ni pai changwad rũe?	รถนี้ไปจังหวัดหรือ
That's very kind of you.	Phõm khob-khun maak.	ผมขอบคุณมาก
Where do you live?	Khun you thi nãi?	คุณอยู่ที่ไหน

220

Do you live alone or with your family?	Khun you khon-diao rũe you kap khrob-khrũa?	คุณอยู่คนเดียวหรืออยู่กับครอบครัว
Do you live here?	Khun you thi-ni rũe?	คุณอยู่ที่นี่หรือ
What is the name of this road?	Thanõn-ni shue thanõn a-rai?	ถนนนี้ชื่อถนนอะไร
Do you have the correct time?	Vela khõng-khun trong mãi?	เวลาของคุณตรงไหม
Are you sure your watch is right?	Nalika khun trong nae rũe?	นาฬิกาคุณตรงแน่หรือ
It may be a few minutes slow.	Art chah-sha sõng-sãrm nathi.	อาจช้าสองสามนาที
Excuse me for troubling you.	Phõm khãw a-bhai thi rob-kuan khun.	ผมขออภัยที่รบกวนคุณ
What's the matter?	Mi a-rai rue khrap?	มีอะไรหรือครับ
My car has broken down.	Khreuang yont phõm mai tham-ngarn.	เครื่องยนต์ผมไม่ทำงาน
Do you have a telephone?	Khun mi thorasab mãi?	คุณมีโทรศัพท์ไหม
May I use your phone, please?	Khãw phõm shai thorasab dai mãi?	ขอผมใช้โทรศัพท์ได้ไหม

221

LIVING

I think there's something wrong with the......	Phõm wa khong penh thi......	ผมว่าคงเป็นที่......
– carburettor	– carburettor	– คาร์บูเรเตอร์
– ignition system	– rabob karn choud fai	– ระบบการจุดไฟ
– transmission	– karn thaai kamlang	– การถ่ายกำลัง
Where is the nearest filling station?	Raan narm-manh klai-klai mi mãi?	ร้านน้ำมันใกล้ๆ มีไหม
I'd like to see Mr. Jackson.	Karuna khãw-phob Mr. .Jackson.	กรุณาขอพบ มิสเตอร์แจ๊กสัน
He is out at the moment.	Khun Jackson pai khang-nawk.	คุณแจ๊กสันไปข้างนอก
May I leave a message for him?	Anuyart phõm khĩan a-rai faak wai dai mãi?	อนุญาตผมเขียนอะไร ฝากไว้ได้ไหม
Please tell him that Suraphong came.	Karuna bawk wa Suraphong ma hã.	กรุณาบอกว่า สุรพงศ์มาหา
I hope I am not disturbing you.	Wang-wa phõm khong mai rob-kuan khun.	หวังว่าผมคงไม่รบกวน คุณ
I'll come again tomorrow.	Phroung-ni phõm chah ma ik.	พรุ่งนี้ผมจะมาอีก

222

What's your name, please?	Khāw-thode, khun shue a-rai?	ขอโทษ, คุณชื่ออะไร
My name is Suraphong Kanchananaga.	Phŏm shue Suraphong Kanchananaga.	ผมชื่อ สุรพงศ์ กาญจนนาค
What a long name! Would you repeat it?	Shue khun yao chang! Karuna phoud ik khrang?	ชื่อคุณยาวจัง กรุณาพูดอีกครั้ง
I am glad to meet you.	Phŏm yindi thi phob khun.	ผมยินดีที่พบคุณ
Would you care to come inside?	Shern khun khao ma khang nai.	เชิญคุณเข้ามาข้างใน
Please sit down.	Shern nang.	เชิญนั่ง
Do you smoke?	Khun soub bouri mãi?	คุณสูบบุหรี่ไหม
Would you like to drink some-thing?	Khun yaak duem a-rai mãi?	คุณอยากดื่มอะไรไหม
Shall I bring you some coffee?	Phŏm hã kafae hai khun tham aow mãi?	ผมหากาแฟให้คุณทานเอาไหม
Thank you, that would be nice.	Khob-khun maak khrap.	ขอบคุณมากครับ
Do you like your coffee black or with milk?	Khun shob kafae damh rũe sai-nom?	คุณชอบกาแฟดำหรือใส่นม

LIVING

Do you want to drink whisky?	Khun duem whisky mãi?	คุณดื่มวิสกี้ไหม
Do you drink plain or with soda?	Duem pure-pure rue term soda?	ดื่มเพียว-เพียวหรือเติมโซดา
Let's go out to eat.	Pai hã a-rai tharn khang nawk.	ไปหาอะไรทานกันข้างนอก
I want to eat Thai food.	Phõm yaak tharn a-hãrn Thai.	ผมอยากทานอาหารไทย
I want to eat something simple.	Phõm tharn a-rai kaw-dai thi ngai-ngai.	ผมทานอะไรก็ได้ที่ง่าย-ง่าย
Have you ordered food?	Khun sang a-hãrn laew rũe yang?	คุณสั่งอาหารแล้วหรือยัง
Please let me pay for everything.	Karuna hai phõm chaai.	กรุณาให้ผมจ่าย
It's very kind of you.	Khob khun maak.	ขอบคุณมาก
I'm leaving early tomorrow for Singapore.	Phõm pai Singkhapo phrung-ni shao.	ผมไปสิงคโปร์พรุ่งนี้เช้า
I'm going for business reasons.	Pai tham kich-thurah.	ไปทำกิจธุระ
How will you travel, by bus, train or plane?	Pai doai a-rai, rot tour, rot-fai rue khreuang-bin?	ไปโดยอะไร? รถทัวร์, รถไฟ หรือเครื่องบิน
Most likely I'll go by train.	Khong chah pai doai rot-fai maak-kwa.	คงจะไปโดยรถไฟมากกว่า

Why don't you fly direct to Singapore?	Thammai khun mai binh trong-pai Singkhapo?	ทำไมคุณไม่บินตรงไป สิงคโปร์
Frankly, it is less expensive to go by train.	Pai rot-fai thouk-kwa maak.	ไปรถไฟถูกกว่ามาก
And it happens that I have much more time than I have money.	Phõm mi vela maak-kwa mi ngoen.	ผมมีเวลามากกว่ามีเงิน
When shall I see you again?	Meua-rai chah mi o-kas phob khun ik?	เมื่อไรจะมีโอกาสพบ คุณอีก
In the next few months, probably.	Ik pramarn song-sãrm deuan.	อีกประมาณสองสาม เดือน
Can you show me some cotton cloth for making dresses?	Phõm khãw dou pha-faai sãmrab tat seua?	ผมขอดูผ้าฝ้ายสำหรับ ตัดเสื้อ
Do you have the famous Madmee Thai silk fabric?	Khun mi pha Madmee Thai mãi?	คุณมีผ้ามัดหมี่ไทยไหม
Could I have a look at it?	Khãw shom dai mãi?	ขอชมได้ไหม
Can you show me the one in the window?	Khãw shom thi you nai tou-show?	ขอชมที่อยู่ในตู้โชว์

225

LIVING

I want something like this.	Phõm tong-karn thi khlai-khlai kanh ni.	ผมต้องการที่คล้ายๆ กันนี้
I want another one like this.	Phõm tongkarn yang diao kanh.	ผมต้องการอย่างเดียวกัน
I don't want anything too expensive.	Phõm mai tong-kam shanid phaeng.	ผมไม่ต้องการชนิดแพง
How much is that a metre?	Khun khid met-lah thao-rai?	คุณคิดเมตรละเท่าไร
I would like to see your material for a suit.	Khun mi pha tat-seua di-di mãi.	คุณมีผ้าตัดเสื้อดีๆ ไหม
What will a suit cost me?	Khun khid shout-lah thao rai?	คุณคิดชุดละเท่าไร
Make me two pairs of trousers.	Tham kang-keng khã yao hai song tua.	ทำกางเกงขายาวให้ สองตัว
The trousers are a little too short.	Kang-keng khã sanh pai.	กางเกงขาสั้นไป
Will you lengthen them by at least two centimetres?	Kae hai yao ik yang-noi sõng cent chah dai mãi?	แก้ให้ยาวอีกอย่างน้อย สองเซนต์จะได้ไหม
How much is this/ that?	Ni thao-rai/Nanh thao-rai?	นี่เท่าไร/นั่นเท่าไร
I'll take this one.	An-ni phõm sue.	อันนี้ผมซื้อ

226

Will you take a traveller's cheque?	Khun rab traveller's cheque mãi?	คุณรับแทรเวลเลอร์เช็ค ไหม
Can you wrap it up for me?	Haw hai phõm dai mãi?	ห่อให้ผมได้ไหม
Have you got a carrier bag?	Khun mi thõung mãi?	คุณมีถุงไหม
Where are you going?	Khun chah pai nãi?	คุณจะไปไหน
Are you waiting for someone?	Khun khoi khrai rũe?	คุณคอยใครหรือ
Where do you live?	Khun you thi-nãi?	คุณอยู่ที่ไหน
Is it far from here?	Klai chaak ni maak mãi?	ไกลจากนี่มากไหม
Can I ride you home?	Phom pai song khun thũeng baan dai mãi?	ผมไปส่งคุณถึงบ้าน ได้ไหม
You didn't eat. Aren't you hungry?	Khun mai-dai tharn a-rai. Mai hĩew rũe?	คุณไม่ได้ทานอะไร ไม่หิวหรือ
Can we stop to eat something somewhere?	Yout hã a-rai tharn konn di mãi?	หยุดหาอะไรทานก่อน ดีไหม
Please order me a cup of black coffee.	Karuna sang kafae-damh hai nueng thuai.	กรุณาสั่งกาแฟดำให้ หนึ่งถ้วย

LIVING

What will you drink?	Khun chah duem a-rai?	คุณจะดื่มอะไร
Are you free this evening?	Khuen-ni khun waang-mãi?	คืนนี้คุณว่างไหม
Would you like to go for a drive?	Nang rot thiao kin-lom kanh di mãi?	นั่งรถเที่ยวกินลมกัน ดีไหม
Shall we go to the cinema?	Pai dou pharb-phayont kanh mãi?	ไปดูภาพยนตร์กันไหม
Would you like to go dancing?	Pai tenh disco kanh mãi?	ไปเต้นดิสโก้กันไหม
Don't go home now, please.	Ya-pheu klab baan nah.	อย่าเพิ่งกลับบ้านนะ
Is there any inexpensive accommodation near here?	Thi klai-klai ni mi rongraem rakha yaow bang mãi?	ที่ใกล้ๆ นี้มีโรงแรม ราคาเยาบ้างไหม

Short Phrases

After you	Shern konn, shern khun	เชิญก่อน, เชิญคุณ
All right	Di-laew; Thouk-laew	ดีแล้ว, ถูกแล้ว
Anything else?	Mi a-rai ik mãi?	มีอะไรอีกไหม

Nah (นะ) particle used to make an utterance gentler, milder. Nah (นะ) is often comparable to English "May I?"

228

Anything special?	Mi a-rai phisesh rũe?	มีอะไรพิเศษหรือ
Anything will do	Arai-kaw-dai	อะไรก็ได้
Are you joking?	Phoud-lenh rue-plao?	พูดเล่นหรือเปล่า
As you like	Tarm-chai, laew-tae khun	ตามใจ, แล้วแต่คุณ
Are there any coaches to……?	Mi rot pai…… mãi?	มีรถไป……ไหม
Are you free today?	Wan-ni khun waang mãi?	วันนี้คุณว่างไหม
Another cup please.	Khaw ik thuai.	ขออีกถ้วย
A little more	Ik nid	อีกนิด
Are you ready?	Phromm rũe yang?	พร้อมหรือยัง
Be careful!	Ra-wang!	ระวัง!
Be quick!	Reow! Reow-noi!	เร็ว! เร็วหน่อย
Be quiet! Shut up!	Ngiap! Houp-paak sĩa!	เงียบ หุบปากเสีย
Best of luck.	Shoke di nah.	โชคดีนะ
Bring me……	Aow……ma hai shan	เอา……มาให้ฉัน
Call a taxi for me, please.	Karuna riak taxi.	กรุณาเรียกแท็กซี่
Can/Cannot	Dai/Mai-dai	ได้/ไม่ได้
Can I have this?	Khãw dai mãi?	ขอได้ไหม

LIVING

Can I buy……?	Khãw sue dai mãi?	ขอซื้อได้ไหม
Can I come in?	Phõm khow-pai dai mai?	ผมเข้าไปได้ไหม
Can you come?	Khun ma dai mãi?	คุณมาได้ไหม
Can you help me?	Shuai phõm dai mãi?	ช่วยผมได้ไหม
Can you tell me?	Bawk phõm dai-mãi?	บอกผมได้ไหม
Can I see……?	Khaw phõm dou dai mãi?	ขอผมดูได้ไหม
Can I try it?	Hai phõm lawng dai-mãi?	ให้ผมลองได้ไหม
Can I use……?	Anuyart phõm shai dai mãi?	อนุญาตผมใช้ได้ไหม
Can you lend me?	Hai phõm yuem dai mãi?	ให้ผมยืมได้ไหม
Can you wait?	Khoi dai mãi?	คอยได้ไหม
Can you wash ……?	Laang……hai-dai mãi?	ล้าง……ให้ได้ไหม
Can you go to……?	Pai thi…… dai mãi?	ไปที่……ได้ไหม
Can I park my car here?	Khãw chawd-rot thi-ni dai mãi?	ขอจอดรถที่นี่ได้ไหม
Can you repair this?	Khun somm-saem ni dai mãi?	คุณซ่อมแซมนี้ได้ไหม
Can I occupy this seat?	Phõm nang dai mãi?	ผมนั่งได้ไหม

230

Come. Come over here.	Ma sih. Ma ni.	มาซิ มานี่
Come back quick!	Klab reow-reow noi!	กลับเร็วเร็วหน่อย
Congratulations to you.	Khãw sadaeng khwam yin-di.	ขอแสดงความยินดี
Damn!	Ba ra-yamh!	บ้า ระย้า!
Disgusting!	Thu-resh! Na-beau!	ทุเรศ! น่าเบื่อ!
Do you understand what he said?	Khun khaow-chai khõw phoud wa a-rai mãi?	คุณเข้าใจเขาพูดว่า อะไรไหม
Do you have......?	Khun mi...... mai?	คุณมี......ไหม
Do you have a mosquito net?	Khun mi moung mãi?	คุณมีมุ้งไหม
Do you think so?	Hẽn duai mãi?	เห็นด้วยไหม
Do you understand?	Khow-chai mãi?	เข้าใจไหม
Do it like this.	Tham yang ni.	ทำอย่างนี้
Don't do like that.	Ya tham yang nanh.	อย่าทำอย่างนั้น
Don't be crazy!	Ya ba noi leui!	อย่าบ้าหน่อยเลย
Don't be late!	Ya sha nah!	อย่าช้านะ
Don't be silly!	Ya seur! Ya ngo noi leui!	อย่าเซ่อ อย่าโง่หน่อยเลย
Don't disturb!	Ya kuan!	อย่ากวน

LIVING

Don't fool me!	Ya lawk shãn! Ya law shan!	อย่าหลอกกัน/อย่าล้อฉัน
Don't forget!	Ya luem!	อย่าลืม
Don't go yet!	Ya pheu pai!	อย่าเพ่อไป!
Don't lie!	Ya ko-hok!	อย่าโกหก
Don't mention it.	Mai penh rai.	ไม่เป็นไร
Don't pay any attention.	Ya pai sõnh.	อย่าไปสน
Don't trouble yourself.	Ya rob-kuan khun leui.	อย่ารบกวนคุณเลย
Don't wait for me.	Mai-tong khoi phõm.	ไม่ต้องคอยผม
Don't worry.	Mai penh rai. Ya khid maak.	ไม่เป็นไร อย่าคิดมาก
Drive to the airport.	Khab pai sanãrm-bin.	ขับไปสนามบิน
Forget it.	Luem sia therd.	ลืมเสียเถิด
Forgive me, please.	Proad a-phai phõm.	โปรดอภัยผม
For me? For you!	Khõng phõm rũe? Khong khun!	ของผมหรือ ของคุณต่างหาก
Funny! It's funny!	Khãm! Khãm philuek!	ขำ/ขำพิลึก
Get out! Get out of the way!	Pai! Pai hai phon!	ไป ไปให้พ้น
Give me......	Khãw phõm nah......	ขอผมนะ......

232

Give me another ……	Khãw ……phõm ik.	ขอ……ผมอีก
Go ahead! Go straight on!	Pai dai! Trong pai!	ไปได้! ตรงไป
Go back!	Thõi lãng! Thõi!	กลับหลัง ถอยหลัง ถอย
Go faster!	Pai reow-reow!	ไปเร็วเร็ว
Go further on!	Pai ik!	ไปอีก
Go that way!	Pai thaang nanh!	ไปทางนั้น
Go there!	Pai thi-nanh!	ไปที่นั่น
Good for you!	Sõm narm-na!	สมน้ำหน้า
Good heavens!	Mae-chao weui!	แม่เจ้าโวย
Good luck!	Shoke-di nah!	โชคดีนะ
Have/Don't have	Mi/Mai-mi	มี/ไม่มี
Have you any?	Mi bang mãi?	มีบ้างไหม
Have you many more?	Mi maak mãi?	มีมากไหม
Happy birthday	Suk-sãnt wan kerd	สุขสันต์วันเกิด
Happy New Year	Sawadi pi mai	สวัสดีปีใหม่
He's a handsome man.	Khãow penh khon roup-law.	เขาเป็นคนรูปหล่อ
Here's my address.	Ni thi-you phõm.	นี่ที่อยู่ผม
Here it is.	Ni-ngai-laow.	นี่ไงเล่า
How about you?	Laew khun lah?	แล้วคุณล่ะ
How do you say that in Cantonese?	Kwangtung riak yang-rai?	กวางตุ้งเรียกอย่างไร
How much a pair?	Khou-lah thaorai?	คู่ละเท่าไร
Hurry up!	Réow-noi!	เร็วหน่อย

233

LIVING

English	Phonetic	Thai
How much if I buy three?	Tha sue sãrm chah aow thaorai?	ถ้าซื้อสามจะเอาเท่าไร
How long must I wait?	Tong khoi narn thaorai?	ต้องคอยนานเท่าไร
I am looking for......	Phõm kamlang hã......	ผมกำลังหา......
I am ashamed.	Shãn kradaak/ Shãn khãai na.	ฉันกระดาก/ฉันขายหน้า
I am busy.	Phõm mai waang.	ผมไม่ว่าง
I am going to	Phõm chah pai thi......	ผมจะไปที่......
I am hard up.	Phõm thãng-taek.	ผมถังแตก
I am hungry.	Phõm hĩew.	ผมหิว
I am thirsty.	Phom krahãai.	ผมกระหาย
I am much annoyed.	Phõm ram-kharn tem-thi.	ผมรำคาญเต็มที
I am not so sure.	Phõm mai-nae chai.	ผมไม่แน่ใจ
I am not feeling well.	Phõm mai sabaai.	ผมไม่สบายใจ
I am sleepy.	Phõm nguang.	ผมง่วง
I am sorry. I am glad	Phõm sĩa-chai. Phõm di-chai.	ผมเสียใจ ผมดีใจ
I am sorry I have troubled you so much.	Phõm sĩa chai thi rob-kuan khun maak.	ผมเสียใจที่รบกวนคุณมาก
I am tired.	Phõm phlia/mai-mi raeng.	ผมเพลีย/ไม่มีแรง

234

English	Phonetic	Thai
I beg your pardon.	Phŏm khãw a-phai.	ผมขออภัย
I can't find any.	Phŏm hã mai dai.	ผมหาไม่ได้
I can't help it.	Shuai mai dai.	ช่วยไม่ได้
I don't care.	Phŏm mai sõnh.	ผมไม่สน
I don't have time.	Phŏm mai mi vela.	ผมไม่มีเวลา
I don't know.	Phŏm mai saab.	ผมไม่ทราบ
I don't like it.	Phŏm mai shob.	ผมไม่ชอบ
I like this one.	Phŏm shobb ann-ni.	ผมชอบอันนี้
I don't mind.	Phŏm mai rang-kiat.	ผมไม่รังเกียจ
I don't remember.	Phŏm cham mai dai.	ผมจำไม่ได้
I don't think so.	Phŏm mai hẽnh duai.	ผมไม่เห็นด้วย
I don't understand.	Phŏm mai khow-chai.	ผมไม่เข้าใจ
I don't want it.	Phŏm mai tongkarn.	ผมไม่ต้องการ
I doubt it.	Phŏm sõng-sãi.	ผมสงสัย
I forgot.	Phŏm luem-pai.	ผมลืมไป
I guarantee it.	Phŏm rab-rong.	ผมรับรอง
I give you this……	Ni phŏm hai khun……	นี่ผมให้คุณ……
I have already paid you.	Phŏm chaai hai laew.	ผมจ่ายให้แล้ว

LIVING

English	Transliteration	Thai
I know that.	**Phõm saab/Phom rou laew.**	ผมทราบ/ผมรู้แล้ว
I love you.	**Phõm rak khun/ Shãn rak theu.**	ผมรักคุณ/ฉันรักเธอ
I must apologize.	**Phõm tong khãw-thode.**	ผมต้องขอโทษ
I want it. I want more.	**Phõm tongkam/ Aow ik.**	ผมต้องการ/เอาอีก
I will buy it.	**Phõm chah sue.**	ผมจะซื้อ
I will wait here.	**Phõm chah khoi thi-ni.**	ผมจะคอยที่นี่
I will think it over.	**Phõm khid dou konh.**	ผมคิดดูก่อน
I will try.	**Phõm chah phaya-yarm.**	ผมจะพยายาม
I will come back later.	**Laew-phõm chah klab-ma.**	แล้วผมจะกลับมา
If you don't mind.	**Tha khun mai rang-kiat.**	ถ้าคุณไม่รังเกียจ
If you like.	**Laew-tae khun.**	แล้วแต่คุณ
Is that made in Thailand?	**Tham nai meuang Thai shai mãi?**	ทำในเมืองไทยใช่ไหม
Is it hand made?	**Tham duai mue shai-mãi?**	ทำด้วยมือใช่ไหม
Is there a discount?	**Mi suan-lod mãi?**	มีส่วนลดไหม
Is this seat free?	**Thi-nang ni waang mãi?**	ที่นั่งนี่ว่างไหม

It doesn't matter.	Mai penh rai.	ไม่เป็นไร
It's rotten luck!	Shoke mai di. Suai!	โชคไม่ดี ซวย
It's very annoying.	Ram kham chang.	รำคาญจัง
It just makes me sick!	Shān beua tem-thonh!	ฉันเบื่อเต็มทน
Is everything alright?	Thouk-yang riab-roi mãi?	ทุกอย่างเรียบร้อยไหม
Is this yours?	Khõng khun shai-mãi?	ของคุณใช่ไหม
It can't be done.	Tham mai-dai.	ทำไม่ได้
It is an awful nuisance!	Ram-kharn thi sout!	รำคาญที่สุด
It doesn't make sense.	Mai dai khwam.	ไม่ได้ความ
It gets on my nerves!	Chah ba taai!	จะบ้าตาย
It's getting late.	Sãai laew.	สายแล้ว
It is no use.	Mai mi prayote.	ไม่มีประโยชน์
It is all the same to me.	Kaw mẽuan-kanh.	ก็เหมือนกัน
It is too noisy!	Nouak-hou chang!	หนวกหูจัง
Just a minute, please.	Khãw vela dĩao. Dĩao konn.	ขอเวลาเดี๋ยว, เดี๋ยวก่อน
Kiss me, please.	Choup-shãn sih.	จูบฉันซิ
Let us go!	Pai kanh therd!	ไปกันเถอะ
Look here!	Dou ni!	ดูนี่

237

LIVING

English	Transliteration	Thai
Look out!	Ra-wang!	ระวัง
Let me pass, please.	Khăw-thang phŏm noi.	ขอทางผมหน่อย
Meet me here at six o'clock.	Phob thi ni vela hok mong yenh.	พบที่นี่เวลาหกโมงเย็น
Mind the motor cars!	Rawang rot!	ระวังรถ
Mind your head!	Rawang sĭ-sah!	ระวังศีรษะ
Mind your own business!	Khon-uen ya young!	คนอื่นอย่ายุ่ง
More! A little more!	Ik! Ik nid!	อีก อีกนิด
Never again!	Mai laew! Khed laew!	ไม่แล้ว เข็ดแล้ว
Never mind!	Mai penh rai!	ไม่เป็นไร
Not now. Not this time.	Mai shai dĭao ni.	ไม่ใช่เดี๋ยวนี้
Nothing else? Nothing more?	Mi a-rai ik măi?	มีอะไรอีกไหม
Not yet.	Yang.	ยัง
Of course!	Nae lah!	แน่ละ
Oh dear! What a stupid!	Chao-prakhun! Ngo chang!	เจ้าประคุณ โง่จัง
Just only one night.	Khuen-diao thao nanh.	คืนเดียวเท่านั้น
Please buy some for me.	Karuna sue ma faak phŏm duai.	กรุณาซื้อมาฝากผมด้วย

238

Please come this way.	**Karuna ma thaang-ni.**	กรุณามาทางนี้
Please do me a favour.	**Karuna tham a-rai hai noi.**	กรุณาทำอะไรให้หน่อย
Please sit down.	**Proad nang.**	โปรดนั่ง
Please take a chair.	**Shern nang bonh kao-ee.**	เชิญนั่งบนเก้าอี้
Please excuse me while I change.	**Khãw-thode, phõm khãw-plian seua-pha.**	ขอโทษ ผมขอเปลี่ยนเสื้อผ้า
Pleased to meet you.	**Yin-di thi phob khun.**	ยินดีที่พบคุณ
Pleasant journey to you.	**Khãw hai dern-thang plawd phai.**	ขอให้เดินทางปลอดภัย
Poor thing!	**Na song-sarn na som-phesh!**	น่าสงสาร น่าสมเพช
See you later.	**Phob kanh mai.**	พบกันใหม่
Shall I wait?	**Phõm tong khoi mãi?**	ผมต้องคอยไหม
Shame on you!	**Na mai aye!**	หน้าไม่อาย
She's a pretty girl.	**Theu penh são na-rak.**	เธอเป็นสาวน่ารัก
So cheap! So expensive!	**Thouk-chang! Phaeng-chang!**	ถูกจัง, แพงจัง
Sorry, I have a date.	**Sia-chai, wan-ni shãn mi natt.**	เสียใจวันนี้ฉันมีนัด

239

LIVING

English	Transliteration	Thai
Speak a little louder.	Phoud dang-dang noi.	พูดดัง-ดัง หน่อย
Stop! Stop here!	Yout! Yout thi-ni!	หยุด หยุดที่นี่
Take care!	Rawang!	ระวัง
Take it easy!	Chai yen-yenh!	ใจเย็นเย็น
Take it away!	Aow pai!	เอาไป
Thank you very much!	Khob-khun maak!	ขอบคุณมาก
That's all wrong!	Phid thang phe!	ผิดทั้งเพ
That's enough!	Phaw laew! Phaw kanh-thi!	พอแล้ว พอกันที
That's going too far!	Awk chah maak pai! Kern pai!	ออกจะมากไป เกินไป
That is for me.	Nanh samrab shān.	นั่นสำหรับฉัน
That is yours.	Nanh khŏng khun.	นั่นของคุณ
There it is.	Nanh ngai laow.	นั่นไงเล่า
This seat is engaged.	Thi-ni mi khon nang laew.	ที่นี่มีคนนั่งแล้ว
This seat is vacant.	Thi-ni yang waang.	ที่นี่ยังว่าง
This is very urgent.	Ni penh reuang duan.	นี่เป็นเรื่องด่วน
Trust in me, sweetheart.	Sheua shān sih, thi-rak.	เชื่อฉันซิ-ที่รัก
Very well, that's all!	Di-laew; thao-nanh laeh!	ดีแล้ว, เท่านั้นแหละ

240

Wait for me here!	Khoi shãn you thi-ni!	คอยฉันอยู่ที่นี่
Walk faster!	Dern reow-reow noi!	เดินเร็วเร็วหน่อย
Well done!	Tham di! Riab-roi di!	ทำดี-เรียบร้อยดี
What? What is it?	A-rai? Penh a-rai?	อะไร เป็นอะไร
What are you doing?	Khun tham a-rai?	คุณทำอะไร
What did you say?	Meua-ki khun wa a-rai?	เมื่อกี้คุณว่าอะไร
What is going on here?	Tham a-rai kanh thi-ni?	ทำอะไรกันที่นี่
What is the matter?	Reuang a-rai?	เรื่องอะไร
What is the trouble?	Mi reuang a-rai?	มีเรื่องอะไร
What is the fare to...?	Kha doai-sãrn pai......thaorai?	ค่าโดยสารไป......เท่าไร
What is that for?	Nanh sãmrab tham a-rai?	นั่นสำหรับทำอะไร
What is the use?	Mi pra-yote a-rai?	มีประโยชน์อะไร
What is to be done?	Tham yang-rai dai?	ทำอย่างไรได้
What do you want?	Khun tongkarn a-rai?	คุณต้องการอะไร
What would you have me do?	Chah hai phõm tham yang-rai?	จะให้ผมทำอย่างไร
What a character!	Khon a-rai!	คนอะไร

241

LIVING

What a horrible smell!	Mēhn chang!	เหม็นจังเ
What a pity!	Na sŏngãrn/Na sīa-daai!	น่าสงสาร, น่าเสียดาย
What did you buy?	Khun sue a-rai ma?	คุณซื้ออะไรมา
What do I care?	Phŏm mai sŏhn? Mai-shai reuang phŏm?	ผมไม่สนไม่ใช่เรื่องผม
What is wrong?	Phid a-rai? Phid trong-nãi?	ผิดอะไร ผิดตรงไหน
When will it be ready?	Meua-rai chah set?	เมื่อไรจะเสร็จ
Where can I buy it?	Phŏm chah sue dai thi-nai?	ผมจะซื้อได้ที่ไหน
Where did you buy it?	Khun sue chaak nãi?	คุณซื้อจากไหน
Where are you going?	Khun pai nãi?	คุณไปไหน
Where is the W.C.?	Hong-suam you thi nãi?	ห้องส้วมอยู่ที่ไหน
Where is the urinal?	Thi nãi mi thi passã-wah?	ที่ไหนมีที่ปัสสาวะ
Where is the bus stop?	Paai chawd-rot you nãi?	ป้ายจอดรถอยู่ไหน
Which will you buy?	Khun chah sue ann-nãi?	คุณจะซื้ออันไหน

242

English	Transliteration	Thai
Which do you like?	Khun shobb ann-nãi?	คุณชอบอันไหน
Which way out?	Awk thang nãi?	ออกทางไหน
Who told you?	Khrai bawk khun?	ใครบอกคุณ
Will it be alright?	Shai dai mãi?	ใช้ได้ไหม
Will you help me?	Shuai phõm dai mãi?	ช่วยผมได้ไหม
With pleasure.	Yin di, duai khwam tem chai.	ยินดี ด้วยความเต็มใจ
Won't you change seats with me?	Plian thi-nang kap phõm mãi?	เปลี่ยนที่นั่งกับผมไหม
Will you call a policeman for me?	Riak tamruat hai dai mãi?	เรียกตำรวจให้ได้ไหม
Will you show me?	Hai phõm dou sih?	ให้ผมดูซิ
Who are you?	Khun penh khrai?	คุณเป็นใคร
Who is that man?	Khon nanh khrai?	คนนั้นใคร
Whose is it?	Khõng khrai?	ของใคร
Who knows?	Khrai saab? Khrai rou?	ใครทราบ ใครรู้
Write it down in Thai.	Proad khĩan penh bhasã Thai.	โปรดเขียนเป็นภาษาไทย
You are pretty and nice.	Khun sũai na-rak.	คุณสวยน่ารัก
You are beautiful.	Khun sũai.	คุณสวย
You are divine.	Khun sũai mẽuan thep-thida.	คุณสวยเหมือนเทพธิดา

243

LIVING

You are mistaken.	Khun khowchai phid.	คุณเข้าใจผิด
You are a real flatterer.	Khun ni-yaw keng.	คุณนี่ยอเก่ง
You are very kind.	Khun ni-chai di.	คุณนี่ใจดี
You are right!	Thouk khõng khun!	ถูกของคุณ
You are so stupid!	Khun ni ngo chang!	คุณนี่โง่จัง
You are very stubborn!	Khun due chang!	คุณนี่ดื้อจัง
You are talking nonsense.	Phoud leow-lãi mai dai khwam.	พูดเหลวไหลไม่ได้ความ
You are welcome.	Khãw tonn-rab duai khwam yin-di.	ขอต้อนรับด้วยความยินดี
You look very lovely.	Dou khun sũai maak.	ดูคุณสวยมาก
You speak English very well.	Khun phoud Angkrit keng.	คุณพูดอังกฤษเก่ง
You misunderstand me.	Khun mai khow-chai phõm.	คุณไม่เข้าใจผม

244

Tips for Travellers and Residents

The Thais are very hospitable, and a visitor is always welcome. Greetings and compliments are essential, and an offered cup of coffee or at least a glass of cold drinking water should not be turned down.

Thais don't normally shake hands when they greet one another, but instead press the palms together, in a prayer-like gesture called a *wai*. Generally, the younger person *wais* the older, who returns it. Watch how the Thais do it, and you'll soon catch on.

While Thailand is a Land of Smiles and a country where almost every visitor greatly enjoys himself, it should be remembered that the King and Queen as well as the Buddha are all sacred and are not to be subjects of even the most innocuous joke.

The Thai people have a deep, traditional reverence for their Royal Family, and a visitor should also be careful to show respect for the King, the Queen, and the Royal Children. In a cinema, for example, a portrait of the King is shown during the playing of the national anthem, and the audience is expected to stand. When attending some public event at which a member of the Royal Family is present, the best guide as to how to behave is probably to watch the crowd and do what it does.

Dress neatly. Don't go shirtless, or in shorts, hot pants, or other unsuitable attire. If you look at the Thais around you, you'll see the way they would prefer you to be dressed which, in fact, is probably not very different from the way you'd dress in a similar place back home.

TRAVEL TIPS

Buddhist priests are forbidden to touch or to be touched by a woman or to accept anything from the hand of one. If a woman has to give anything to a monk or novice, she first hands it to a man, who then presents it. Or in the case of a woman who wants to present it with her hand, the monk or novice will spread out a piece of saffron robe or handkerchief in front of him, and the woman will lay down the material on the robe which is being held at one end by the monk or novice.

It's all right to wear shoes while walking around the compound of a Buddhist temple, but not inside the chapel where the principal Buddha image is kept. Don't worry about dirt when you have to take your shoes off; the floors of such places are usually very clean.

All Buddha images, large or small, ruins or not, are regarded as sacred objects. Hence, don't climb up on one to take a photograph or generally speaking, do anything that might show a lack of respect.

It's considered rude to point your foot at a person, so try to avoid doing so when sitting opposite anyone, and following the concept that the foot is a low limb, don't point with your foot, but use your fingers instead. It is the custom in Thailand to remove one's shoes before entering a temple or a private residence.

Do not touch the head of an adult as the Thais regard it as the highest part of the body. As a result they don't approve of patting anyone there, even in a friendly gesture.

In a Moslem mosque in Thailand, visitors should wear hats and women should be well-covered with a long skirt, a long-sleeved blouse buttoned to the neck, and a scarf over the hair. All should remove their shoes before entering the mosque and not pass near, especially directly in front of, anyone kneeling in prayer. Muslims are devout and answer the call to prayer five times a day. Friday is the Sabbath for all Muslims.

For Your Own Protection

Always bargain the price before getting in the taxi; use the taxi service provided by the hotel; use roving taxis rather than ones that are standing near the hotels, check with the desk clerk at your hotel, as to the distance and what the price should be.

Always find out who is knocking before opening your door. When returning home have your key ready before you get to the door. Be aware of where an attacker might hide: under stairs, between buildings, etc. If someone is watching you, avoid having him see where you live.

When walking or going out alone, maintain a secure grip on your purse. Money and wallets are safer in an inside pocket. Unless absolutely necessary, never carry expensive jewellery or large amounts of money. At night, walk near the curb and avoid passing close to shrubbery, doorways and other places of concealment.

Avoid dark streets. Don't take short-cuts through alleys, backstreets or deserted areas. Girls are urged to walk in groups. If going out alone or returning home late at night, arrange for someone to escort you.

Avoid riding in lifts alone, if possible. Don't enter a lift with any male stranger. Should he enter a lift after you, get out immediately and take the lift later when it is safe.

TRAVEL TIPS

If you stay in a house or an apartment don't leave your doors open, or you will attract strangers. Also do not hang up your trousers or leave any valuables near windows. They could be easily "fished" out.

Never resist an armed man, if it is between money and life, choose life without hesitation.

It is certainly a traumatic experience to be in the confines of a lift with a desperate armed man whose intention is to rob you. Don't start screaming your head off — that would be dangerous. Try not to let panic seize you. Give him your valuables but take a good look at him. Your ample description of the criminal could be invaluable in helping police to track him down.

If you happen to come face-to-face with a burglar, don't play hero. Shut up and do what he tells you — unless he seems intent upon doing you bodily harm. Then scream, fight and try to get away. The more noise you make the better. Most burglars would just as soon clear out fast if you act up.

If you think someone is following you, do not hesitate to turn around and check. To verify it, walk faster, or cross the street, or walk down the middle of the street. If you are being followed, head for the closest inhabited or lighted area. Or you might try to run — do it suddenly, as fast as you can, and shouting as you go.

Today the safest way to travel with money is with traveller's cheques or credit cards.

REFERENCE SECTION

The Weather

It's warm today.	Wanni-ronn.	วันนี้ร้อน
The weather is cold.	Akas yen.	อากาศเย็น
It's bad weather today.	Wanni akas mai di.	วันนี้อากาศไม่ดี
It's nice weather today.	Wanni akas sabaai di.	วันนี้อากาศสบายดี
It's beginning to rain.	Fõn rerm tok/ Fõn tang khow.	ฝนเริ่มตก ฝนตั้งเค้า
It's raining.	Fõn kamlang tok.	ฝนกำลังตก
It rained yesterday.	Waan-ni fõn tok.	วานนี้ฝนตก
It rains almost every day.	Fõn tok keuap thouk wan.	ฝนตกเกือบทุกวัน
I need an umbrella.	Phõm tongkarn rom.	ผมต้องการร่ม
I need a raincoat.	Phõm tongkarn seua-fõn.	ผมต้องการเสื้อฝน
I am afraid of the thunder.	Phõm klua fa-rong/fa-pha.	ผมกลัวฟ้าร้อง/ฟ้าผ่า

Division of Time

Morning	Shao	เช้า
This morning	Shao-ni	เช้านี้
Every morning	Thouk-thouk shao	ทุกๆ เช้า

249

REFERENCE SECTION

Noon	Thiang/Thiang-wan	เที่ยง/เที่ยงวัน
This afternoon	Baai ni	บ่ายนี้
This evening	Yenh-ni	เย็นนี้
Night/tonight	Klang-khuen/Khuen-ni	กลางคืน/คืนนี้
Last night	Meua-khuen	เมื่อคืน
All night long	Talawd khuen	ตลอดคืน
Minute	Nathi	นาที
Hour	Shua-mong	ชั่วโมง
Day (24 hours)	Wan (yisib-si shua-mong)	วัน (ยี่สิบสี่ชั่วโมง)
Today	Wan-ni	วันนี้
Yesterday	Waan-ni	วานนี้
Day before yesterday	Waan-suen ni	วานซืนนี้
Day after day	Wan laew wan laow	วันแล้ววันเล่า
The whole day	Talawd thang-wan	ตลอดทั้งวัน
Three days ago	Sãrm wan ma-laew	สามวันมาแล้ว
Tomorrow	Phrung-ni	พรุ่งนี้
Day after tomorrow	Wan maruen ni	วันมะรืนนี้
Week	Sapda, Athit	สัปดาห์, อาทิตย์
This week	Sapda ni, Athit-ni	สัปดาห์นี้, อาทิตย์นี้
Next week	Sapda na, Athit-na	สัปดาห์หน้า, อาทิตย์หน้า

250

REFERENCE SECTION

Last week	**Sapda konn, Athit konn**	สัปดาห์ก่อน, อาทิตย์ก่อน
Twice a week	**Sapda lah song khrang**	สัปดาห์ละสองครั้ง
Month	**Deuan**	เดือน
This month	**Deuan-ni**	เดือนนี้
Next month	**Deuan-na**	เดือนหน้า
Last month	**Deuan konn, Deuan thi-laew**	เดือนก่อน, เดือนที่แล้ว
At the beginning of the month	**Tonh deuan**	ต้นเดือน
At the end of the month	**Plaai deuan**	ปลายเดือน
Year	**Pi**	ปี
This year, next year	**Pi ni, Pi na**	ปีนี้, ปีหน้า
Last year	**Pi konn, Pi klaai**	ปีก่อน, ปีกลาย
It's early	**Tae-shao, tae-wan, reow pai**	แต่เช้า, แต่วัน, เร็วไป
It's late	**Sāai, Sāai-laew**	สาย, สายแล้ว
Every day	**Thouk-thouk wan**	ทุกๆ วัน
Every night	**Thouk-thouk khuen**	ทุกๆ คืน
Every other day	**Wan wenh wan**	วันเว้นวัน
On Sunday	**Nai Wan Athit**	ในวันอาทิตย์
A long time ago	**Naan ma laew**	นานมาแล้ว
How long ago?	**Naan thao-rai laew?**	นานเท่าไรแล้ว

REFERENCE SECTION

Just now	Meua khru ni	เมื่อครู่นี้
A moment ago	Khru thi laew	ครู่ที่แล้ว
Another time	Vela uen	เวลาอื่น

The Hours of the Day*

1:00 p.m.	Baai-mong	บ่ายโมง
3:55 p.m.	Sărm-mong ha-sib-ha nathi	สามโมงห้าสิบห้านาที
4:57 p.m.	Si-mong ha-sib-ched nathi	สี่โมงห้าสิบเจ็ดนาที
6:15 p.m.	Hok-mong sib-ha nathi (yenh)	หกโมงสิบห้านาที (เย็น)
8:30 p.m.	Paed-mong-khrueng (or Sŏng thoum khrueng)	แปดโมงครึ่ง (สองทุ่มครึ่ง)
9:45 p.m.	Kaow-mong si-sib-ha nathi	เก้าโมงสี่สิบห้านาที
12 o'clock (midnight)	Thiang khuen (or Sŏng yarm)	เที่ยงคืน (สองยาม)
3:10 a.m.	Sărm-mong sib nathi	สามโมงสิบนาที
6:50 a.m.	Hok-mong ha-sib nathi (shao)	หกโมงห้าสิบนาที (เช้า)

* Although official time is based on the twenty-four-hour clock, the twelve-hour system is used in conversation.

252

8:23 a.m.	**Paed-mong yi-sib-sārm nathi**	แปดโมงยี่สิบสามนาที
11:33 a.m.	**Sib-ed-mong sārm-sib-sārm nathi**	สิบเอ็ดโมงสามสิบสามนาที
11:45 a.m.	**Sib-ed-mong si-sib-ha nathi**	สิบเอ็ดโมงสี่สิบห้านาที
12 o'clock (noon)	**Thiang-Wan**	เที่ยงวัน

The Days of the Week

Monday	**Wan Chand**	วันจันทร์
Tuesday	**Wan Angkharn**	วันอังคาร
Wednesday	**Wan Phud**	วันพุธ
Thursday	**Wan Pharuehat**	วันพฤหัส
Friday	**Wan Souk**	วันศุกร์
Saturday	**Wan Sāow**	วันเสาร์
Sunday	**Wan Athit**	วันอาทิตย์

The Months

January	**Mokara-khom**	มกราคม
February	**Kumbha-phand**	กุมภาพันธ์
March	**Mina-khom**	มีนาคม
April	**Mesa-yon**	เมษายน
May	**Phrueksapha-khom**	พฤษภาคม
June	**Mithuna-yon**	มิถุนายน
July	**Karakada-khom**	กรกฎาคม

REFERENCE SECTION

August	**Sĭnghã-khom**	สิงหาคม
September	**Kanya-yon**	กันยายน
October	**Tula-khom**	ตุลาคม
November	**Phrueksachika-yon**	พฤศจิกายน
December	**Thanwa-khom**	ธันวาคม

Numbers

0	zero	**sŏon**
1	one	**nueng**
2	two	**sŏng**
3	three	**sãrm**
4	four	**si**
5	five	**ha**
6	six	**hok**
7	seven	**ched**
8	eight	**paed**
9	nine	**kao**
10	ten	**sib**
11	eleven	**sib-ed**
12	twelve	**sib-sŏng**
13	thirteen	**sib-sãrm**
14	fourteen	**sib-si**
15	fifteen	**sib-ha**
16	sixteen	**sib-hok**
17	seventeen	**sib-ched**
18	eighteen	**sib-paed**
19	nineteen	**sib-kao**

REFERENCE SECTION

20	twenty	**yi-sib**
21	twenty-one	**yi-sib ed**
22	twenty-two	**yi-sib sõng**
23	twenty-three	**yi-sib sãrm**
24	twenty-four	**yi-sib si**
25	twenty-five	**yi-sib ha**
26	twenty-six	**yi-sib hok**
27	twenty-seven	**yi-sib ched**
28	twenty-eight	**yi-sib paed**
29	twenty-nine	**yi-sib kao**
30	thirty	**sãrm-sib**
40	forty	**si-sib**
50	fifty	**ha-sib**
60	sixty	**hok-sib**
70	seventy	**ched-sib**
80	eighty	**paed-sib**
90	ninety	**kao-sib**
100	one hundred	**nueng roi**
200	two hundred	**sõng-roi**
300	three hundred	**sãrm-roi**
400	four hundred	**si-roi**
500	five hundred	**ha-roi**
1000	one thousand	**phan/nueng phan**
5000	five thousand	**ha-phan**
10,000	ten thousand	**muen /nueng muen**
100,000	hundred thousand	**sãen/nueng sãen**
1,000,000	one million	**laan/nueng laan**

REFERENCE SECTION

Some Official Titles

His Majesty The King	Phra Baht Sõm-dech Phra Chao You Hũa	พระบาทสมเด็จพระเจ้า-อยู่หัว
Her Majesty The Queen	Phra Borom Rajini Nath	พระบรมราชินีนาถ
The Prime Minister	Nayok Ratha-montri	นายกรัฐมนตรี
Deputy Prime Minister	Rong Nayok Ra-tha-montri	รองนายกรัฐมนตรี
Provincial Governor	Phu-wa Rajakarn Changwad	ผู้ว่าราชการจังหวัด
Provincial Clerk	Cha Changwad	จ่าจังหวัด
Personnel & Procurement Officer	Samĩan-tra Changwad	เสมียนตราจังหวัด
Commune Headman	Kamnan	กำนัน
Village Headman	Phuyai Baan	ผู้ใหญ่บ้าน
District Officer	Nai Ampheu	นายอำเภอ
Deputy District Officer	Palad Ampheu	ปลัดอำเภอ
Minister Secretary to Minister	Ratha-montri Lekhã-nukam Ratha-montri	รัฐมนตรี เลขานุการรัฐมนตรี
Under Secretary of State	Palad Krasuang	ปลัดกระทรวง

REFERENCE SECTION

Deputy Under Secretary of State	Rong Palad Kra-suang	รองปลัดกระทรวง
Director General	Athibodi	อธิบดี
Deputy Director	Rong Athibodi	รองอธิบดี
Chief of Division	Hŭa-na Kong	หัวหน้ากอง
Chief of Section	Hŭa-na Pha-naek	หัวหน้าแผนก

VOCABULARY

Vocabulary

The following list of words and phrases has been selected as those you are likely to use most often in solving small problems of understanding. If you are hesitant about the pronunciation, you should either *repeat* those words or *point* to the word. The person with whom you are trying to talk will invariably pronounce it promptly and correctly. Do not be self-conscious if your speech is halting and awkward.

In the Thai translation, the words are pronounced as in the French or Italian language.

> *a* as in *father*
> *e* as in *enemy*
> *i* as in *police, machine*
> *o* as in *original*
> *u* as in *pull, full*

able	**sã-mart**	สามารถ
about (more or less)	**pramarn**	ประมาณ
above (position over)	**nĕua;** **khang-bonh**	เหนือ ข้างบน
accent	**sãm-niang**	สำเนียง
accept, to	**rap; yomm-rap**	รับ ยอมรับ
accident	**u-batti-het**	อุบัติเหตุ
accompany, to	**pai duai**	ไปด้วย
account (bill)	**banshi ngoen**	บัญชีเงิน

accustomed to	khun-kheui	คุ้นเคย
ache	puad	ปวด
acquaintance	khon rou-chak	คนรู้จัก
across	kharm	ข้าม
active	khlong-khlaew; wong-wai	คล่องแคล่ว ว่องไว
actor; actress	dara shaai; dara yǐng	ดาราชาย ดาราหญิง
address	thi-you	ที่อยู่
admire, to	leuam-sǎi; shom-shob	เลื่อมใส ชมชอบ
admit, to	a-nuyart hai khow	อนุญาตให้เข้า
adopt, to	liang wai; liang dou	เลี้ยงไว้ เลี้ยงดู
advance (of money)	ngoen luang-na	เงินล่วงหน้า
advantage	dai-priab	ได้เปรียบ
advise, to	nae-namh	แนะนำ
advertise, to	khosana	โฆษณา
afraid	klua; kreng	กลัว เกรง
after (later on)	thi-lǎng; phaai-lǎng	ทีหลัง ภายหลัง
again	ik	อีก
age (length of)	a-yuh	อายุ
– old age	– kae	แก่
agent	tua-thaen	ตัวแทน
agree, agreed	tok long	ตกลง
agreement	sǎnya tok-long	สัญญาตกลง

VOCABULARY

agriculture	karn kaset	การเกษตร
aid	khwam shuai-lẽua	ความช่วยเหลือ
air	a-kas	อากาศ
air-conditioned	prab a-kas	ปรับอากาศ
airplane	khreuang-binh	เครื่องบิน
airport	sanãrm-binh	สนามบิน
airmail	praisani a-kas	ไปรษณีย์อากาศ
alien	tang-daow	ต่างด้าว
almost	keuap	เกือบ
allow, to	a-nuyart; yin-yomm	อนุญาต ยินยอม
alms; giving alms	tharn; tham tharn	ทาน ทำทาน
alphabet	tua nãng-sẽu	ตัวหนังสือ
also	ik duai; duai	อีกด้วย ด้วย
although	mae-wa	แม้ว่า
altogether	thang-mod	ทั้งหมด
always	samẽu	เสมอ
ambassador	ek-akkha rajathout	เอกอัครราชทูต
ambulance	rot phaya-barn	รถพยาบาล
among	nai rawaang; ban-da	ในระหว่าง ในบรรดา
amount	cham-nuan	จำนวน
amulet	khreuang-rang; Khõng-khlãng	เครื่องรางของขลัง
amusement	khwam a-phirom	ความอภิรมย์
ancestor	banh-bourus	บรรพบุรุษ
angry	krode	โกรธ

260

announce	prakas	ประกาศ
announcer	phu prakas	ผู้ประกาศ
annoy, to	rob-kuan	รบกวน
annual, annually	pracham-pee; thouk-pee	ประจำปี ทุกปี
answer to	tobb	ตอบ
anthem (national)	phleng-shart	เพลงชาติ
anyone, anybody	khrai kaw-dai; khrai-khrai	ใครก็ได้ ใครๆ
apartment	hong-shoud	ห้องชุด
appetite	yaak a-hãrn	อยากอาหาร
apologize to	khãw khama; khãw-thode	ขอขมา ขอโทษ
apply, to	samak	สมัคร
application	bai samak	ใบสมัคร
appoint, to	taeng-tang	แต่งตั้ง
appreciate, to	phaw-chai	พอใจ
apprentice	phu fuek-ngarn	ผู้ฝึกงาน
approve, to	hẽn-duai	เห็นด้วย
arena	sãng-vian	สังเวียน
argue, to	toh-thĩang	โต้เถียง
arm (of body)	khãen	แขน
army, armed forces	kawng-thap	กองทัพ
arrest, to	chab-koum	จับกุม
arrive, to	ma-thũeng	มาถึง
arsenal	khlang sãnbhavudh	คลังสรรพาวุธ

VOCABULARY

ashamed	kradaak-chai	กระดากใจ
ask, to	thãrm	ถาม
assault, to	chu-chome tham-laai	จู่โจมทำลาย
assembly hall	sãla prashakhom	ศาลาประชาคม
assist, to	shuai-lẽua	ช่วยเหลือ
associate	phu ruam ngarn	ผู้ร่วมงาน
astrology	hõra-sast	โหราศาสตร์
assure, to	rap-prakanh	รับประกัน
astronaut	nak-binh a-wakas	นักบินอวกาศ
athlete, athletics	nak kila; karn kila	นักกีฬา การกีฬา
attaché	phu-shuai thout	ผู้ช่วยทูต
attack, to	chome-tee	โจมตี
attempt	khwam phaya-yarm	ความพยายาม
attendant	khon dou-lae	คนดูแล
auction	le-lãng	เลหลัง
audience	khon dou; khon fang	คนดู คนฟัง
author	phu praphand	ผู้ประพันธ์
authority	amnach na-thi	อำนาจหน้าที่
automatic	attano-mat	อัตโนมัติ
average	doai sha-lia	โดยเฉลี่ย
avoid, to	leek-liang	หลีกเลี่ยง
awaken	plouk; plouk hai tuen	ปลุก ปลุกให้ตื่น
award	rang-wanh	รางวัล

262

aware	saab; rou-tua	ทราบ รู้ตัวดี
awkward	ngoum-ngarm	งุ่มง่าม
bachelor	shaai sode	ชายโสด
bad	mai di; leow raai	ไม่ดี เลวร้าย
bail, to	prakanh tua	ประกันตัว
bank	thana-kharn	ธนาคาร
bankrupt	lom la-laai	ล้มละลาย
barbarian	khon-pa; a-naraya shon	คนป่า อนารยชน
barber	shang tat phŏm	ช่างตัดผม
bargain	taw ra-kha	ต่อราคา
basement	phuen shanh lang	พื้นชั้นล่าง
bastard	louk mai-mi phaw	ลูกไม่มีพ่อ
bathroom	hong narm	ห้องน้ำ
battle	karn rob; song-khram	การรบ/สงคราม
beach	shai haad	ชายหาด
beautiful	sŭai	สวย
beauty salon	hong sĕrm-sŭai	ห้องเสริมสวย
beggar	khăw-tharn	ขอทาน
bed; bedroom	thi-nonn; hong-nonn	ที่นอน/ห้องนอน
believe, to	sheua	เชื่อ
beloved	khon-rak	คนรัก
benefit	pra-yote	ประโยชน์
beverage	khreuang duem	เครื่องดื่ม
bigamy	mi-mia sawng	มีเมียสอง

VOCABULARY

birth; birthday	karn-kerd; wan-kerd	การเกิด วันเกิด
birth control	khum kamnerd	คุมกำเนิด
bite, to	kadd-kin	กัดกิน
blame, to	tamnih; klaow-thode	ตำหนิ กล่าวโทษ
blackmail	hak-lãng	หักหลัง
black market	talad mued	ตลาดมืด
blind	ta-bawd; lõng-phid	ตาบอด หลงผิด
blood	lo-hit	โลหิต
blood pressure	khwam-danh lohit	ความดันโลหิต
boarder	nak-rian kin-nonn	นักเรียนกินนอน
boardinghouse	hãw-phak	หอพัก
boat; motor boat	reua; reua-tit khreuang	เรือ เรือติดเครื่อง
bodyguard	khon khum-kanh	คนคุ้มกัน
border	shaai daen	ชายแดน
borrow, to	yuem	ยืม ขอยืม
boss	nai hang; hũa-na-ngarn	นายห้าง หัวหน้างาน
bother, to	rob-kuan	รบกวน
boundary	khet-daen	เขตแดน
bourgeois	shon shanh klang	ชนชั้นกลาง
boxing (Thai)	muai Thai	มวยไทย
brag, to; braggart	khui-mo; khon khee-mo	คุยโม้ คนขี้โม้

264

brainwash	laang samõng	ล้างสมอง
brave	kla; kla-hãrn	กล้า กล้าหาญ
breakfast	a-hãrn shao	อาหารเช้า
bribe, to; bribery	hai sĩn-bonh; sĩn-bonh	ให้สินบน สินบน
bride	chao-sãow	เจ้าสาว เจ้าบ่าว
bridegroom	chao-baow	
broadcast, to	krachai sĩang	กระจายเสียง
broad-minded	chai-kwang	ใจกว้าง
broker	nai-na; tua-thaen sue khãai	นายหน้า ตัวแทนซื้อขาย
brothel; brothel keeper	song sõpheni; mae-laow	ช่องโสเภณี แม่เล้า
brunette	yĩng phĩew-khlam ta-damh	หญิงผิวคล้ำตาดำ
budget	ngob-pramarn	งบประมาณ
building	a-kharn	อาคาร
bullet	louk-puen	ลูกปืน
busboy	dek rab-shai raan a-hãrn	เด็กรับใช้ร้านอาหาร
business	thurah-kich	ธุรกิจ นักธุรกิจ
businessman	nak thura-kich	
bus stop	thi chawd-rot pracham thang	ที่จอดรถประจำทาง
bystander	phuak thai-moung	พวกไทยมุง
capable	sãmart	สามารถ
capital (finance)	ngoen-thoun	เงินทุน

VOCABULARY

career	ar-sheep	อาชีพ
caretaker	khon dou-lae	คนดูแล
cargo	sīnkha	สินค้า
car-park	thi chawd-rot	ที่จอดรถ
carpet	phrom	พรมปูพื้น
cassette tape	talab tape	ตลับเทป
cat-burglar	teen-maew	ตีนแมว
celebrate, to	shalōng	ฉลองรื่นเริง
cemetery	pa-sha; su-sārn	ป่าช้า สุสาน
century	sattavat	ศตวรรษ
ceremony	phi-thee	พิธี
certificate	bai rab-rong	ใบรับรอง
certify, to	rab-rong	รับรอง
chairman	pratharn	ประธาน
challenge, to	tha; tha-thaai	ท้า ท้าทาย
champion	phu shanah-lert	ผู้ชนะเลิศ
chance	o-kas	โอกาส
change, to	plian-plaeng	เปลี่ยนแปลง
channel (TV)	shong	ช่อง (ทีวี)
charitable	chai-boon	ใจบุญ
charlatan	nak tomh; māw theuan	นักต้ม หมอเถื่อน
charm; charming	saneh; mi saneh	เสน่ห์ มีเสน่ห์
chauffeur	khon khap-rot	คนขับรถ
cheap	rakha thouk	ราคาถูก
cheat	khon khee-kong	คนขี้โกง
childbirth	klawd-louk	ตลอดลูก

266

VOCABULARY

childish	tham mĕuan dek	ทำเหมือนเด็ก
Chinatown	thin shao-chine	ถิ่นชาวจีน
cinema	rong pharbhayont	โรงภาพยนตร์
citizen	phol-meuang; prasha-korn	พลเมือง ประชากร
citizenship	sãn-shart	สัญชาติ
city	nakhorn; meuang	นคร เมือง
civilian	phol-reuan	พลเรือน
clean	sa-ard	สะอาด
clear	sãi sa-ard; chaem-sai	ใสสะอาด แจ่มใส
clerk	sa-mĩan	เสมียน
clever	shalĩao shalard; keng	เฉลียวฉลาด เก่ง
climate	a-kas; lom-fa a-kas	อากาศ ลมฟ้าอากาศ
close, to	pid	ปิด
clothes	seua-pha	เสื้อผ้า
co-education	saha sueksã	สหศึกษา
coexist	you ruam-kanh	อยู่ร่วมกัน
coffin	heep-soph	หีบศพ
colleague	phu ruam ngarn	ผู้ร่วมงาน
collect, to	keb, ruab-ruam	เก็บ รวบรวม
college	vithayalai	วิทยาลัย
colony	ana-nikhom	อาณานิคม
colour	sẽe/sĩ	สี

267

VOCABULARY

combine, to	ruam-kanh; ruam-khow duai-kanh	ร่วมกัน รวมเข้าด้วยกัน
come, to	ma	มา
– come a long way	– ma thang-klai	– มาทางไกล
– come back	– klab ma	– กลับมา
– come along	– ma duai kanh	– มาด้วยกัน
comfortable	sabaai	สบาย
commander	phu bang-khab bansha	ผู้บังคับบัญชา
commander in chief	phu bansha-karn tha-hãrn	ผู้บัญชาการทหาร
commerce	phanich-karn	พณิชยการ
commission	kha nai-na	ค่านายหน้า
commodity	sĩn-kha	สินค้า
common sense	sãmanh sãmnuek	สามัญสำนึก
community	shoum-shon	ชุมชน
companion	pheuan	เพื่อน
complain	bonh; rong-thouk	บ่น ร้องทุกข์
complete	set sõmboon	เสร็จสมบูรณ์
concession	sãmpa-tham	สัมปทาน
condition	sapharb; ngeuan-khãi	สภาพ เงื่อนไข
condom	thõung-yang a-namai	ถุงยางอนามัย
conduct	khwam praphruet	ความประพฤติ
connect, to	sheuam; tit-taw	เชื่อม ติดต่อ
consent, to	a-nuyart	อนุญาต

268

consider, to	phicha-rana	พิจารณา
consonant	phayan-shanah	พยัญชนะ
constitution	rattha-thammanoon	รัฐธรรมนูญ
construction	karn kaw-sang	การก่อสร้าง
consult, to	pruek-sã	ปรึกษา
contest	karn khaeng-khãnh	การแข่งขัน
continuation	karn taw-neuang	การต่อเนื่อง
contract	sãnya; khaw tok-long	สัญญา ข้อตกลง
contradict	toh-yaeng	โต้แย้ง
contrary	trong kanh-kharm	ตรงกันข้าม
– contrary to fact	– trong kanh-kharm kap khwam ching	ตรงกันข้าม กับความจริง
contribute, to	borichaak ngoen	บริจาคเงิน
contributor	phu borichaak	ผู้บริจาค
control, to	khuab-khum	ควบคุม
convention	karn prashum	การประชุม
convict	nak-thode	นักโทษ
cook, to	proung a-harn	ปรุงอาหาร
copyright	likhasit	ลิขสิทธิ์
corpse	soph	ศพ
corruption	sĩn-bonh	สินบน
cosmetics	khreuang sãm-ang	เครื่องสำอาง
cost	rakha tonh thoun	ราคาต้นทุน

269

VOCABULARY

costume	**khreuang taeng-kaai**	เครื่องแต่งกาย
council	**sabha**	สภา
counterfeit	**plomm**	ปลอม
country	**prathesh**	ประเทศ
– up country	**– shonnabot; baan-nawk**	– ชนบท บ้านนอก
court (law)	**săl/ sărn**	ศาล
– magistrate court	**– săl khwăeng**	– ศาลแขวง
– civil court	**– săl phaeng**	– ศาลแพ่ง
– criminal court	**– săl a-yar**	– ศาลอาญา
– appeal court	**– săl utthom**	– ศาลอุทธรณ์
– military court	**– săl tha-hărn**	– ศาลทหาร
– supreme court	**– săl dika**	– ศาลฎีกา
courtesy	**mara-yart**	มารยาท
cousin	**louk-phi louk-nong; yati**	ลูกพี่ลูกน้อง ญาติ
coward	**khon khee-khlad**	คนขี้ขลาด
crackpot	**khon mai tem-teng**	คนไม่เต็มเต็ง
creditor	**chaow-nee**	เจ้าหนี้
cremate, to	**phăow-soph**	เผาศพ
criminal	**a-shaya-korn**	อาชญากร
cultivate, to	**phoh-plouk**	เพาะปลูก
culture	**wathanatham**	วัฒนธรรม
custom	**prapheni**	ประเพณี
customer	**louk-kha**	ลูกค้า

270

dance, to	tenh-ramh	เต้นรำ
– dance hostess	– khou tenh-ramh	– คู่เต้นรำ
danger	anta-raai	อันตราย
dark	mued	มืด
dead	taai	ตาย
debt; debtor	nee; chao-nee	หนี้ เจ้าหนี้
decease	phu-taai	ผู้ตาย
deceive, to	lawk-luang	หลอกลวง
declare, to	pra-kass	ประกาศ
decide, to	tok long; tat-sĭn-chai	ตกลง ตัดสินใจ
delegate	phu-thaen	ผู้แทน
defendant	chamleui	จำเลย
delighted	yindi	ยินดี
deliver, to	mobb song	มอบส่ง
demand, to	riak-rong	เรียกร้อง
democracy	prasha thipatai	ประชาธิปไตย
department	krom	กรม กอง
– department store	– hang sanpha-sĭnkha	– ห้างสรรพสินค้า
deport, to	nera-thesh	เนรเทศ
deposit (money)	faak pracham	ฝากประจำ
– deposit account	– banshi ngoen-faak	– บัญชีเงินฝาก
desire	tongkarn	ต้องการ
destroy, to	tham-laai	ทำลาย
detail	raai la-iat	รายละเอียด

VOCABULARY

devil	pi-sast; phẽe	ปีศาจ ผี
difficult	yaak; lam-bark	ยาก ลำบาก
diligent	kha-yãnh	ขยัน
diplomat	nak-karn thout	นักการทูต
disappoint	phid-wãng; mai som-wãng	ผิดหวัง ไม่สมหวัง
discount	suan-lod	ส่วนลด
disgrace	khwam abb-aye; khwam seuam-sĩa	ความอับอาย ความเสื่อมเสีย
dispute, to	to-thĩang	โต้เถียง
distance	rayah-thang	ระยะทาง
drug	ya septit	ยาเสพติด
– drug addict	– phu tit ya septit	– ผู้ติดยาเสพติด
dry cleaning	sak haeng	ซักแห้ง
duty	phasĩ/phasẽe	ภาษี
– duty free shop	– raan plawd phasĩ	– ร้านปลอดภาษี
east	tawan-awk	ตะวันออก
eat, to	kin; rappratharn	กิน รับประทาน
elevator	lift	ลิฟต์
embassy	sathãrn ek-akkha rajathout	สถานเอกอัครราชทูต
embezzle, to	yak-yawk	ยักยอก
emigrate, to	awk pai you tang-prathesh	ออกไปอยู่ต่างประเทศ
employer; employee	nai chang; louk-chang	นายจ้าง ลูกจ้าง

272

enemy	sattrou; kha-suek sattrou	ศัตรู ข้าศึกศัตรู
energy	phlang-ngarn	พลังงาน
engage, to	manh	หมั้น
– engagement ring	– waen manh	– แหวนหมั้น
engineer	visava-korn	วิศวกร
enlarge, to	kha-yāi	ขยาย
enterprise	kich-karn	กิจการ
entrance	thang-khow	ทางเข้า
entrepreneur	nak visāhakich	นักวิสาหกิจ
entry	thang khow	ทางเข้า
environment	sing waed-lomm	สิ่งแวดล้อม
equal	samēu kanh; thaow-thiam kanh	เสมอกัน เท่าเทียมกัน
equipment	u-pakorn	อุปกรณ์
entrust, to	wai waang chai	ไว้วางใจ
error	khwam-phid	ความผิด
escalator	bandai leuan	บันไดเลื่อน
escape	lop-nēe	หลบหนี
escort	khum-kanh	คุ้มกัน
espionage	chara-kamh	จารกรรม
etiquette	sōmbat phu-dee	สมบัติผู้ดี
Eurasian	louk-khrueng farang	ลูกครึ่งฝรั่ง
evidence	lak-thārn	หลักฐาน

VOCABULARY

examine, to	truad sobb	ตรวจสอบ
example	tua-yang	ตัวอย่าง
expenditure	kha shai-chaai	ค่าใช้จ่าย
expensive	rakha phaeng	ราคาแพง
experience	prasob-karn	ประสบการณ์
expert	phu shiao-sharn	ผู้เชี่ยวชาญ
expire	mod a-yuh	หมดอายุ
export, to	song awk tang prathesh	ส่งออกต่างประเทศ
expressway	thang-duan	ทางด่วน
extravagant	surui-suraai	สุรุ่ยสุร่าย
factory	rong-ngarn	โรงงาน
fair	yuti-tham	ยุติธรรม
faithful	sue-satt	ซื่อสัตย์
familiar	khun-kheui	คุ้นเคย
family	khrob-khrua	ครอบครัว
famous	mi shue-sĭang	มีชื่อเสียง
fare	kha doai-sărn	ค่าโดยสาร
– return fare	– kha doai-sărn pai-klab	– ค่าโดยสารไปกลับ
farm	farm; rai na	ฟาร์ม ไร่นา
farmer	shao-na; shao-rai	ชาวนา ชาวไร่
fate	shoke sha-ta	โชคชะตา
fated	tarm duang; laew-tae duang	ตามดวง แล้วแต่ดวง
favour, to	karuna	กรุณา
fear	klua; khwam-klua	กลัว ความกลัว

274

VOCABULARY

fee	kha tham-niam	ค่าธรรมเนียม
feel, to	rou-suek; sămnuek	รู้สึก สำนึก
festival	wan shalŏng; thesakarn	วันฉลอง เทศกาล
fiancé; fiancée	khu-rak shaai; khu-rak yĭng	คู่รักชาย คู่รักหญิง
fierce	duh-raai	ดุร้าย
fight	taw-sou	ต่อสู้
finance	karn ngoen	การเงิน
financier	phu shiao-sharn karn ngoen	ผู้เชี่ยวชาญการเงิน
fine (police)	kha-prab	ค่าปรับ
fingerprint	laai-phim mue	ลายพิมพ์มือ
fisherman	shao pramong	ชาวประมง
flight (aviation)	thiao-binh	เที่ยวบิน
fly, to	binh	บิน
flying saucer	chaan-binh	จานบิน
food	a-hărn	อาหาร
foreigner	shao tang-prathesh	ชาวต่างประเทศ
forget, to	luem	ลืม
forgetful	khee-luem	ขี้ลืม
free	penh issarah	เป็นอิสระ
freight	kha rawang khŏn-song	ค่าระวางขนส่ง
frontier	shaai daen	ชายแดน
fruit market	talad phŏlamai	ตลาดผลไม้

275

VOCABULARY

funeral	ngarn soph	งานศพ
future	a-nakhot	อนาคต
garden	sũan	สวน
gasoline	narm-manh sheua phloeng	น้ำมันเชื้อเพลิง
gems	petch phloi	เพชรพลอย
generous	chai kwang	ใจกว้าง
ghost	pisast	ปีศาจ
glad	dee-chai	ดีใจ
glutton	ta-klah	ตะกละ
go-between	khon klang; mae-sue	คนกลาง แม่สื่อ
goldsmith	shang-thong	ช่างทอง
government	ratthabarn	รัฐบาล
governor	phu-wa rajakarn	ผู้ว่าราชการ
graduate	bandid	บัณฑิต
grateful	khob-khun	ขอบคุณ
grenade	louk raberd	ลูกระเบิด
group	mou; mou-thi	หมู่ หมู่ที่
grumble	bonh	บ่น
grumbling	mai phaw-chai	ไม่พอใจ
guarantee	rap-rong; rap-prakanh	รับรอง รับประกัน
guard	yaam	ยาม
guardian	phu pok-khrong	ผู้ปกครอง
guerrilla	rob baeb-kong-chone	รบแบบกองโจร

276

VOCABULARY

guest	phu dai-rab shoen; khaek	ผู้ได้รับเชิญ/แขก
guesthouse	baan phak shua-khrao	บ้านพักชั่วคราว
guide	makkhu-thesh	มัคคุเทศก์
guided missile	khĕe-panavudh namh vithĩ	ขีปนาวุธนำวิถี
guilty	mi khwam-phid	มีความผิด
gunman	mue-puen	มือปืน
habit	nis-saĩ	นิสัย
haircut	tat-phõm	ตัดผม
hairdresser	shang taeng phõm	ช่างแต่งผม
handcuff	kunchae mue	กุญแจมือ
handicraft	karn fĩ-mue	การฝีมือ
handsome	roup-law	รูปหล่อ
handwriting	laai mue	ลายมือ
hang, to	khwãen	แขวน
happy	suk-sabaai	สุขสบาย
harbour	tha-reua	ท่าเรือ
hardship	yaak lam-baak	ยาก ลำบาก
harvest	kep-kiao	เก็บเกี่ยว
hate, to	kliad	เกลียด
head	sĩ-sah	ศีรษะ
– headman	– kamnan; phuyai baan	– กำนัน ผู้ใหญ่บ้าน
headquarters	sãmnak-ngarn yai	สำนักงานใหญ่

277

VOCABULARY

headmaster	**a-chaan yai**	อาจารย์ใหญ่
health	**sukkha-pharb;**	สุขภาพ อนามัย
	a-namai	
hear, to	**dai-yin**	ได้ยิน
heart	**hũa-chai**	หัวใจ
– heartbroken	**– sĩachai maak**	– เสียใจมาก
– heartache	**– cheb-chai**	– เจ็บใจ
– heartless	**– mai pranee**	– ไม่ปรานี
hell	**narok**	นรก
help, to; helper	**shuai-lẽua; phu**	ช่วยเหลือ ผู้ช่วยเหลือ
	shuai-lẽua	
here	**trong-ni; thi-ni**	ตรงนี้ ที่นี่
– hereafter	**– taw chaak ni**	– ต่อจากนี้
– herein	**– nah thi-ni**	– ณ ที่นี้
– hereby	**– duai prakarn**	– ด้วยประการฉะนี้
	shani	
– heretofore	**– konn na ni**	– ก่อนหน้านี้
hide, to; hiding	**thi-sonn**	ซ่อน ที่ซ่อน
place		
hire, to	**shaow**	เช่า
history	**pravat-sast**	ประวัติศาสตร์
highways	**thang-lũang**	ทางหลวง
hill	**noen lek-lek**	เนินเล็ก-เล็ก
hilltribes	**shao khõw**	ชาวเขา
hold, to	**chab, thũe**	จับ ถือ
home	**baan**	บ้าน

278

VOCABULARY

– home sick	– **khid thũeng baan**	– คิดถึงบ้าน
homosexual	**rak ruam-phesh**	รักร่วมเพศ
honest	**sue-satt**	ซื่อสัตย์
honour	**kiati-yot; shue-sĩang**	เกียรติยศ ชื่อเสียง
hooligan	**anthapharn; nak-leng**	อันธพาล นักเลง
hope	**khwam wãng**	ความหวัง
horse	**ma**	ม้า
– horse racing	– **khaeng ma**	– แข่งม้า
– horsepower	– **raeng-ma**	– แรงม้า
hospital	**rong phaya-barn**	โรงพยาบาล
hostage	**tua prakanh**	ตัวประกัน
hot	**ronn**	ร้อน
house	**baan**	บ้าน
– house-keeper	– **khon dou-lae baan**	– คนดูแลบ้าน
– house-wife	– **mae baan**	– แม่บ้าน
hungry	**hĩew**	หิว
hypocrite	**na-wai lãng-lawk**	หน้าไหว้หลังหลอก
idea	**khwam-khid**	ความคิด
ideal	**udom khati**	อุดมคติ
identity	**ek-laksana**	เอกลักษณ์
– identity card	– **batt pracham-tua**	– บัตรประจำตัว

279

VOCABULARY

idiot	khon ngoh	คนโง่
idol	watthu busha	วัตถุบูชา
ignorant	mai rou; mai sonh-chai	ไม่รู้ ไม่สนใจ
ill	puai-cheb; mai sabaai	ป่วยเจ็บ ไม่สบาย
illegal	phid kod-mãai	ผิดกฎหมาย
imagination	chintana-karn	จินตนาการ
imitate	lian baeb	เลียนแบบ
immediate	than-thi	ทันที
immigrant	khon khow-prathesh	คนเข้าประเทศ
immoral	phid sĩla-tham	ผิดศีลธรรม
immortal	mai-taai	ไม่ตาย
import	sĩnkha-khow	สินค้าเข้า
impolite	mai supharb	ไม่สุภาพ
impotent	mai-mi samattha-pharb	ไม่มีสมรรถภาพ
imprison	cham-khouk	จำคุก
important	sãm-khanh	สำคัญ
incurable	raksã mai hãai	รักษาไม่หาย
indecent	yaab-khaai	หยาบคาย
indigestion	a-hãrn mai yoi	อาหารไม่ย่อย
induce, to	shak-namh	ชักนำ
inexperienced	mai-mi prasob-karn	ไม่มีประสบการณ์
infant	tha-rok	ทารก

280

VOCABULARY

inferior	doi-kwa	ด้อยกว่า
information	khwam rou; khao	ความรู้ ข่าว
informer	phu chaeng khao	ผู้แจ้งข่าว
inhabitant	phu you a-sai	ผู้อยู่อาศัย
injection	sheed-ya	ฉีดยา
injustice	khwam a-yuti-thamh	ความอยุติธรรม
innocent	borisut	บริสุทธิ์
insane	penh ba	เป็นบ้า
insolent	mai-mi marayart	ไม่มีมารยาท
instalment (pay by)	sham-rah penh nguad	ชำระเป็นงวด
insufficient	mai-phaw	ไม่พอ
insure, to	rap-prakanh	รับประกัน
insult, to	dou-minh	ดูหมิ่น
integrity	khwam sue-satt sucharit	ความซื่อสัตย์สุจริต
interest (on money)	dawk-bia	ดอกเบี้ย
interesting	na-thueng; na-sanuk	น่าทึ่ง น่าสนุก
international	rawaang prathesh; sākol	ระหว่างประเทศ สากล
interpreter	laam; phu plae bhasā	ล่าม ผู้แปลภาษา
interrupted	khad-khwāng	ขัดขวาง
interview, to	sam-phas	สัมภาษณ์
introduce, to	naeh-namh	แนะนำ

281

VOCABULARY

investment	karn long-thoun	การลงทุน
invite, to	sheua-shearn	เชื้อเชิญ
jail	khouk tarang	คุก ตาราง
jealous	it-shã ris-sayã	อิจฉา ริษยา
joint-venture	ruam long-thoun	ร่วมลงทุน
jolly	ra-rerng	ร่าเริง
journalist	nak nãngsũe phim	นักหนังสือพิมพ์
judge	phu phiphaak-sã	ผู้พิพากษา
just (fair)	yuti-thamh	ยุติธรรม
justice	khwam yuti-thamh	ความยุติธรรม
juvenile	dek; yaowa-shon	เด็ก เยาวชน
keep, to	kep; rak-sã	เก็บ รักษา
kick, to	teh	เตะ
kidnap	lak-pha pai	ลักพาไป
kill, to	kha; kha-hai-taai	ฆ่า ฆ่าให้ตาย
kind-hearted	chai metta	ใจเมตตา
king	phrachao-you-hũa	พระเจ้าอยู่หัว
kiss, to	choub; hõmm-kaem	จูบ หอมแก้ม
kitchen	khrua	ครัว
– kitchen maid	– khon-khrua	– คนครัว
– kitchen utensils	– khreuang-shai nai khrua	– เครื่องใช้ในครัว
kite	waow	ว่าว
know, to	saab; rou	ทราบ รู้
knowledge	khwam rou	ความรู้

282

labour	raeng ngarn	แรงงาน
labourer	kamma-korn; khon-ngarn	กรรมกร คนงาน
land, landlord	thi-dinh; chao-khõng thi din	ที่ดิน เจ้าของที่ดิน
lane	trock; soi	ตรอก ซอย
language	bhasã	ภาษา
large	kwang; yai	กว้างใหญ่
last (final)	sud-thaai	สุดท้าย
late	sãai	สาย ล่าช้า
laundry	sathãrn rap sak-reed	สถานรับซักรีด
lavatory	hong sham-rah	ห้องชำระ
law; lawyer	kod-maai; thanai-khwam	กฎหมาย ทนายความ
leader	phu-namh	ผู้นำ
learn, to	rian; sueksã	เรียน ศึกษา
lease, to; lessor	shaow; phu-hai-shaow	เช่า ผู้ให้เช่า
lend, to	hai yuem	ให้ยืม
let, to	hai shaow	ให้เช่า
letter (anonymous)	batt sõnh-theh	บัตรสนเท่ห์
liaison officer	chaow-nathi tit-taw	เจ้าหน้าที่ติดต่อ
licence	bai a-nuyart	ใบอนุญาต
linoleum	phrom narm-manh	พรมน้ำมัน
listeners	phu-fang	ผู้ฟัง

283

VOCABULARY

literature	wanh-kha-di	วรรณคดี
loan (of money)	ngoen-kou	เงินกู้
loin cloth	pha-khão-ma	ผ้าขาวม้า
love; lovely	rak; na-rak	รัก น่ารัก
love letter	khanõm thong-muan	ขนมทองม้วน
love potion	saneh; ya-faed	เสน่ห์ ยาแฝด
love-sick	roke rak tromm chai	โรครักตรอมใจ
luck; lucky	shoke; shoke di	โชค โชคดี
luggage	krapãow dern thang	กระเป๋าเดินทาง
lunch	a-hãm klang-wan	อาหารกลางวัน
maiden	são-phring; yĩng são	สาวพริ้ง หญิงสาว
maintenance	karn bamrung raksã	การบำรุงรักษา
make, to	thamh	ทำ
manage, to	chat-karn	จัดการ
manager	phu-chat-karn	ผู้จัดการ
maniac	sĩa cha-rit	เสียจริต
manicure	tham-lep; taeng-lep	การทำเล็บ-แต่งเล็บ
mannequin	houn sadaeng baeb	หุ่นแสดงแบบ
marathon	wing-thonh thang klai	การวิ่งทนทางไกล

market	**talad**	ตลาด
– black market	**– talad mued**	– ตลาดมืด
– market (day & night)	**– talad toh-roung**	– ตลาดโต้รุ่ง
marry, to; marriage	**taeng-ngarn; sŏm-rot**	แต่งงาน สมรส
massage, to	**nuad**	นวด
masseur; masseuse	**maw-nuad shaai; maw-nuad yĭng**	หมอนวดชาย หมอนวดหญิง
matches	**mai-khide-fai**	ไม้ขีดไฟ
match-maker	**mae-sue**	แม่สื่อ แม่ชัก
matinee	**robb-baai**	รอบบ่าย
medicine	**ya raksă-roke**	ยารักษาโรค ยา
meditation	**vi-pasna**	วิปัสสนา
medium (spiritualistic)	**khon-song**	คนทรง
melody	**tham-nong phleng**	ทำนองเพลง
memorize, to	**thong-chamh**	ท่องจำ
memory	**khwam song-chamh**	ความทรงจำ
menu	**raai-shue a-harn**	รายชื่ออาหาร
merchandise	**sĭn-kha**	สินค้า
merchant	**phaw-kha**	พ่อค้า คนค้าขาย
messenger	**phu-namh khao**	ผู้นำข่าว คนส่งข่าว
middleman	**khon klang**	คนกลาง
midwife	**phaed phadung-khan**	แพทย์ผดุงครรภ์

VOCABULARY

military	kich-karn tha-harn	กิจการทหาร
millionaire	sreshthī ngoen laan	เศรษฐีเงินล้าน
mischievous	souk-sonh	ซุกซน
miserly	tra-nee	ตระหนี่
missile	khēe-pa-navudh	ขีปนาวุธ
mistakes	khwam-phid phlad	ความผิดพลาด
mistress	mia-keb; mia-shaow	เมียเก็บ เมียเช่า
misunderstand	khow-chai phid	เข้าใจผิด
modern	thanh sa-māi	ทันสมัย
monastery	wat-wa a-rarm	วัดวาอาราม
monk	bhik-khu; sõng	ภิกษุ สงฆ์
money	ngoen-thong	เงินทอง
money-lender	phu hai ku-yuem ngoen	ผู้ให้กู้ยืมเงิน
moon (full)	phra-chand (wan-phen)	พระจันทร์ (วันเพ็ญ)
moonshine	laow theuan	เหล้าเถื่อน
moral	sīla-tham	ศีลธรรม
mortgage, to	cham-nawng	จำนอง
mosque	suraow; masjid	สุเหร่า มัสยิด
Moslem	shaow muslim	ชาวมุสลิม
musician	nak don-tri	นักดนตรี
naked (the body)	pleu-i	เปลือย (ร่าง)
narcotics	ya sep-tit	ยาเสพติด

narrator	phu ban-yaai	ผู้บรรยาย
narrow	khab-khaeb	คับแคบ
nation; national	shart; haeng shart	ชาติ แห่งชาติ
nationality	sãn-shart	สัญชาติ
native	khon thawng-thin	คนท้องถิ่น
natural	tham-mashart	ธรรมชาติ
necessary	cham-penh	จำเป็น
neglect, to	mai-aow chai-sai	ไม่เอาใจใส่ เพิกเฉย
neighbour	pheuan-baan	เพื่อนบ้าน
neighbourhood	boriven klai-khiang	บริเวณใกล้เคียง
negotiator	phu chera-cha	ผู้เจรจา
news; newsman	khao; nak-khao	ข่าว นักข่าว
– news agency	– sãmnak khao	– สำนักข่าว
– newspaper	– nãngsue phim	– หนังสือพิมพ์
nick-name	shue-lenh; shã-ya	ชื่อเล่น ชื่อล้อ ฉายา
night club	samo-sõrn khon klang-khuen	สโมสรคนกลางคืน
nominate, to	taeng-tang	แต่งตั้ง
nonsensical	lẽow-lãi mai-dai khwam	เหลวไหลไม่ได้ความ
Northerner	shaow-nẽua	ชาวเหนือ
north-eastern people	shaow i-sãrn	ชาวอีสาน
notorious	khon-raai; khon-leow	คนร้าย คนเลว

VOCABULARY

nouveau riche	sresh-thĭ na mai	เศรษฐีหน้าใหม่
nude	khon mai-nung pha	คนไม่นุ่งผ้า
nuisance	tham khwam ram-kharn	ทำความรำคาญ กวนใจ
number plate	phaen-paai thabian	แผ่นป้ายทะเบียน
nun; nunnery	mae-shi; sămnak shi	แม่ชี สำนักชี
nurse	nang phaya-barn	นางพยาบาล
– wet nurse	– mae-nom	– แม่นม
nursery	sathărn liang dou dek	สถานเลี้ยงดูเด็ก
object	watthu prasŏng	วัตถุประสงค์
oblige, to	cham-tong	จำต้อง
obscene	la-mok; a-nacharn	ลามก อนาจาร
– obscene picture	– pharb la-mok	– ภาพลามก
observer	phu săng-ket kam	ผู้สังเกตการณ์
obtain, to	hă ma hai-dai	หามาให้ได้
occasion	o-kas	โอกาส
occupation	ar-sheep	อาชีพ
ocean	mahă-samudh	มหาสมุทร
office (work place)	sămnak-ngarn	สำนักงาน
office (position)	tamnaeng-nathi	ตำแหน่งหน้าที่
officer	chao nathi; phanak-ngarn	เจ้าหน้าที่ พนักงาน
– liaison officer	– phanak-ngarn tit-taw	– พนักงานติดต่อ

old (of people)	a-yuh maak; kae	อายุมาก แก่
old maid	são kae	สาวแก่ สาวทึนทึก
operation (surgical)	karn pha-tat	การผ่าตัด
operator	sãlya-bhaed; phu tham-ngarn	ศัลยแพทย์ ผู้ทำงาน
opinion	khwam-hẽnh	ความเห็น
opportunity	o-kas; changwah; shong-thang	โอกาส จังหวะ ช่องทาง
oppose to	taw-tarn; khad-kharn	ต่อต้าน คัดค้าน
order, to	sang; sang-sue	สั่ง สั่งซื้อ
ordinary	tham-mada	ธรรมดาโดยทั่วไป
ore	sĩn-rae	สินแร่
origin	tonh kamnerd	ต้นกำเนิด
ornament	sing pradab-kaai	สิ่งประดับกาย
orphan	kamphra	กำพร้า
out-of-date	la-samãi	ล้าสมัย
overseas	phone tha-le	โพ้นทะเล
overtime	luang vela	ล่วงเวลา
ownership	chao-khõng	เจ้าของ
pack, to	haw; houm	ห่อ หุ้ม
paddy-field	thong-na; na-khao	ท้องนา นาข้าว
pagoda	sathoup chedi	สถูปเจดีย์
parcel	phassa-duh	พัสดุ
palace	nives; phra rajawang	นิเวศน์ พระราชวัง
pantry	hong phak a-hãrn	ห้องพักอาหาร

VOCABULARY

parachute; parachutist	romh; nak-dode-romh	ร่ม นักโดดร่ม
partner in love	khou-nonn	คู่นอน
party	khanah; phak	คณะ พรรค
– political party	– phak karn meuang	– พรรคการเมือง
parliament	rattha-sabha	รัฐสภา
partner	hoon-suan	หุ้นส่วน
passenger	phu doai-sārn	ผู้โดยสาร
passport	nāngsūe dern-thang	หนังสือเดินทาง
patient	khon-khai	คนไข้
pawnshop	rong rap-chamnamh	โรงรับจำนำ
pay, to	chaai hai	จ่ายให้
peace	sāntipharb	สันติภาพ
peasant farmer	shao-na shao-rai	ชาวนาชาวไร่
pedestrian	khon dern-thaow	คนเดินเท้า
permanent wave	dadd-phom baeb thavorn	ตัดผมแบบถาวร
people	khon; fõong shon	คน ฝูงชน
person; personal	khon; suan buk-khon	คน ส่วนบุคคล
permit, to; permit	a-nuyart; bai a-nuyart	อนุญาต ใบอนุญาต
persuade, to	shak-shuan	ชักชวน
photograph, to	thaai-pharb	ถ่ายภาพ

290

picture	**pharb**	ภาพ
pickpocket	**nak-luang**	นักล้วง
pimp	**maeng-da**	แมงดา (ค้าสวาท)
pistol	**puen-phok**	ปืนพก
placard	**paai pra-kass**	ป้ายประกาศ
place	**sathãrn-thi**	สถานที่
platform	**sharn sha-la**	ชานชาลา
police constable	**phol tamruat**	พลตำรวจ
police officer	**nai tamruat**	นายตำรวจ
politician	**nak karn-meuang**	นักการเมือง
politics	**karn-meuang**	การเมือง
polite	**su-pharb**	สุภาพ
poor	**chonh**	จน
population	**phol-meuang**	พลเมือง
pornography	**nãngsũe/pharb la-mok**	หนังสือ/ภาพ ลามก
post, to	**song thang praisani**	ส่งทางไปรษณีย์
porter	**khon-karn**	คนการ (ขนสัมภาระ)
post code	**rahat praisani**	รหัสไปรษณีย์
postman	**burus-praisani**	บุรุษไปรษณีย์
postmaster	**nai-praisani**	นายไปรษณีย์
pray, to	**suad-monh**	สวดมนต์ภาวนา
present (gift)	**khõng-khwãn**	ของขวัญ
pretend, to	**saeng-thamh/**	แสร้งทำ
pretended deafness	**tham hõu thuan-lom**	ทำหูทวนลม ทำไม่รู้ไม่ชี้

VOCABULARY

princess	chao-fa yĭng	เจ้าฟ้าหญิง
printing; printing press	karn-phim; rong-phim	การพิมพ์ โรงพิมพ์
prison; prisoner	reuan-chamh; nak-thode	เรือนจำ นักโทษ
prize	rang wanh	รางวัล
produce	phlit; phlit-phŏi	ผลิต ผลิตผลจากวัตถุดิบ
products	phlit-phanh	ผลิตภัณฑ์
professor	sastra-charn	ศาสตราจารย์
profile	shiva-pravat bukkhon	ชีวประวัติย่อของบุคคล
profit	phŏl kam-rai	ผลกำไร
promissory note	bai-sănya shamrah-ni	ใบสัญญาชำระหนี้
propaganda	khosana shuan-sheua	โฆษณาชวนเชื่อ
prosecute	fong-rawng	ฟ้องร้อง
programme	kam-nod karn	กำหนดการ
prostitute	sŏpheni	โสเภณี
proprietor	chaow-khŏng; thaow-kae	เจ้าของ เถ้าแก่
province	chang-wad	จังหวัด
pseudonym	narm-făeng	นามแฝง
pursue, to	tit-tarm reuang	ติดตามเรื่อง
quack	theuan	เถื่อน
– quack doctor	– măw-theuan	– หมอเถื่อน

quality	khuna-pharb	คุณภาพ
qualification	khùna-sõmbat	คุณสมบัติ
quantity	pari-marn	ปริมาณ
quarrel, to	thalawh; vivadh	ทะเลาะ วิวาท
queen	rajini	ราชินี
– beauty queen	– rajini haeng khwam ngarm	– ราชินีแห่งความงาม
question; questionnaire	kham-thãrm; khaw-thãrm	คำถาม ข้อถาม
quick	reow; ruad-reow	เร็ว รวดเร็ว
quiet	ngiap; sa-ngop	เงียบ สงบ
quota	rabob quota	ระบบโควต้า
race	sheua-shart	เชื้อชาติ
– race horse	– ma-khaeng	– ม้าแข่ง
raid, to	ob-lomm, lomm	โอบล้อม
railway	rot-fai	รถไฟ
ranger (forest)	phran-pa (phu raksa-pa)	พรานป่า (รักษาป่า)
rank (dignity)	yosh	ยศ
rape, to	khom-khũen sham-raow	ข่มขืนชำเรา
rascal	khon ke-re	คนเกเร
rate	attra	อัตรา
– rate of exchange	– attra laek-plian	– อัตราแลกเปลี่ยน
read, to	arn/ann	อ่าน
ready	phromm-laew	พร้อมแล้ว
– ready made	– thamh set-laew	– ทำเสร็จแล้ว

VOCABULARY

– ready mixed	– phasŏm set-laew	– ผสมเสร็จแล้ว
– ready to wear	– sŭam-sai dai than-thi	– สวมใส่ได้ทันที
reason	het-phol	เหตุผล
reassure, to	rapprakanh; rap-rong	รับประกัน รับรอง
rebate	suan-lod	ส่วนลด
rebel	penh-kabot	เป็นกบฎ
recall	ra-luek	ระลึก
receive, to	rap	รับ
reception	karn tonn-rap	การต้อนรับ
recipé	tamrap a-hārn	ตำรับอาหาร
recipient	phu-rap	ผู้รับ
refreshment	khreuang-duem bao-baow	เครื่องดื่มเบาๆ
reconcile, to	prani pranomm	ประนีประนอม
recognize, to	cham-daai	จำได้
recommend, to	naeh-namh	แนะนำ
recover, to	dai khuen ma; hăai-puai	ได้คืนมา หายป่วย
recreation	karnphak-phonn yonn-chai	การพักผ่อนหย่อนใจ
rendez-vous	sathārn-thi nat-phob	สถานที่นัดพบ
refuse, to	pati-seth	ปฏิเสธ
reply, to	tobb; toh-tobb	ตอบ โต้ตอบ
report, to	raai-ngarn	รายงาน

reporter	phu raai-ngarn	ผู้รายงาน
representative	phu-thaen	ผู้แทน
resident	phol-meuang phu you a-sãi	พลเมืองผู้อยู่อาศัย
resign, to	la awk	ลาออก
restaurant	phat-ta-kharn	ภัตตาคาร
responsibility	khwam rap-phid-shobb	ความรับผิดชอบ
reserve, to	sãm-rong wai	สำรองไว้
rest-house	baan-phak shua-khrao	บ้านพักชั่วคราว
restriction	khaw chamkat	ข้อจำกัด
revenge	phouk phaya-bart	ผูกพยาบาท
reward	rang-wanh	รางวัล
road	tha-nõnh	ถนน
robber	kha-moai	ขโมย
rogue	antha-pharn	อันธพาล
romance	ni-yaai rak	นิยายรัก
room	hong	ห้อง
rubber	yang phara	ยางพารา
– plantation	– sũan-yang phara	– สวนยางพารา
– planter	– shao-sũan yang	– ชาวสวนยาง
– tapper	– kam-ma-korn kride yang	– กรรมกรกรีดยาง
rubbish	kha-yah	ขยะ
runways	thaang wing	ทางวิ่ง (ของเครื่องบิน)
sabotage	kaw vinass-kamh	ก่อวินาศกรรม

VOCABULARY

saint	nak-boun	นักบุญ
salary	ngoen-deuan	เงินเดือน
salon	hong rab-khaek	ห้องโถงรับแขก
sample	tua-yang	ตัวอย่าง
sanitation	karn sukhã-phibal	การสุขาภิบาล
savages	khon-pa	คนป่า
satellite	dao-thiam	ดาวเทียม
safety	khwam plawd phai	ความปลอดภัย
scare	tham hai tok-chai	ทำให้ตกใจ
schedule	kamnod raai-karn	กำหนดรายการ
science	vithaya-sastr	วิทยาศาสตร์
scoundrel	wai-raai	วายร้าย
search, to	khon-hã	ค้นหา
season	rue-dou karn	ฤดูกาล
security	khwam manh-khong plawd phai	ความมั่นคงปลอดภัย
secret	khwam-lap; khled-lap	ความลับ เคล็ดลับ
self-service	borikarn tonh-eng	บริการตนเอง
self-supporting	liang tua-eng	เลี้ยงตนเอง
selfish	hẽnh kae-tua	เห็นแก่ตัว
sell, to	khãai; cham-naai	ขาย จำหน่าย
seniority	avu-sõ	อาวุโส
sensation	khwam rou-suek tuen-tenh	ความรู้สึกที่ตื่นเต้น

sense	khwam rou-suek; sâm-nuek	ความรู้สึก สำนึก
sentence	pra-yoke	ประโยค
separation	yaek awk-chaak kanh	การแยกออกห่างจากกัน
servant	khon-shai	คนใช้
serve, to	rap-shai	รับใช้
service	borikarn rap-shai	บริการรับใช้
serious; seriously	nak-nuang; ching-chang	หนักหน่วง จริงจัง
shake, to	kha-yaow	เขย่า
shaman	mãw sãi-ya-sastr	หมอไสยศาสตร์
shamed	appayosh od-sõu, abb-aye	อัปยศอดสู อับอาย
shameless	na-darn; mai abb-aye	หน้าด้าน ไม่อับอาย
shape	sãn-thãrn roup-baeb	สัณฐาน รูปแบบ
share, to	mi suan ruam	มีส่วนร่วม
sharp-shooter	khon maen-puen	คนแม่นปืน
shoot, to	ying puen	ยิงปืน
show-window	tou-show sĩn-kha	ตู้โชว์ สินค้า
shop; shop-assistant	raan; phu-shuai-raan	ร้าน ผู้ช่วยร้าน
shut, to	pid	ปิด
signature	laai-sen	ลายเซ็น

VOCABULARY

sign (road)	khreuang-mãai chara-chonn	เครื่องหมายจราจร
sin; sinful	bab; penh-bab	บาป เป็นบาป
skill	shiao-sham	เชี่ยวชาญ
slum; slum area	laeng seuam-some; boriven seuam-some	แหล่งเสื่อมโทรม บริเวณ แหล่งเสื่อมโทรม
smart	praad-preuang	ปราดเปรื่อง
smell; smelly	klinh; klinh-mẽhn	กลิ่น กลิ่นเหม็น
smuggle, to (in)	lak-lobb aow khow ma	ลักลอบเอาเข้ามา
soldier	tha-hãrn	ทหาร
smoke, to	soub buri	สูบบุหรี่
souls	vin-yarn	วิญญาณ
south; Southerner	thit-taai; khon phaak-tai	ทิศใต้ คนภาคใต้
souvenir	khõng thi ra-luek	ของที่ระลึก
space	neua-thi waang	เนื้อที่ว่าง
specialist	phu shiao-sharn phiseth	ผู้เชี่ยวชาญพิเศษ
spectacles	waen-ta	แว่นตา
speed	khwam reow	ความเร็ว
spend, to	shai ngoen; shai-chaai	ใช้เงิน ใช้จ่าย
spinster	yĩng sode; sãow-kae	หญิงโสด สาวแก่

spirit	**chetaphout; vin-yarn**	เจตภูต วิญญาณ
spokesman	**kho-sok thalāeng khao**	โฆษกแถลงข่าว
sport	**kila**	กีฬา
stay, to	**a-sãi you**	อาศัยอยู่
stall	**raan phāeng-loi**	ร้านแผงลอย ร้านเล็กๆ
stamina	**narm-od narm-thon**	น้ำอดน้ำทน พละกำลัง
standard	**mattra-thãrn**	มาตรฐาน
statement	**thalāeng-karn**	แถลงการณ์
statue	**a-nussã-vari**	อนุสาวรีย์
steamer	**reua-kon-fai**	เรือกลไฟ
steal; stolen	**kha-moai; khamoai-pai**	ขโมย ขโมยไปแล้ว
stone deaf	**hõu-nuak**	หูหนวก
straight-forward	**trong-pai; trong-ma**	ตรงไปตรงมา
stranger	**burus plaek-na**	บุรุษแปลกหน้า
strategy	**kol-yudh; yuddha-vithi**	กลยุทธ์ ยุทธวิธี
street (one way)	**thanõn-yai**	ถนนกว้าง ถนนใหญ่
strike, to	**strike; youd-ngam**	สไตร๊ค์ หยุดงาน
strip-tease	**rabamh-pleu-i**	ระบำเปลือย
stuck up	**ying-ya-sõ**	หยิ่งยโส วางก้าม
study, to; student	**suek-sã; nak suek-sã**	ศึกษา นักศึกษา

VOCABULARY

submarine	reua taai-narm	เรือใต้น้ำ
submit, to	sanēu	เสนอ
subscription	kha-bamrung	ค่าบำรุง
successor	phu rap-shuang	ผู้รับช่วง
suicide	kha-tua-taai	อัตวินิบาตกรรม ฆ่าตัวตาย
summons (court)	awk māai riak	ออกหมายเรียก
superman	manus mahas-sachan	มนุษย์มหัศจรรย์
superstitious	sheua nai sāiya-sast	เชื่อในไสยศาสตร์
support, to	sanab-sanoun; kham-choun	สนับสนุน ค้ำจุน
supreme com-mander	phu banshakarn thahārn	ผู้บัญชาการทหารสูงสุด
swim, to	waai-narm	ว่ายน้ำ
swimming pool	sah waai-narm	สระว่ายน้ำ
swindler	nak-tom toun	นักต้มตุ๋น
talkative	shang-phoud	ช่างพูด
tax; tax collector	phasī; phanak-ngarn phasī	ภาษี พนักงานภาษี
– tax payer	– phu sīa phasi	– ผู้เสียภาษี
– tax exempt	– yok wenh phasī	– ยกเว้นภาษี
– tax evasion	– lop phasī	– หลบภาษี
– tax free shop	– raan plawd phasī	– ร้านปลอดภาษี
teach, to; teacher	sōnn visha; khru	สอนวิชา ครูผู้สอน

tease, to	sappha-yawk	สัพยอก หยอกล้อ
teenager	wai-roun	วัยรุ่น
telecommunica- tions	thora khamana- khom	โทรคมนาคม
temper	a-rom	อารมณ์
temple	bade; vihãrn	โบสถ์ วิหาร
terrible	na saphueng klua; na-klua	น่าสะพึงกลัว
testimonial	nãngsũe rap-rong	หนังสือรับรอง
trade & commerce	karn-kha; karn phanich	การค้าและการพาณิชย์
trade–local	karn-kha phaai-nai	การค้าภายใน
– foreign	– karn-kha kap tang prathesh	– การค้ากับต่างประเทศ
– retail	– karn-kha pleek	– การค้าปลีก
– wholesale	– karn-kha song	– การค้าส่ง
train	rot-fai	รถไฟ
training	fuek; ob-rom	ฝึก อบรม
transportation	karn khõn-song	การขนส่ง
travel, to	thasana-chorn; thong-thiao	ทัศนาจร ท่องเที่ยว
traveller	nak thasana-chorn	นักทัศนาจร
treaty	sãnya rawang prathesh	สัญญาระหว่างประเทศ
trick (confidence)	kam lawk-luang; tom-toun	การหลอกลวงต้มตุ๋น

VOCABULARY

trip	karn dern-thang	การเดินทาง
trouble	khwam young-yaak	ความยุ่งยาก
troublesome	young-yaak; lambaak	ยุ่งยากลำบาก
try to	phaya-yarm	พยายาม
UFO	chaan-binh	จานบิน
ugly	na-kliad	น่าเกลียด
umbrella	rom	ร่ม
unaccustomed	mai-khun-kheu-i	ไม่คุ้นเคย
unarmed	mai-mi avudh	ไม่มีอาวุธ
unbelievable	lẽua-sheua	เหลือเชื่อ
uncertain	mai-nae	ไม่แน่
unclean	mai sa-ard	ไม่สะอาด
undecided	lang-le chai; mai-tok-long	ลังเลใจ ยังไม่ตกลง
undertake, to	khow thamh; a-sã thamh	เข้าทำ อาสาทำ
undertaker	sappa-reu	สัปเหร่อ
under the table	sĩn-bonh taai toh	สินบนใต้โต๊ะ
underworld	khõum na-rok	ขุมนรก อเวจี
undesirable	thi mai phueng prathanã	ที่ไม่พึงปรารถนา
uneasy	kravon-kravaai; krasab-kra saai	กระวนกระวาย กระสับกระส่าย
uneconomical	mai penh karn prayad	ไม่เป็นการประหยัด

302

unexpected	mai-khid mai-fãnh	ไม่คิดไม่ฝัน คาดไม่ถึง
unfair	mai yuti-thamh	ไม่ยุติธรรม
unfaithful	nera-khun; mai-sue satt	เนรคุณ ไม่ซื่อสัตย์
unfamiliar	mai khun-kheu-i	ไม่คุ้นเคย
unfinished	yang mai-seth	ยังไม่เสร็จ
unforgettable	luem sĩa mi-dai	ลืมเสียมิได้
unfounded	mai-mi moul	ไม่มีมูล ปราศจากหลักฐาน
unfriendly	mai penh mit	ไม่เป็นมิตร
unfurnished	mai-mi khreuang reuan hai	ไม่มีเครื่องเรือนให้
unhappy	mai suk sabaai	ไม่สุขสบาย
unhealthy	suk-khapharb mai di	สุขภาพไม่ดี
unheard of	mai kheu-i dai yin	ไม่เคยได้ยิน
union	sahapharb	สหภาพ การรวมกัน
unit	nuai	หน่วย
universe	chak-kraval	จักรวาล
universal	sãkol	สากล ทั่วๆ ไป
university	mahã vithayalai	มหาวิทยาลัย
unlawful	phid kod-mãai	ผิดกฎหมาย
unlimited	mai chamkat	ไม่จำกัด
unlucky	shoke mai-di	โชคไม่ดี ซวย
unreasonable	rai het-phol	ไร้เหตุผล
until	chon-kwa, chon krathang	จนกว่า จนกระทั่ง

VOCABULARY

unwilling	mai tem-chai	ไม่เต็มใจ
up country	shonnabot; baan-nawk	ชนบท บ้านนอก
upkeep, to	bamrung raksã	บำรุงรักษา
upper class	kha-hah bawdi	คหบดี
upset	tham hai young	ทำให้ยุ่ง
urinal	thõ passã-vah	โถปัสสาวะ
use; used	shai; shai laew	ใช้ ใช้แล้ว
useless	rai prayote	ไร้ประโยชน์
useful	mi prayote	มีประโยชน์
vacant	waang	ว่าง ไม่มีใคร
vacation	la-youd phak ngarn	ลาหยุดพักงาน
vaccinate, to	plouk-fẽe	ปลูกฝี
vagabond, vagrant	khon ré-ronn; khon chorn-chat	คนเร่ร่อน จรจัด
valid	yang shai-dai; yang mai-mod ayuh	ยังใช้ได้ ยังไม่หมดอายุ
valuable	mi rakha	มีราคา
value	kha	ค่า
valueless	mai-mi kha	ไม่มีค่า
vandal	phu tham-laai sab-sĩn	ผู้ทำลายทรัพย์สิน
variety	shanid tang-tang	หลายๆ ลักษณะ ชนิดต่างๆ

304

vegetarian	khon kin a-hãrn phak	คนกินอาหารผัก
vehicle	yarn pha-hah-nah	ยานพาหนะ
vengeance	khwam phaya-bart	ความพยาบาท
verdict	kham shi khard	คำชี้ขาด
veteran	tha-hãrn phaan suek	ทหารผ่านศึก
veterinarian	satta-wah phaed	สัตวแพทย์
victim	phuprasop khroh; yeua sãng-hãrn	ผู้ประสบเคราะห์ เหยื่อสังหาร
victory	shai sha-nah	ชัยชนะ
videotape	videotape	วิดีโอเทป
viewpoint	khwam-hẽnh; thasanah-khati	ความเห็น ทัศนคติ
village	mou-baan	หมู่บ้าน
virgin	phrom-machari	พรหมจารี
visible	thi hẽnh dai (duai ta plao)	ที่เห็นได้ (ด้วยตาเปล่า)
vision	sãai-ta	สายตา
visit	karn yiam-yian	การเยี่ยมเยียน
voice	sĩang	เสียง
voluntary	doai samak chai	โดยสมัครใจ
volunteer	a-sã samak	อาสาสมัคร
voyage	karn dern thang	การเดินทาง
vulgar	yaab-lone	หยาบโลน
wages	kha-chang	ค่าจ้าง

VOCABULARY

wait, to; waiter	raw-khoi; phu dou-lae-rapshai	รอคอย ผู้ดูแลรับใช้
wake, to	plouk hai tuen	ปลุกให้ตื่น
walk, to	dern	เดิน
warm	ob-oun	อบอุ่น
warranty	rap-rong; yuen-yanh	รับรอง ยืนยัน
warrior	nak-rop	นักรบ
wash, to	laang	ล้าง
washable	laang awk dai	ล้างออกได้
washroom	hong-narm; hong sham-rah	ห้องน้ำ ห้องชำระ
waste, to	tham hai sia; hai mod pleuang	ทำให้เสีย ให้หมดเปลือง
watch-dog	sunak faow khŏng	สุนัขเฝ้าของ
watchman	khon yarm	คนยาม
waterfall	narm-tok	น้ำตก
water-ski	ski-narm	สกีน้ำ
wealthy	ramh-ruai; mang-khang	ร่ำรวย มั่งคั่ง
weapon	a-vudh	อาวุธ
weather	lom-fa a-kas	ลมฟ้าอากาศ
wedding	karn sŏm-rot	การสมรส
weekend	soud sap-dah	สุดสัปดาห์
weight	narm-nak	น้ำหนัก
welcome	yin-di tonn-rap	ยินดีต้อนรับ
welfare	sawatdi-karn	สวัสดิการ

VOCABULARY

well-done	thamh-di	ทำดี
well-known	mi shue sĩang	มีชื่อเสียง
well-mannered	mara-yart ngarm	มารยาทงาม
well-off	mang-khang; ramh-ruai	มั่งคั่ง ร่ำรวย
wharf	tha-reua	ท่าเรือ
white-collar	ngarn nang-toh	งานประเภทนั่งโต๊ะ
whore	sõ-pheni	โสเภณี
widow; widower	yĩng-maai; shaai- rai-khu	หญิงม่าย ชายไร้คู่
wife	phan-raya	ภรรยา
winner	phu shanah	ผู้ชนะ
wise; wisdom	shalard; shalĩao- shalard	ฉลาดทันคน ความเฉลียวฉลาด
wish; wishful	pra-thanã; khãw hai-som prathanã	ปรารถนา ขอให้สมปรารถนา
witchcraft	saneh	เสน่ห์ยาแฝด
witchdoctor	mãw saneh	หมอเสน่ห์ หมอผี
withdraw, to; withdrawn	thõnn tua awk	ถอนตัวออก
witness	pha-yarn	พยาน
witty	mi wai-phrib; mi waew	มีไหวพริบ มีแวว
wonder	pralard	ประหลาด
wonderful	ma-hassa-chan	มหัศจรรย์
word	kham; thoi-kham	คำ ถ้อยคำ

VOCABULARY

work; worker	**ngarn; kamma-korn**	งาน คนงาน กรรมกร
working class	**shon shan-kanma-sheep**	ชนชั้นกรรมาชีพ
workmanship	**ngarn fi-mue**	งานฝีมือ
workshop	**rong-ngam lek**	โรงงานเล็ก
world	**loke**	โลก
worn-out	**suek-rãw**	สึกหรอ
worry	**nak-chai**	หนักใจ
worse	**leow long**	เลวลง
worship	**bu-sha**	บูชา
worth	**mi-kha**	มีค่า
worth-while	**khoum-kha; khoum-vela**	คุ้มค่า คุ้มเวลา
would; would-be	**ach-chah; ach penh-daai**	อาจจะ อาจเป็นได้
wound; wounded	**bard-phlãe; mi bard-phlãe**	บาดแผล มีบาดแผล
wrap, to; wrapper	**houm-haw**	หุ้มห่อ สิ่งที่ใช้ห่อหุ้ม
wreath	**reed, phuang-reed**	หรีด พวงหรีด
wrinkle	**teen-ka, na-yonh**	ตีนกา หน้าย่น
write, to	**khĩan**	เขียน
wrong, wrongful	**phid; thang thi-phid**	ผิด ทางที่ผิด
yawn, to	**hão**	หาว หาวเรอ
yogi	**yo-khi**	โยคี
yogurt	**nom-priao**	นมเปรี้ยว

VOCABULARY

youngster	**rounh-noum;**	รุ่นหนุ่ม รุ่นสาว
	rounh-sáo	
youth	**yuwa-shon**	ยุวชน
zigzag	**khod-khiao**	คดเคี้ยว
zone	**khet; boriven**	เขต บริเวณ
zoological garden	**sũan-satt**	สวนสัตว์
zoology	**satt-vĩthaya**	สัตว์วิทยา

NOTES